AF605876

FOCUS ON PLAYWRIGHTS

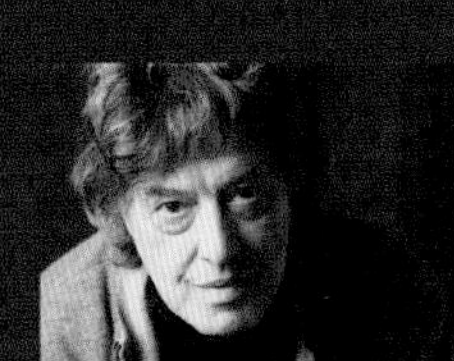

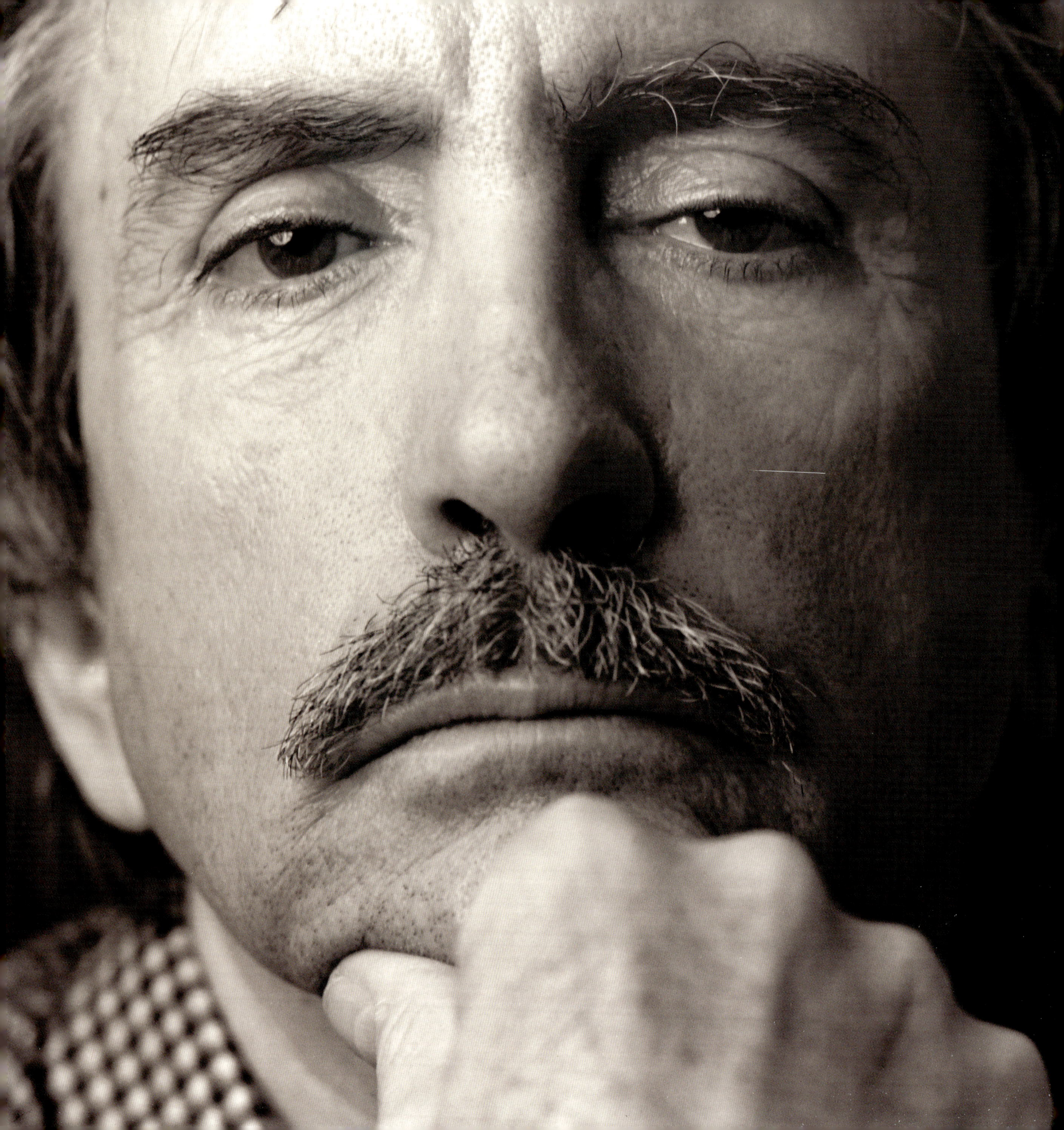

FOCUS ON PLAYWRIGHTS

Portraits and Interviews

SUSAN JOHANN

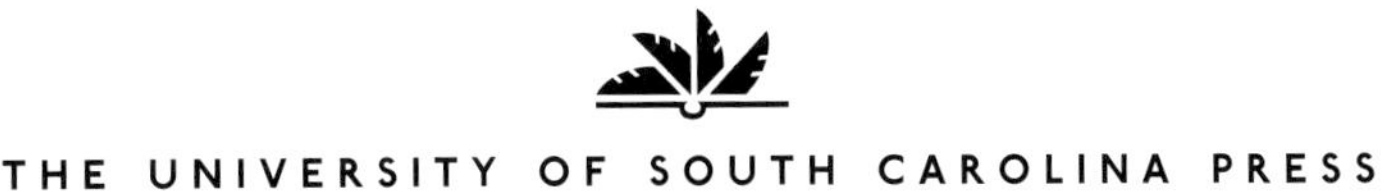

THE UNIVERSITY OF SOUTH CAROLINA PRESS

Library of Congress Cataloging-in-Publication Data can be found
at http://catalog.loc.gov/.

ISBN: 978-1-61117-714 (cloth)

25 24 23 22 21 20 19 18 17 16
10 9 8 7 6 5 4 3 2 1

Design and production by Blue Design

Printed in China

Page 1: Tom Stoppard
Page 2: Edward Albee
Right: Bill Irwin
Page 6: Beth Henley
Page 10: Joan Schenkar

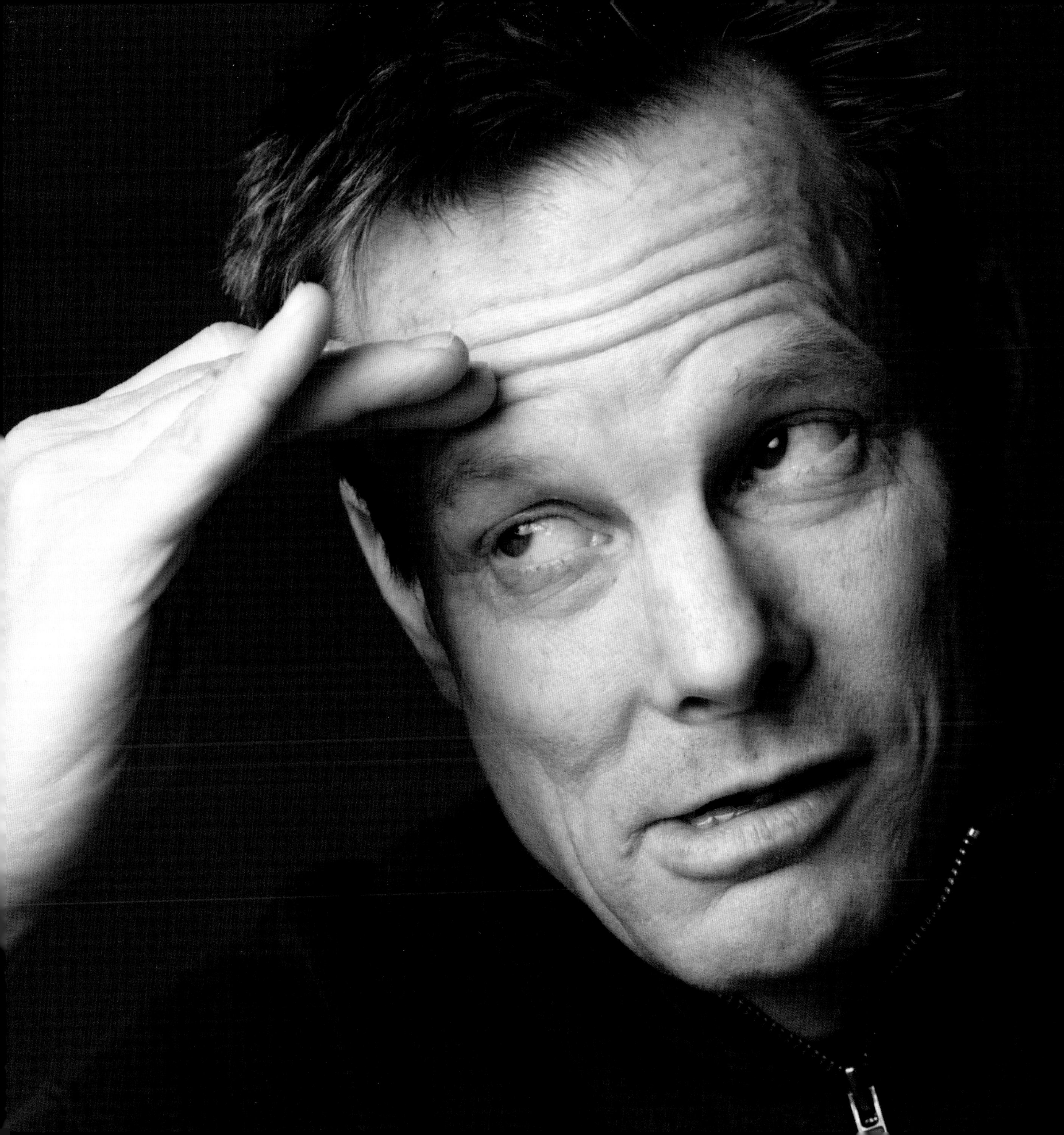

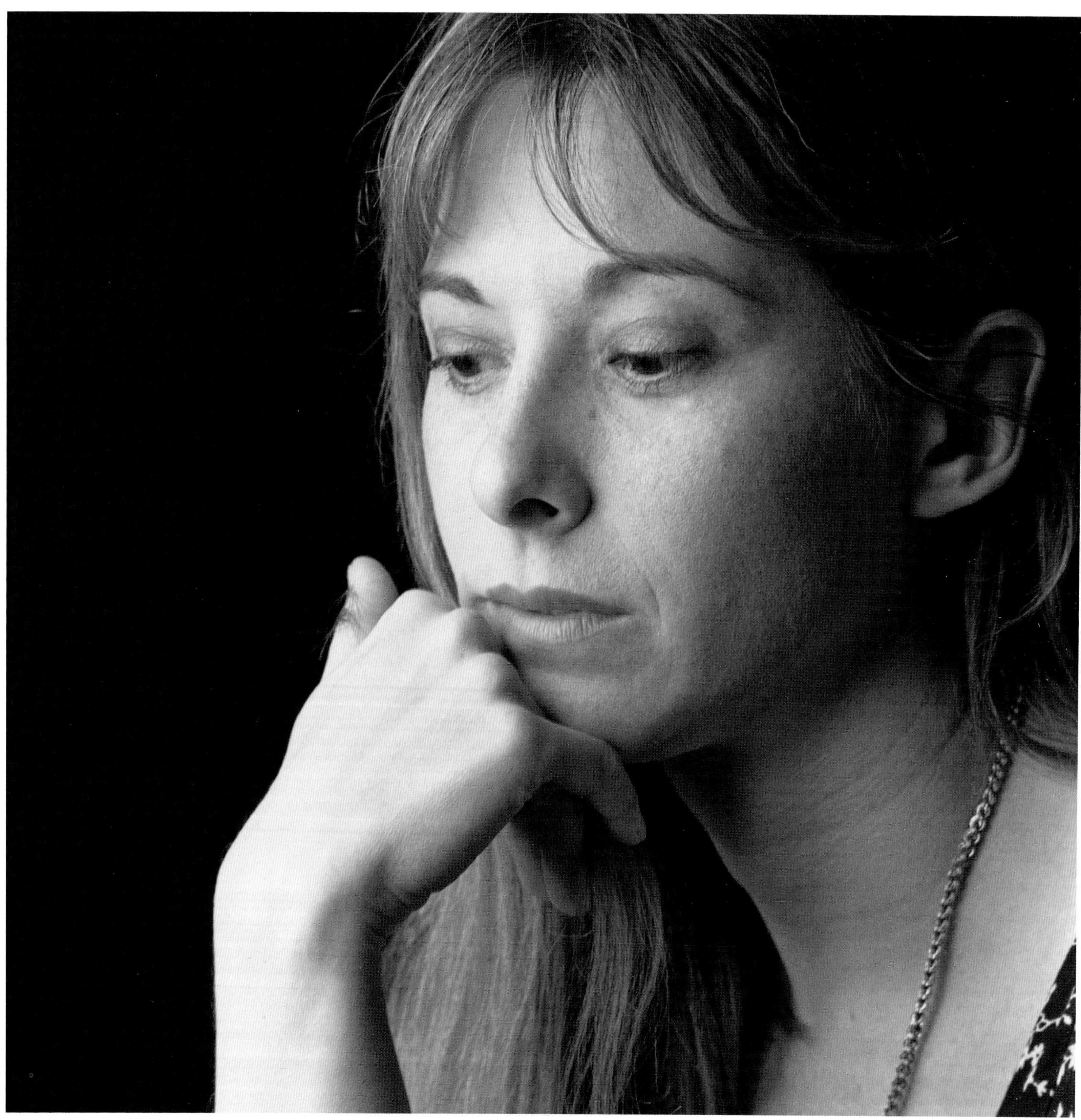

CONTENTS

INTERVIEWS / TEXT

PHOTOGRAPHS

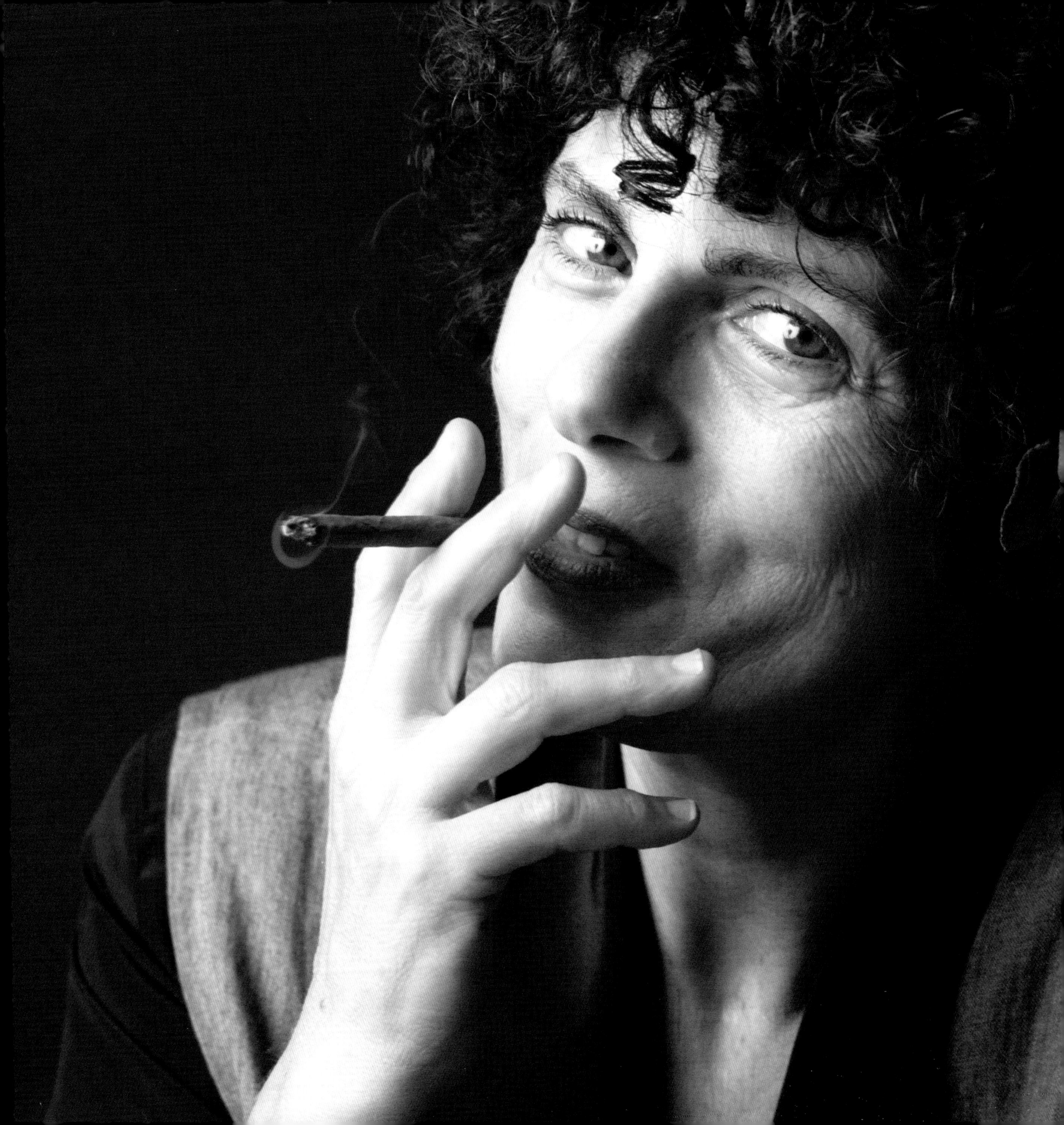

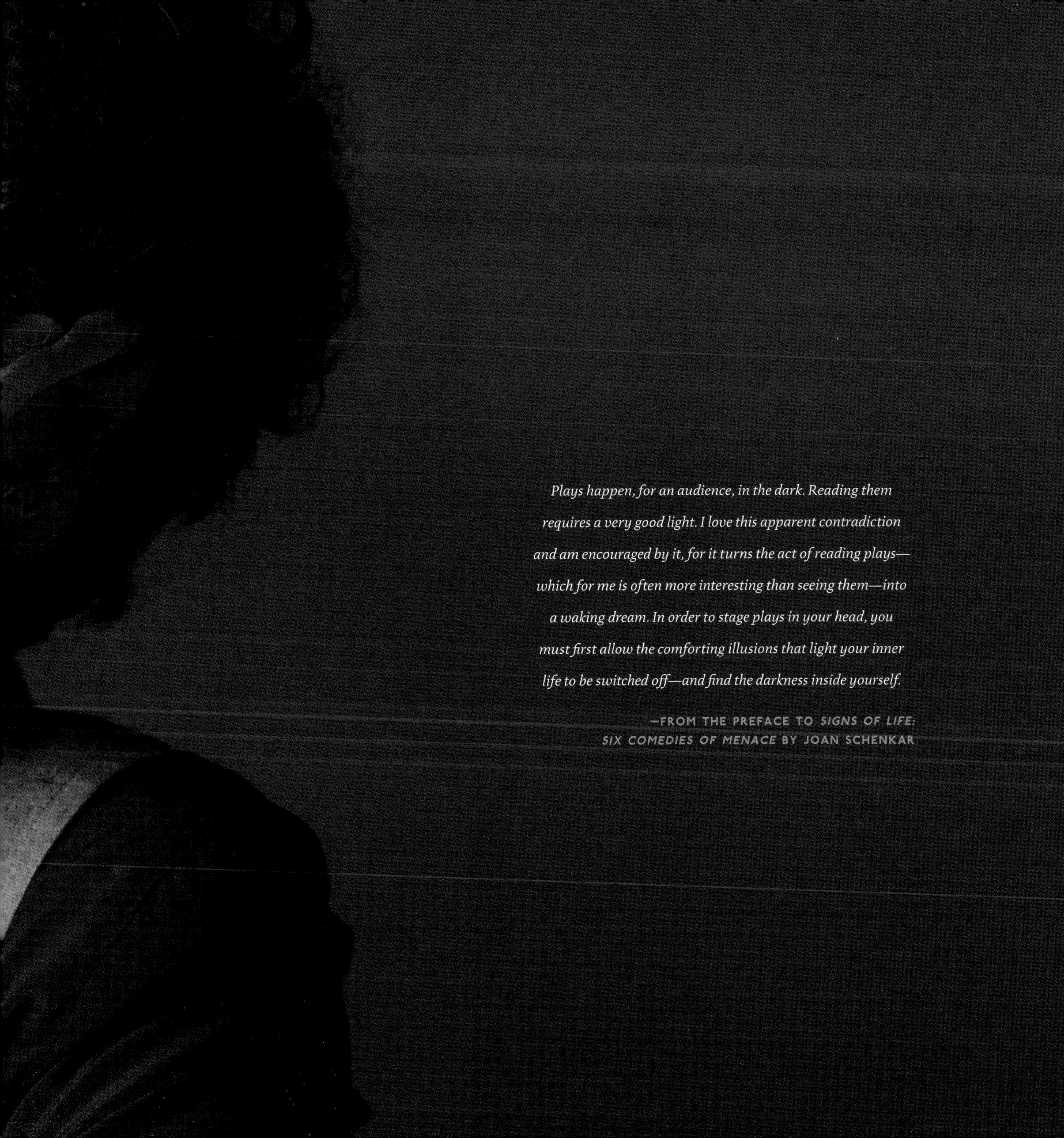

Plays happen, for an audience, in the dark. Reading them requires a very good light. I love this apparent contradiction and am encouraged by it, for it turns the act of reading plays—which for me is often more interesting than seeing them—into a waking dream. In order to stage plays in your head, you must first allow the comforting illusions that light your inner life to be switched off—and find the darkness inside yourself.

—FROM THE PREFACE TO *SIGNS OF LIFE: SIX COMEDIES OF MENACE* BY JOAN SCHENKAR

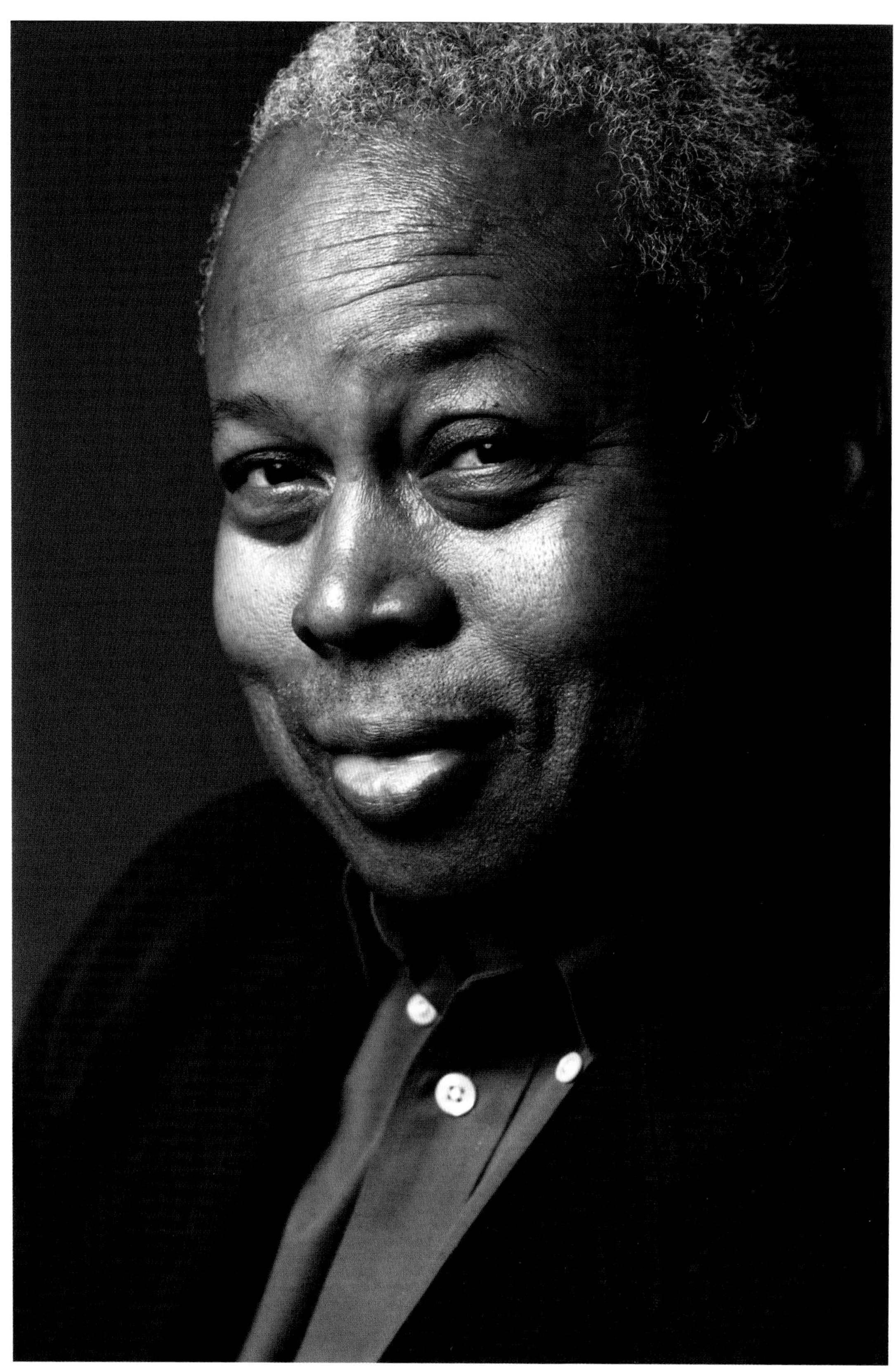

PROLOGUE

Shakespeare called the play "a brief and abstract chronicle of its time." The playwright is chronicler. A mirror. Sometimes through biting satire, sometimes through moments that crystallize our experiences and return them to us clearer, they put themselves in a vulnerable position. If we are uncomfortable with what we see, we may wish to take the light away. Don't buy a ticket. Close the theater. What good is a mirror in the dark? Without a stage, a play can be literature, but not theatre. Theatre—as opposed to film or video—is a three-dimensional mirror in which words and ideas reverberate through time and space with an immediacy that can only happen when living, breathing human beings share an experience.

For decades, I have been intrigued by the idea of bringing to light the highly imaginative, vital people who work behind the scenes—playwrights. Those photographed are a diverse group—ranging in age from twenty-something to one hundred and four. They are often political thinkers, sometimes poets. Some have college degrees and post-graduate degrees and others have less than a high school education. The group crisscrosses ethnic and class lines. They are impassioned artists with a common need to communicate their vision of the world.

The criterion for including a playwright in this series was simple: I wanted playwrights with a body of work, a body of work of distinction. Why are some important names missing? Again it is simple: because we were not in the same place at the same time. No collection can be exhaustive, and there will always be playwrights to photograph and other images that might show us another side.

Each playwright was photographed in studio using the same film, a single light and a plain backdrop. Each portrait chosen is a single frame of many taken—a single instant that in my judgment captures and distills something essential. There is always a full-length portrait, giving us a picture of the bearing and the apparel. The camera moves ever closer and eventually we get a very intimate look. As observers, we have permission to stare back at Edward Albee, August Wilson, or Marsha Norman, to examine them the way they examine us.

In the interviews, we can explore their journeys and their reasons for choosing such a chancy profession—this highly speculative, collaborative, crazy business—the art of making plays.

Ed Bullins (opposite)

It is thanks to these brave men and women who step forward to reveal those truths the rest of us are unwilling or unable to utter, that we as audience can sit in a darkened theater surrounded by others looking for an experience, or answers, or perhaps just amusement—but we will always get something more. If we are lucky, we will be transported into the magical, heightened reality that is theatre. If it is truly great, we will be marked by it forever. These photographs and interviews are a way to remember and celebrate the originating magician—the playwright.

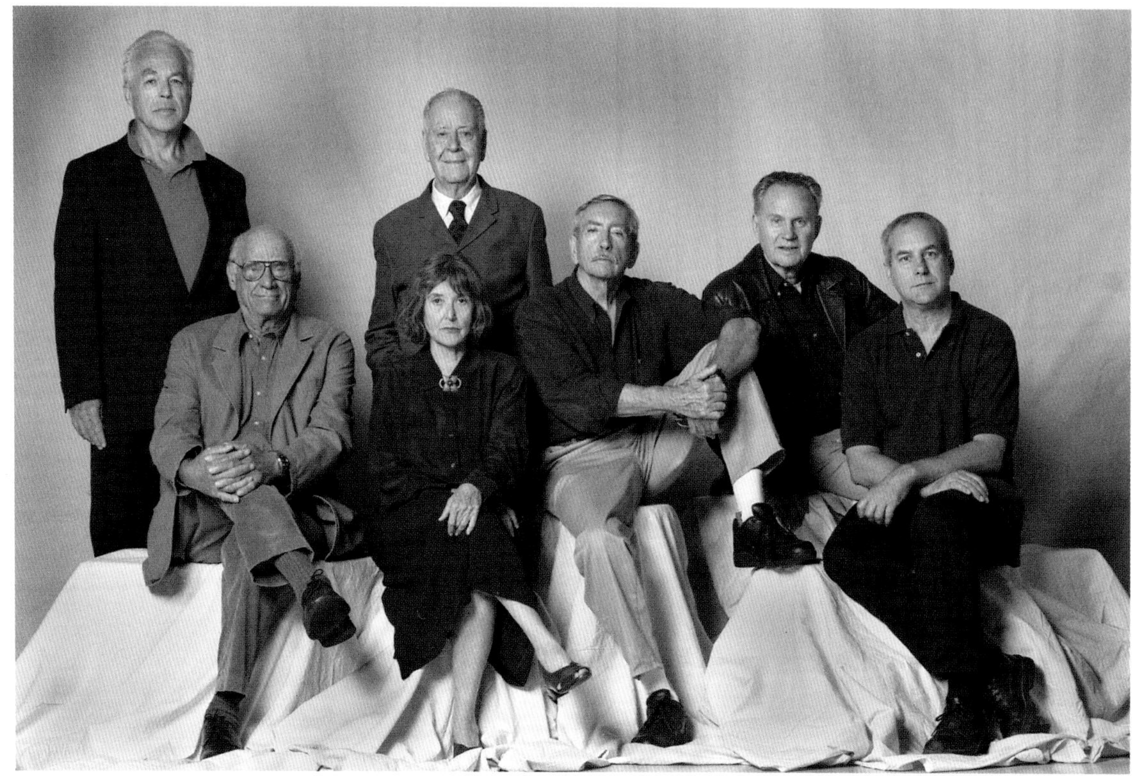

Standing left to right — John Guare and Horton Foote. Seated — Arthur Miller, Maria Irene Fornes, Edward Albee, Romulus Linney, Lee Blessing. Photographed at Signature Theatre in 2000.

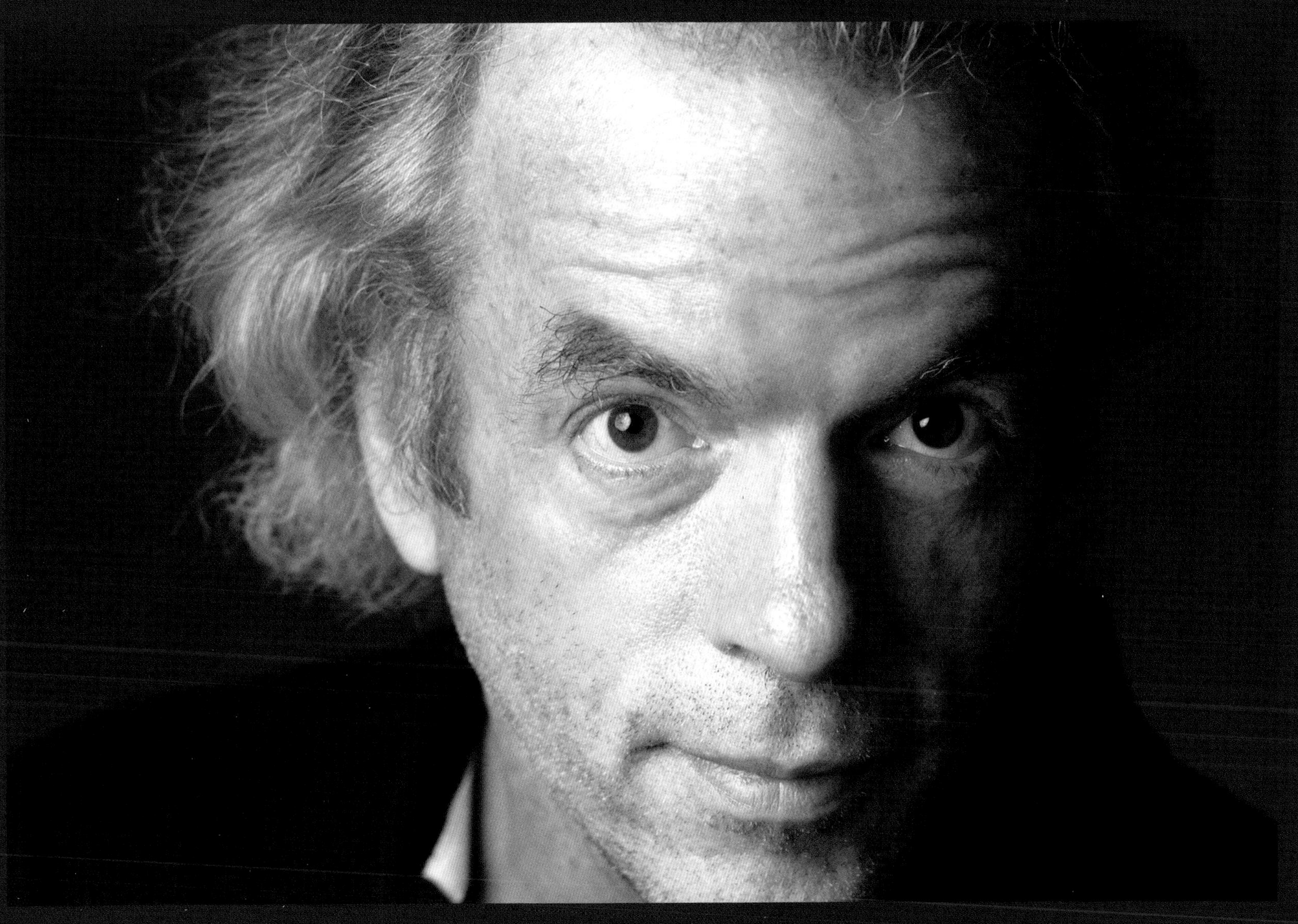

Spalding Gray

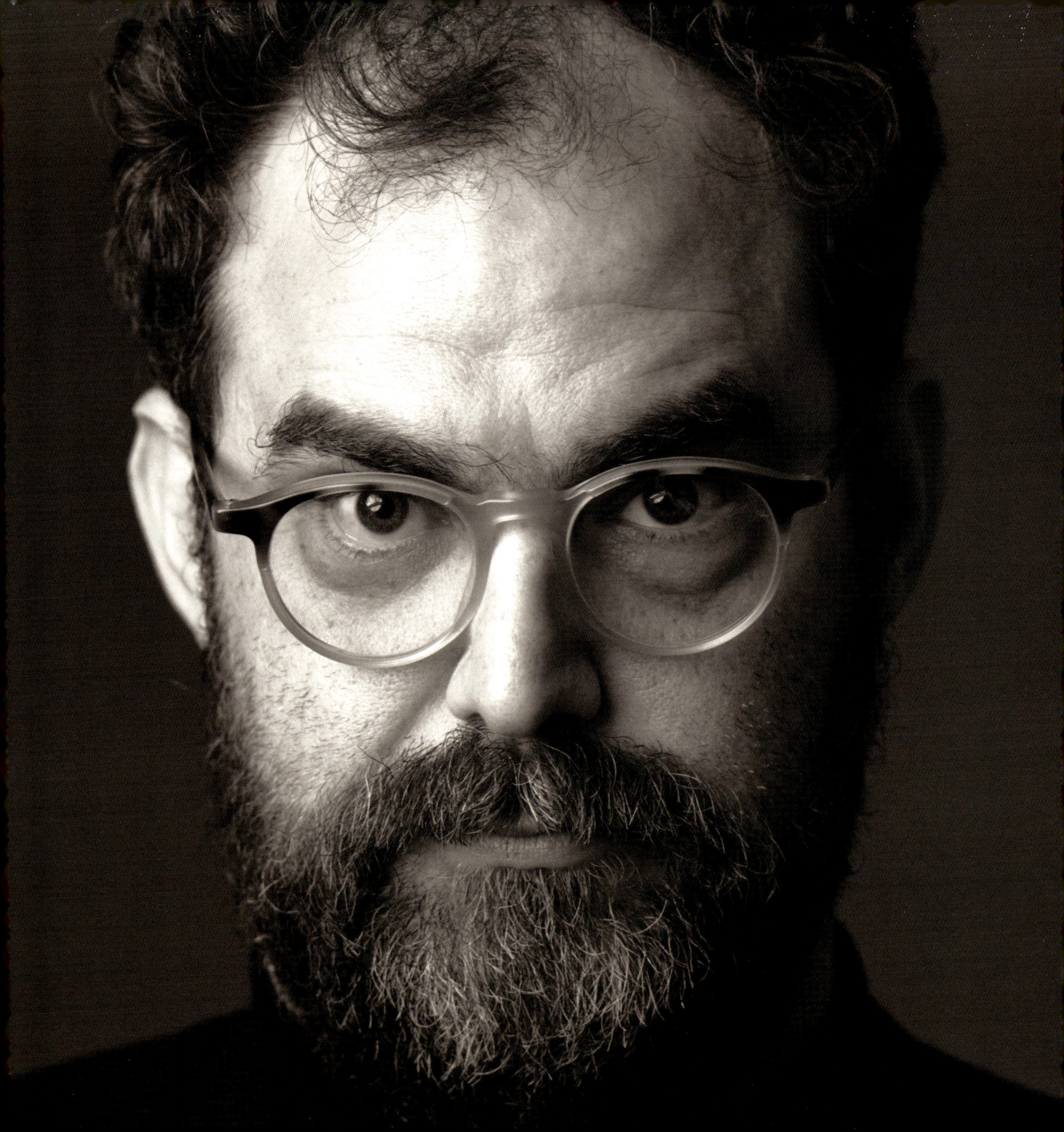

DECEPTIVE SIMPLICITY

An Introduction by Alexandra C. Anderson

Susan Johann has assigned herself an ongoing project for which she is singularly well-prepared. This veteran photographer has been steadily photographing and interviewing playwrights since 1989. As a seasoned performer who began acting for stage and television when she was in her teens, creating portraits of the playwrights of the late 20th and early 21st centuries gradually became her particular obsession. She has documented a large number of those individuals who have crucially nourished the live theatre of our time.

As a portrait photographer, Johann is straightforward, self-effacing, precise. She works, believing that each detail—the subject's gaze, clothing, posture, hands, expression—provides the photographer with documentary and psychological insight into an individual and his or her larger relationship to the community and to audiences. Such purposeful vision produces the deceptive simplicity of a unified style. Her portraits are also immensely sympathetic and revealingly intimate. The result is a record of the specific character of the individuals who stubbornly compose drama's quirky corps of living writers.

American playwriting has possessed a vigor, reach, and range that could well be one of the antidotes we need to help save us from the consequences of being force-fed the entertainment industry's latest merchandising ploy and the clever amateur distractions of YouTube. More than ever, it is vitally important to pay attention to individual creative visions that break through the sleek monotony and trivialization of contemporary culture.

Playwrights are a special breed within the community of writers. Johann seeks to record what is essential about each of her subjects. She enables us to see how each individual is very different within a shared profession. At a moment when unceasing celebrity-wooing and the stasis of the red carpet has more and more photographers acting as court lackeys who package manipulated images of pasteboard pop-culture icons, Johann's fine series of portraits of playwrights—some familiar faces, some nearly forgotten legends, and mostly faces unfamiliar to the public at large—are oxygen in a very stuffy room.

Alexandra C. Anderson is an art and photography critic and a longtime editor who lives and works in New York City and Kinderhook, New York. Formerly the art editor of the *Village Voice*, senior editor of *Smart Magazine*, executive editor of *American Photographer*, and editor in chief of *Art & Antiques Magazine*, she is completing a biography of Baron Adolph de Meyer. An earlier version of this piece appeared in *The Argonaut*, © 2014.

William Finn (opposite)

WHAT WE WERE, WHAT WE ARE

A Dialogue with Marsha Norman and Christopher Durang

People are born with an uncanny ability to read faces. Often a face speaks to us more clearly than words—we can read the emotions. But then many of us spend our adulthoods learning to mask emotion until it is automatic. Unmasking is the job of the portraitist.

It was my great pleasure in November 2013 to sit down with Pulitzer Prize winner Marsha Norman and Tony Award winner Christopher Durang, who together run the Juilliard playwriting program, and share with them the many faces that have been captured in the twenty-five years since I began this series in 1989 with Chris, the first playwright photographed for the series. I brought out a mock-up of the book as we sat at a conference table at Juilliard and immediately they got caught up looking at pictures. I watched them as they responded to the portraits. And we spoke about the series.

I recently read that Tennessee Williams said of photography that it was "frozen literature." Certainly the pictures were frozen moments that took us all back to the years when they and their compatriots had come before my camera.

MN: I remember people the way they looked when I first met them.

SJ: So do I. And you two. You look just the same to me.

MN: I didn't ever know what Neil LaBute looked like.

SJ: Is it important to know what these people look like?

MN: It is.

SJ: What does it mean?

MN: Playwrights don't, in general, take bows at the ends of performances.

CD: That's true.

MN: So even people who have been following Charles Mee for a long time might not know—except from some shot in a newspaper maybe—what he actually looked like.

CD: This is a beautiful photo of Charles Mee and he looks like a Biblical figure or an Abraham Lincoln.

MN: Mm-hmm.

CD: There's something very elegant and smart about his face in this photo. Seeing the photos and the faces that go with the names somehow "finishes" our knowledge of playwrights. We may know—or feel we know—something about them from their work but not what the faces and auras suggest. Yeah, it's just nice to see what they look like. Oh, here's my shot. Or shots. First is despair apparently. The second—happy.

[Laughter.]

SJ: We were talking about the time somebody stopped somebody from getting married or something. That was my part of the conversation. That's what we were sharing—the alcoholism in our families—in my family and in your family. That and interfering relatives.

CD: So I just did those two different faces, or did you say –?

SJ: No, I never tell anybody what to do.

CD: So that was me? Okay. My pictures look like the comedy-tragedy mask. But done unconsciously.

SJ: Tina Howe was nervous about having her picture done, because she said her mother told her every day that she was not beautiful. I said to Tina, "I want one gesture that tells me how you feel right now." And that is what she did.

CD: Wow.

SJ: Yeah.

CD: The very first time I met Tina was when her play *The Art of Dining* was at the Public Theater. And it hadn't opened yet. I went because I'd gotten to be friends with Dianne Wiest at the O'Neill when she was there in my play *A History of American Film*. And she was playing what I will call the "Tina" role in *The Art of Dining*. It's one of my favorite characters ever. It's this young woman who's written short stories and someone wants to publish them. But as played by Dianne she is just so shy and she talks too softly to be heard. And she does things like drop her lipstick into the soup. And when he says, "Your writing is beautiful," she's like, "Oh, no, no, no." And it's this marvelous character. Tina putting her hands to her face is just like that character.

SJ: Do you think that seeing these now, years later, alters the way you look at them?

MN: Yep. I think it's also a family of writers. And I think we think of ourselves very much as a sometimes crabby but deeply loving family. You know we're not all crazy about each other but we certainly do know what it's cost us to do this work and you can see it.

SJ: Talking about playwrights as a group, are they different from other writers?

MN: Wildly different. I think it's because we are subject to criticism that is often so vicious and personal and destructive. Poets know that they can never make a living so they're always going to end up in universities. And in the great competitive struggle of university departments they can survive. We realize from the beginning of our careers that we are under siege. There are so few of us that even if we sometimes don't care for each other's plays or even a particular play, we'll actually be very careful, as a rule, be very careful about what we say. We will support other writers because we are family.

SJ: How does that affect what you say to each other?

MN: We'll say things like, "I just thought that moment in Act 2 where he does the whatever was really fabulous." And without having to say, "I was asleep for the rest of it but that moment in Act 2 was really great." And we're very generous about going to see the work. I think we see more plays than novelists read novels. And we keep up with each other in a weird kind of multi-branched sort of way. I mean I'll know through Tina that So-and-So and So-and-So are okay. Or if somebody's having trouble I will hear it from somebody else.

CD: I really didn't get to know Lanford [Wilson] until the last couple of years of his life. The students—the acting students at Juilliard—were doing several plays of his. *Talley's Folly* was one. He visited our playwriting class and told wonderful stories, some of them a little risqué, I must say. But very honest. And then he had to wait half an hour before his ride was bringing him back to Long Island. I stayed and had a nice chat with him. Maybe that's where it got risqué now that I think of it.

[Laughter.]

CD: But he was very charming and also—well, actually, shared with me that he'd been sober for about fifteen years. And that was a big deal since I grew up with so much alcoholism in my family. One of the things about chatting with Lanford—when he was talking to the students—is his work at Caffé Cino. That was their ground for growing. It was very full of artists and wonderfulness, but not in any way practical. Meaning you couldn't make a living there. But you could write and be seen.

SJ: But what about the new writers? You've been teaching here, Chris was saying, for twenty years. Are you seeing that the students now are bringing in very different kinds of work or are plays still about the conflict of what's going on in society and what's going on in the family?

MN: No, young plays are still young plays. They're still looking for: "What was the matter with my home? Why didn't they give me what I needed or recognize who I was? Why didn't they love me the way I needed to be loved? How am I going to survive when I don't have what I need?"

SJ: How is technology affecting the theater? Are we getting a different kind of theater because of this? Or are plays being written for us to watch in a live space still?

MN: Well, certainly comedies are. Comedies are still being written. Some of our people who have been more serious have had more difficulty getting their work done. The good news is that writers now have more choice. They don't have to make such big decisions about how to support themselves because they can go to TV for a while and then come back to the theater and go back and forth for the middle of their careers. The film industry is by and large closed to playwrights, which is why it's so dull. That's why there aren't many great films—because they're not hiring playwrights to write them. But it's also why there's so much great television. It's practically run by playwrights now.

CD: You know it's really true movies have changed—I remember in recent years when I would go to the movies to see something, particularly if it was in the summer, I would see a movie I wanted to see but then they had coming attractions, about five of them, and some were about super heroes and some were violent and some were gross out comedies—I found being trapped with these trailers really depressed me. The films seemed aimed at fourteen-year-old boys.

MN: [Marsha turns to Chris.] Of course, I'm interested in what your response to this question is. Have the plays changed that people bring us?

CD: I guess I don't think they've changed. It can sound boring to say but family stuff just doesn't go away. And one of the things that Marsha says in class that I like is, "You need to write the story that only you can tell." And it doesn't mean only one person gets to talk about the family and then nobody else. But there are real specifics that only come from you.

SJ: Are there as many students now as there were twenty years ago? Or more people who want to be in this profession?

MN: We certainly get about the same number of applications as we used to, which is around three to four hundred a year. They are generally at a higher level than they used to be. We can take four and five kids from a group of three or four hundred. There's still a great interest. I'm thrilled by the class we have this year. It's very, very brainy and yet—oh, I don't know—a little nutty, a little goofy. But they're very, very smart. One of the other big differences that we've really noticed then and now: many more women have a better chance of being produced—as opposed to none, which was the case when I was coming up. Not enough women are being produced, but the percentage is better than it was.

CD: Oh, that makes me think of Wendy Wasserstein. I met her at Yale and we were close. She smiled so much in life, but I loved the "head-in-the-hand" despairing look you found in her. Day to day she was ebullient, but she did have another overwhelmed side, too. And, of course, Wendy and Marsha and Beth [Henley] all came to prominence as writers at the same time.

MN: Unfortunately, these great women writers we are training will still have to fight to get their plays on the main stage, instead of being consigned to the dustbin of readings and workshops. But their work is staggeringly good.

SJ: So the struggle for productions for women is marginally less overwhelming but still continues. And the great women writers keep coming. Maybe the theatre isn't dead?

CD: I do remember when I was in high school and I'd read the articles in the *New York Times* about "Is theatre dead?" And then they'd still ask that question in my twenties and again in my thirties. So actually once we started teaching here, I started to see students who really wanted to be playwrights. And I thought, "I don't know. I think the live experience is going to continue. There are too many smart young people who still want to write for the living stage." Unless the world comes to an end.

* * *

The world having not yet come to an end, we have a moment to contemplate the faces of the members of this tribe, if not to "finish" our understanding of them, perhaps to advance it, perhaps to thank them for keeping the theatre alive. I am reminded again of the interview with Tennessee Williams where he speaks of the photographer, Imogen Cunningham.

> *All that we have—all that we want—is ephemeral, brief. What we try to do, what we hope to do, is capture it for others and for ourselves. We want and we need to look back and look at something and know what happened, what mattered, what we were, what we are.*[1]

1 Tennessee Williams in conversation with James Grissom, author of *Follies of God: Tennessee Williams and the Women of the Fog*, Alfred Knopf, 2015.

AUGUST WILSON

(1945–2005—American playwright, writer of the ten-play series The Pittsburgh Cycle, *which won two Pulitzer Prizes for Drama and a Tony Award for Best Play.)*

"Her name was Nancy Arlen and Nancy Arlen was the kind of seventh grader that even the third grade boys were in love with. I started writing the poems for Nancy Arlen and leaving them on her desk. From that point on, for the rest of my life, I've written poems for Nancy Arlen. Only her name kept changing and I've since learned to put my name to them."

In repose, August Wilson is positively leonine. It is when he speaks that the face softens and we see the poet behind the warrior.

August Wilson was never one to bow his head. He was the only black student at Central Catholic High School in Pittsburgh, and he ended up in continual fights. "Many a time the principal sent me home in a cab to protect me. I could hold my own against four or five but I couldn't fight the whole school. One day when he sent me home I said to hell with it."

He tried trade school. A teacher pushed him hard enough to knock him off his chair, "I got up, put his head through a blackboard and that was when I left there."

"All the time I'm leaving my neighborhood and going to Catholic school and leaving my neighborhood and going to trade school and directly across the street, absolutely across, is the high school. So I started going to public school. Here I am in tenth grade knowing stuff we did in eighth grade in Catholic school. I found that boring. So this teacher said to write a paper on an historical personage. I said, alrighty, I'll have some fun with this. I decided to write on Napoleon because of Victor Hugo's expression 'Napoleon's will to power.' My sister typed it up, a twenty-page paper, and I turned it in. The teacher brought me up in front of the rest of the class and said he didn't believe I had written it. I didn't feel I had to convince him. He gave me a failing grade, and I took the paper, tore it up, threw it in his wastebasket and walked out. I said to hell with it. I walked out of school and I just never went back."

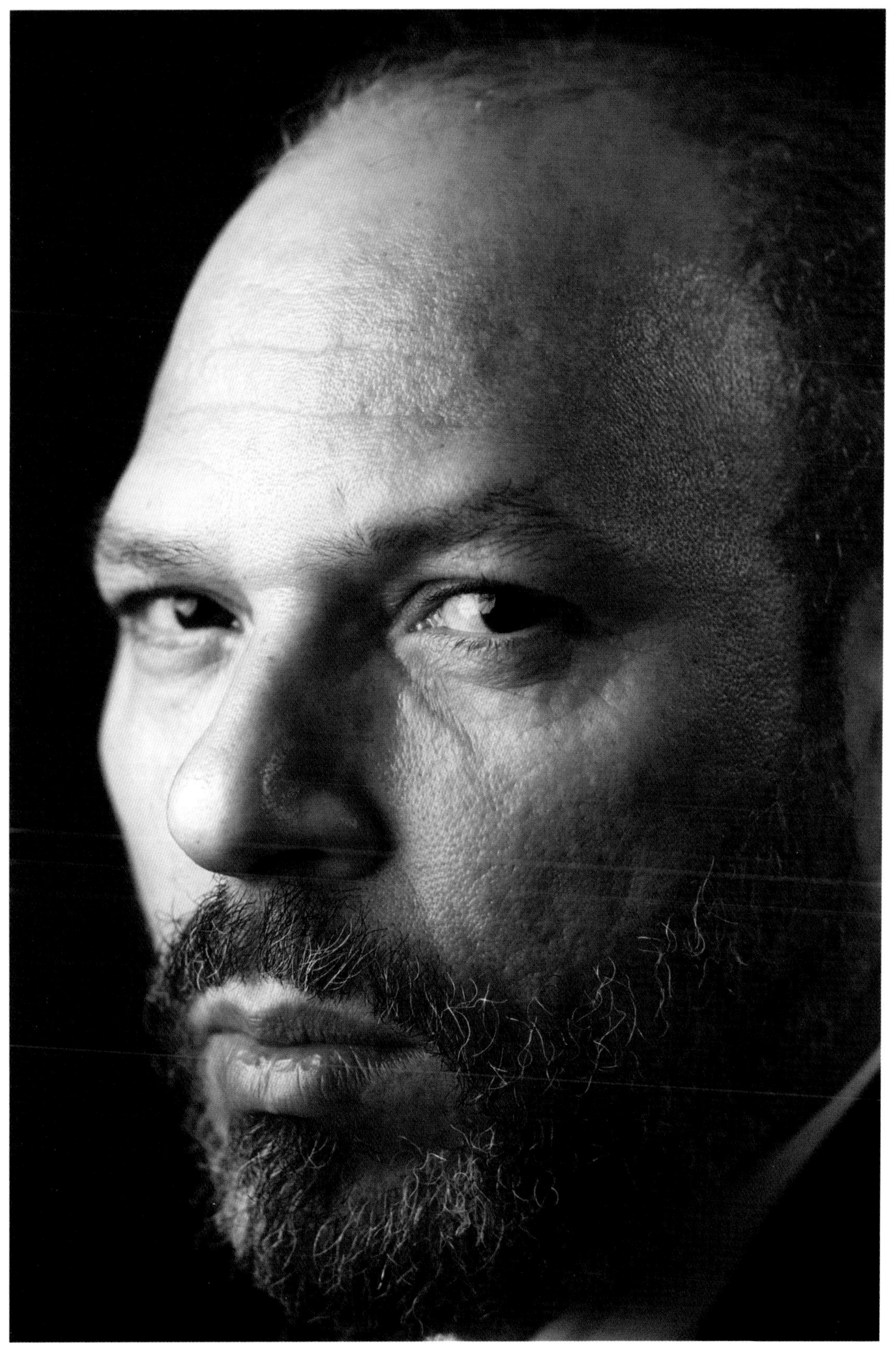

Afraid to tell his mother, August spent months leaving the house and going to the library during school hours. When he finally told her, she just said, "Get a job, you have to do something." He worked for a landscape gardener, at a dairy, and at restaurants, "wherever I could find a job actually."

His sister was the first person to hire him as a writer. She sent him twenty dollars to write her paper for a class at Fordham University on two poets. "I took Robert Frost and Carl Sandburg. I spent the twenty dollars all in one place and bought an old Royal typewriter. I didn't have bus fare home. I got home and I was living in this basement and I put it down on the table. A-U-G. . . . I typed my name, to see how it looked. I'm a writer now, I thought, plus I had just spent this twenty dollars so I'd better be a writer."

He gathered up three of his best poems and sent them to *The Atlantic Monthly*, thinking, "This editor's going to want to see these other two hundred poems I got." When, a few days later, the poems came back in the mail, he sat down and thought, "'Oh, this is serious.' And this has been my reaction to any rejection—'Oh, I see. These are very good, the best I can write, but I'll just have to do better. I've got a lot to learn and the next time I send one out it's not coming back.'"

In 1968, in the middle of the Black Power movement, he started a theatre troupe in Pittsburgh. He liked the idea of "politicizing the community and raising consciousness." It went well. A friend wrote a play and August directed it. "Then I tried to write a play but I couldn't write a play because I couldn't write dialogue." He asked his friend, "How do you make 'em talk?" The friend said, "You don't, you listen." Seven or eight years later, when he moved from Pittsburgh to St. Paul, "I began to listen to them. I couldn't hear the voices I had grown up around all my life for being in the midst of them."

In St. Paul, he worked for the first time in script form, adapting Northwest Indian tales for a troupe of actors at the science museum. He still didn't consider himself a playwright. But after he won a fellowship for his play *Jitney* at the Playwrights Center in St. Paul, he found himself in a room with sixteen other playwrights. "It was very important for me to claim it. I was sitting in the chair, the same chair that O'Neill and Tennessee Williams and Ibsen and Miller sat in. I felt, 'This is great, these guys had a piece of blank paper in front of them, they had to figure out what to write, how to get the characters on the stage. The same problems confronted them as confront me.' And I felt empowered by it."

He sent *Jitney* to the O'Neill Center twice. "And they sent it back twice and it was like getting the poems back . . . what is it I need to learn?" When he sent *Ma Rainey's Black Bottom* they didn't send it back. "If they had accepted the other play, it wouldn't have been as good."

Ma Rainey's Black Bottom went to the Yale Repertory Theatre and to critical acclaim in a Broadway production. His two Pulitzer Prize winners, *Fences* and *The Piano Lesson*, followed the same route. At the time of our interview, Wilson's broad agenda was to write a play for every decade of Black history in the United States, following Baldwin's call for "a profound articulation of the Black tradition," an epic task he set himself on which he worked fiercely for the rest of his life. "I've marked out a ground that I can stand on as a playwright—to show the manners and ritual intercourse Baldwin spoke of that are capable of offering sustenance to the Black American when they go out in the world.

"Since I don't come from a theatre background and I don't know so much about theatre, I've not been influenced by theatre per se. I have what I call my four Bs: Romare Bearden, the artist; Amiri Baraka (until he went into Marxism); the writer Jorge Luis Borges; and the Blues, which is the largest influence. It's the best poetry we have. The music provides you an emotional reference and a cultural response to the world."

August Wilson wrote in bars and restaurants. "It's an old habit from when I was a twenty-year-old poet. You can't, as a twenty-year-old poet, sit at home—you've got to go out and find out about the world. It's the only way I know how to do it. I just take my tablet and go to a bar or restaurant, drink coffee. Maybe the music is playing, maybe a couple come in and charge the atmosphere. But I don't put any obligations on myself. If it feels like I should do something then I do something. Maybe fifteen minutes, maybe half an hour. When it's played itself out, I go up the street to the next bar and repeat the same thing. Then I go home and type it up. Sometimes it's not good stuff, but the initial, seminal stuff is really important. It's really what I want to say so I never throw it out.

"Part of learning about writing is learning how to distinguish your good stuff from your bad stuff. I write some perfectly awful stuff, but ideally no one ever sees it. Somebody asked, 'You write bad lines?' Are you kidding! I write bad scenes, I mean, whole scenes that just don't work, that just don't build, the people don't sound right. If you can recognize them, they won't end up in the play."

When asked to talk more about his ways of working, he responded, "I do things that I'm not conscious of but I'm conscious of the need to do them. So when in *Piano Lesson* Willie Boy walks in and says Sutter fell down the well, it's a surprise to me because I don't know who Sutter is and I have no idea he fell down a well. That's the unconscious part. Consciously I know I need something here in the scene that's going to propel this moment to another."

He said the prizes might have changed his life "but it hasn't changed me. I still consider myself a struggling playwright. I've still got to struggle to get it on the page. I'm still trying to write the best play that's ever been written—no, no, no—no, I'm not. I gave that up when I read a biography of Frank Lloyd Wright, who said, 'I don't want to be the best architect that has ever lived. I want to be the best architect that is ever going to live.' So now I sit down to write the best play that is ever going to be written. I found a way to up my stakes. I still don't have anything to lose. It's still just words on paper and if it doesn't work out, words are free. There are two things that you can always borrow—you can always find a napkin and say, 'Hey, can I borrow your pencil?'"

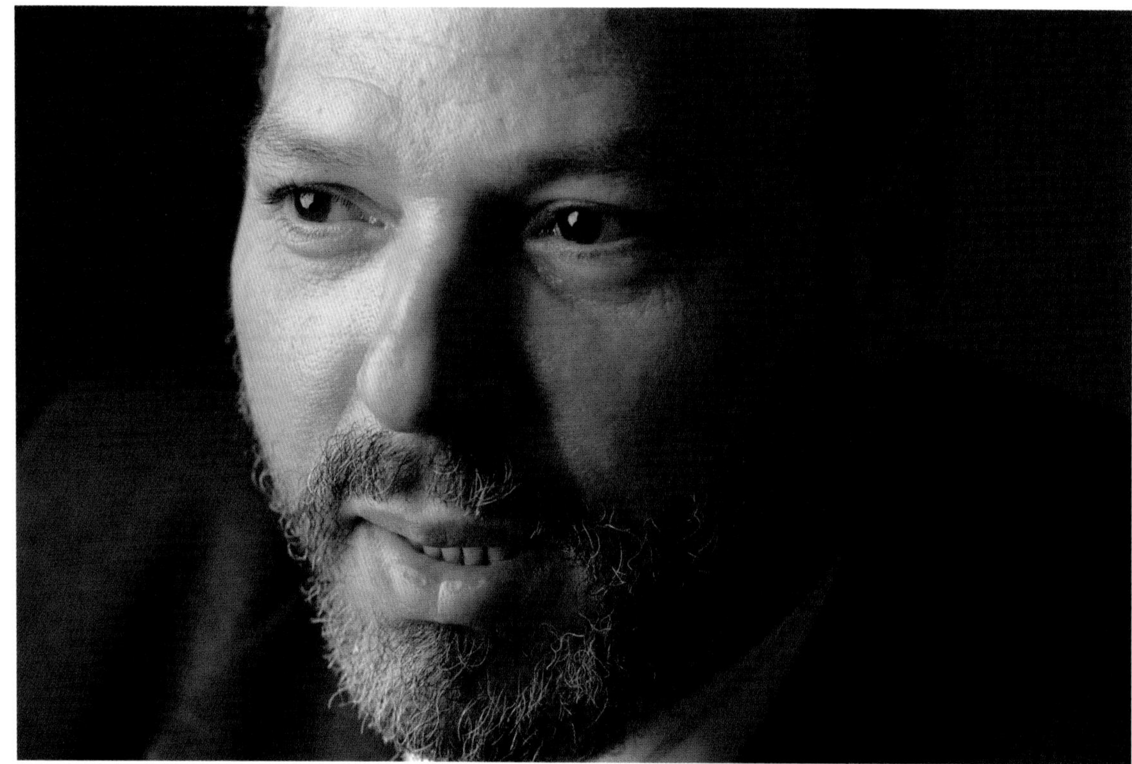

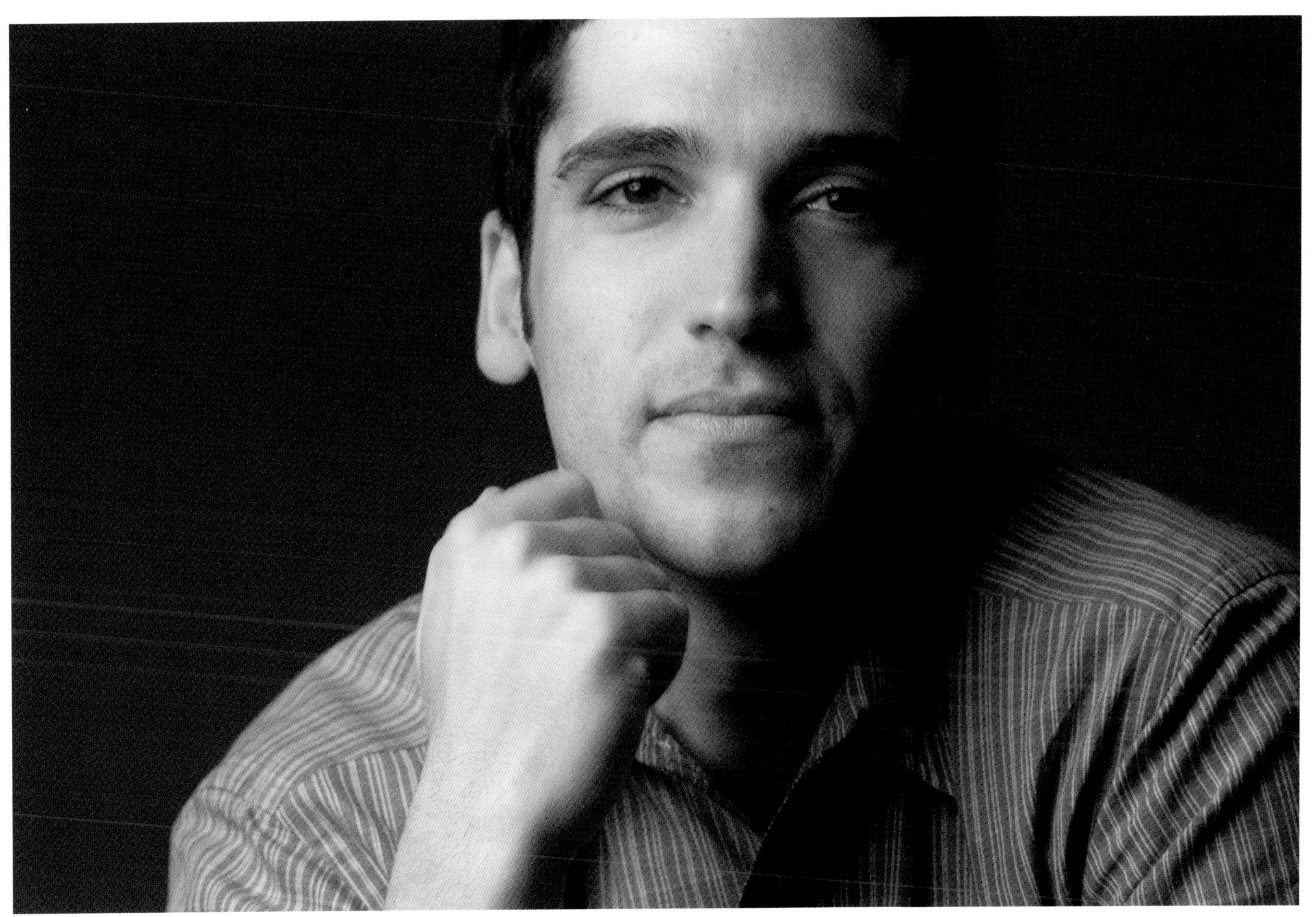

Steven Drukman

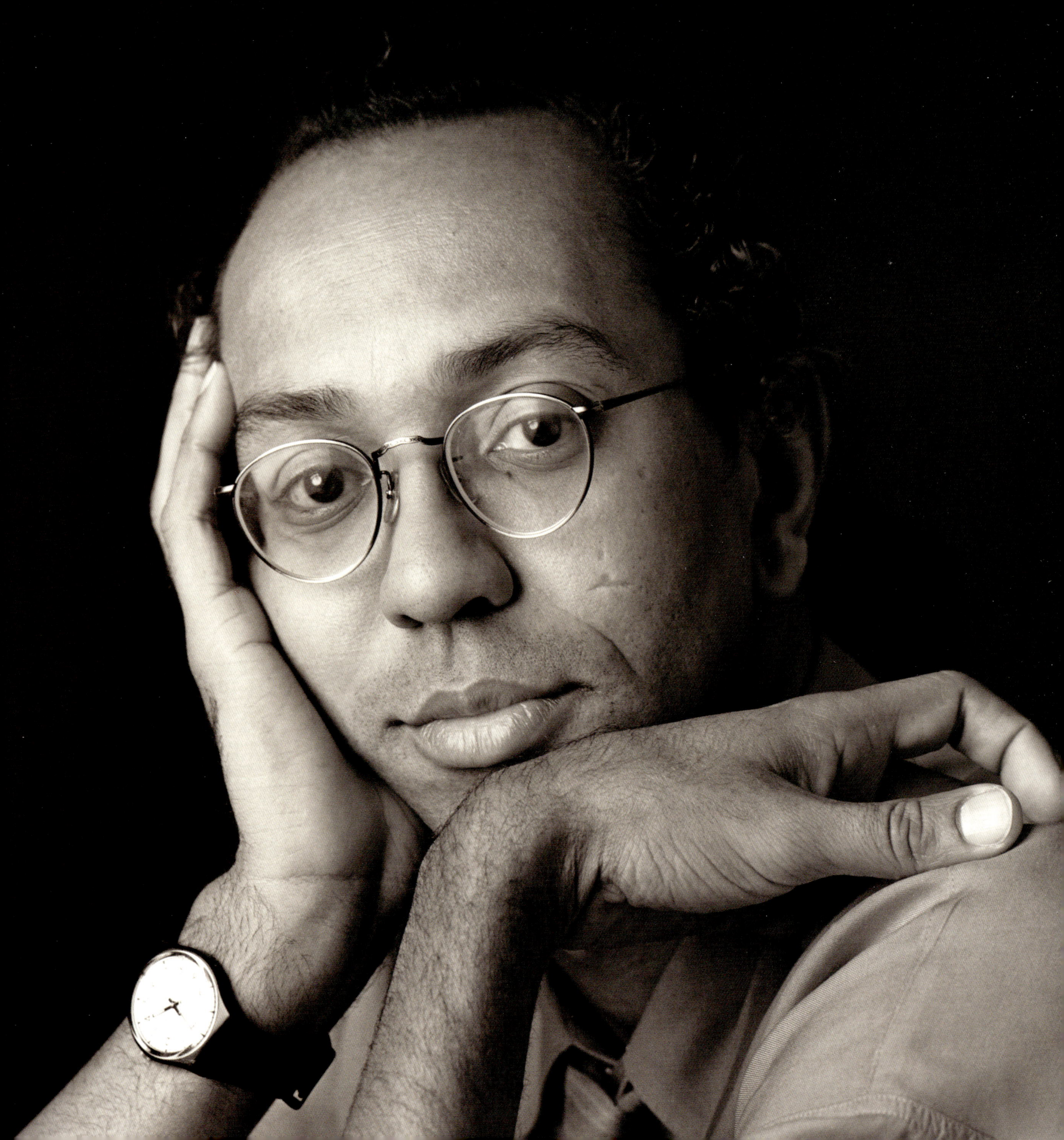

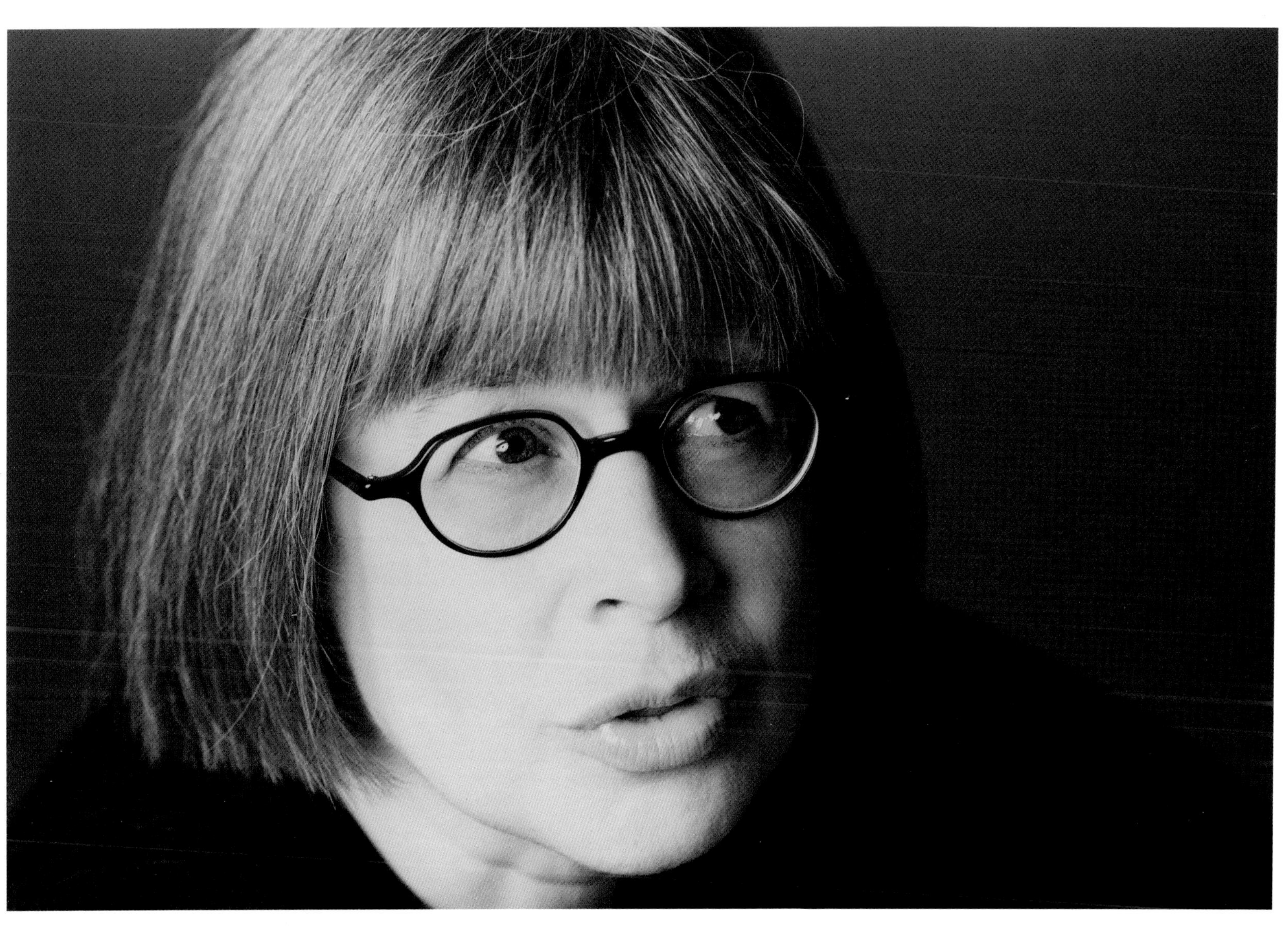

George C. Wolfe (opposite) — Polly Pen

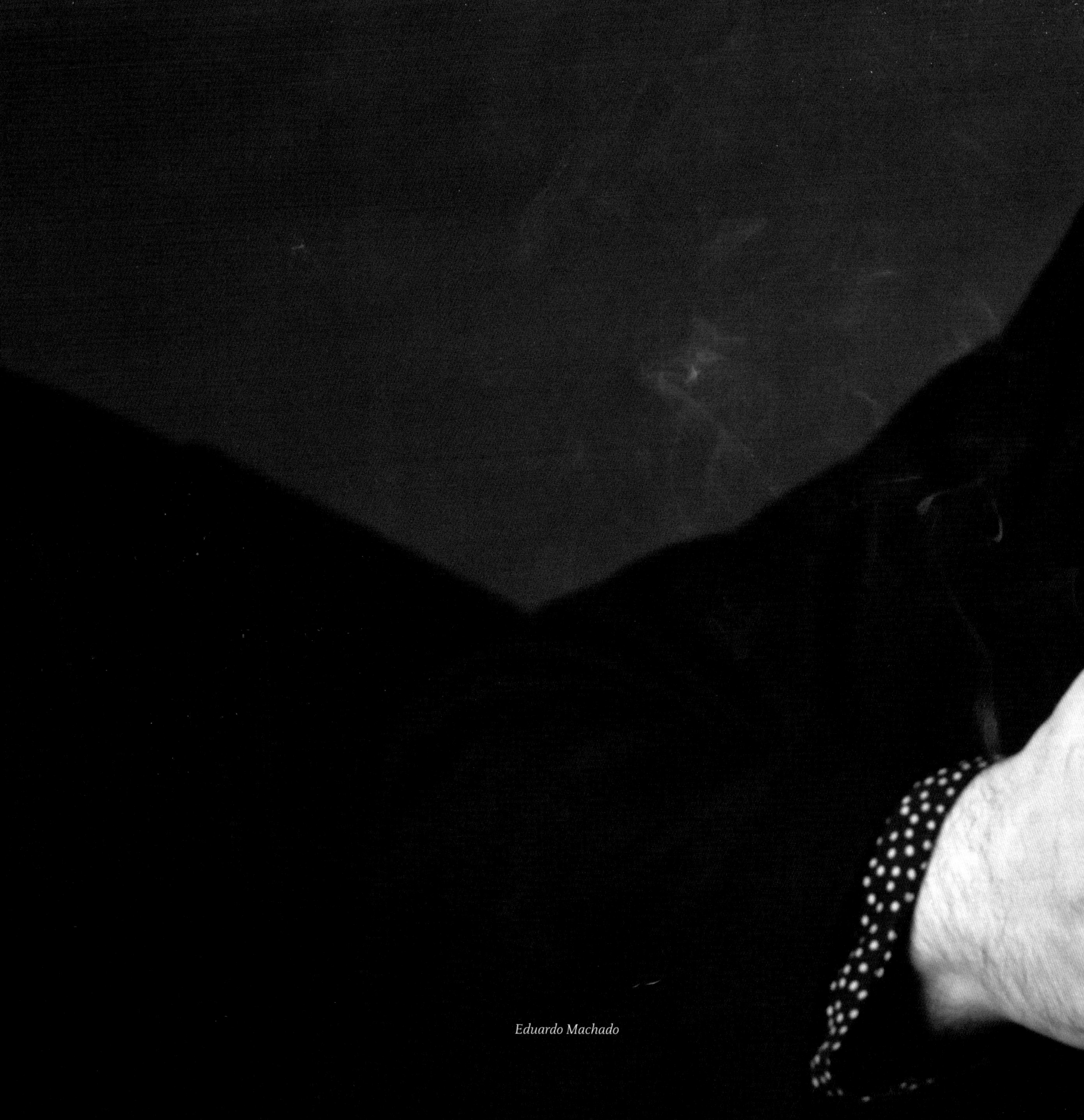

Eduardo Machado

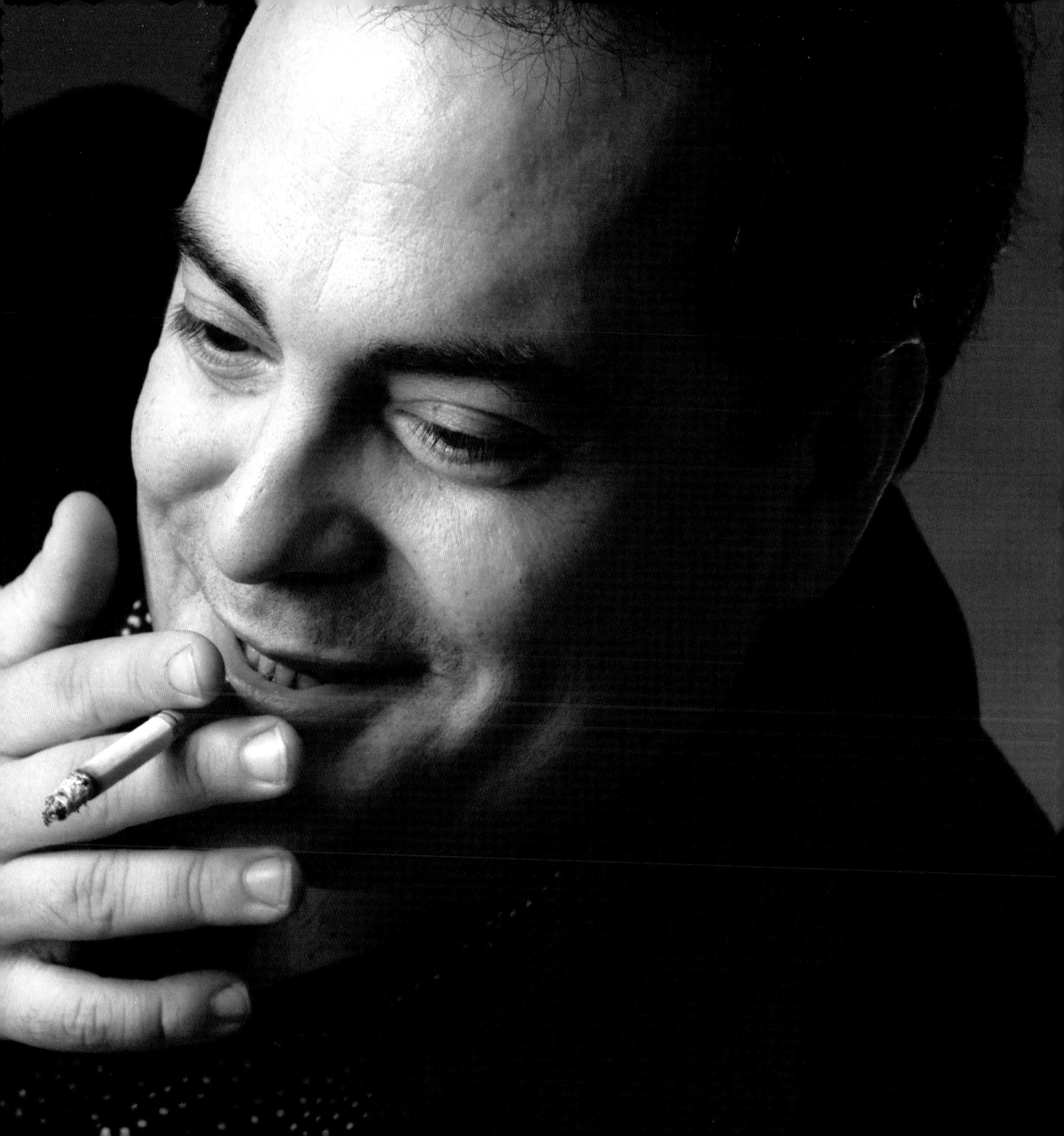

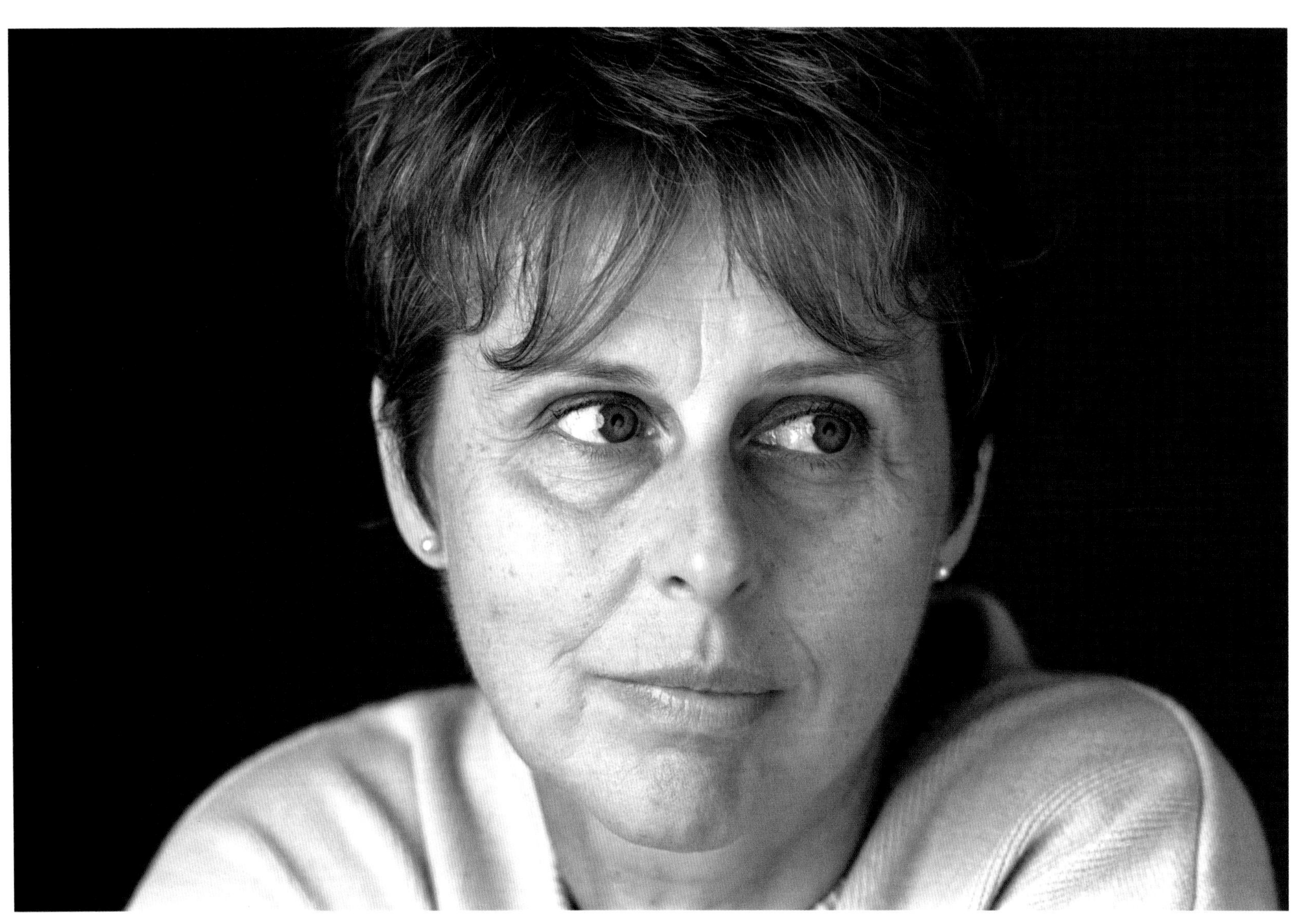

Sybille Pearson — Tom Stoppard (opposite)

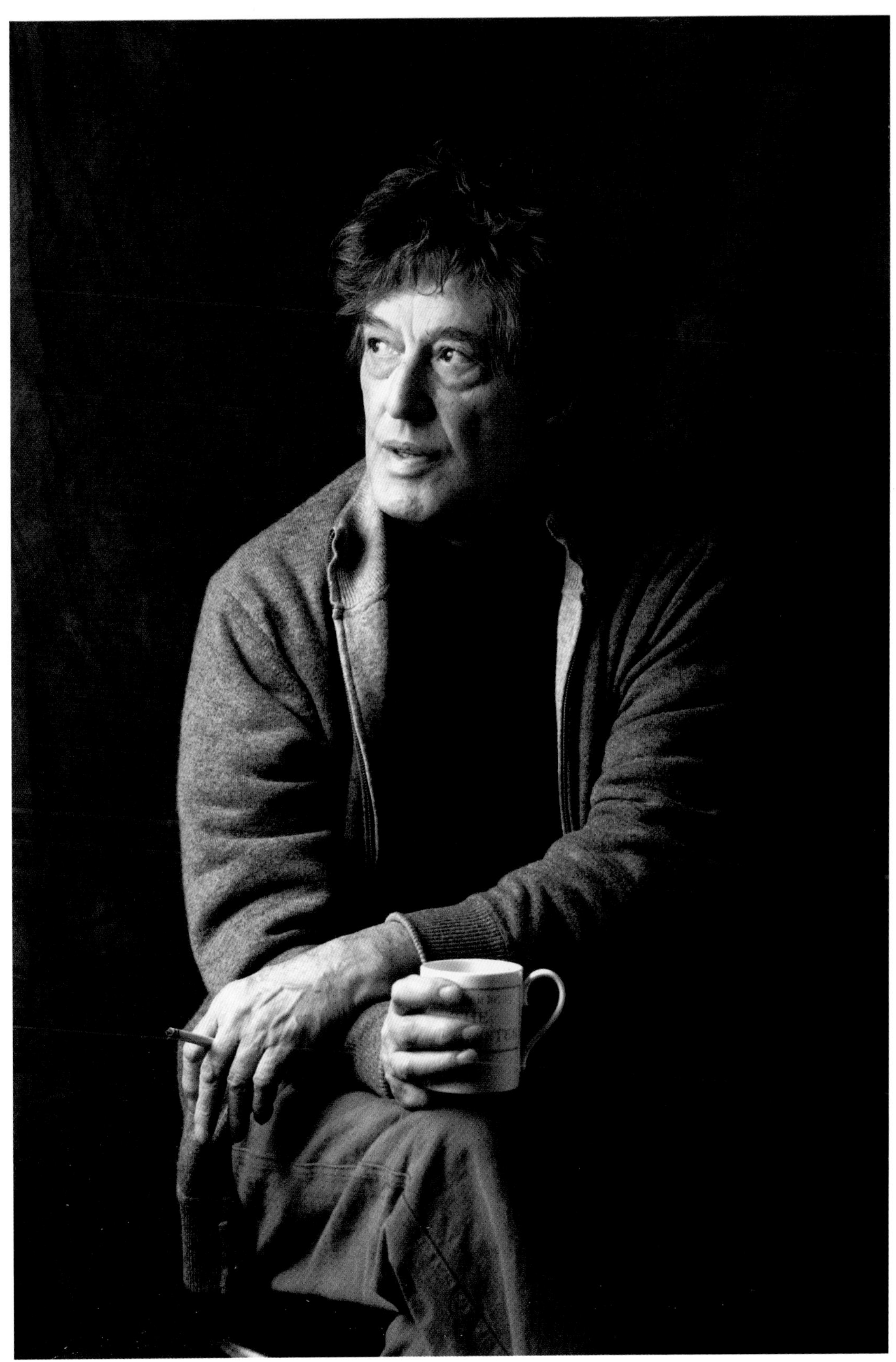

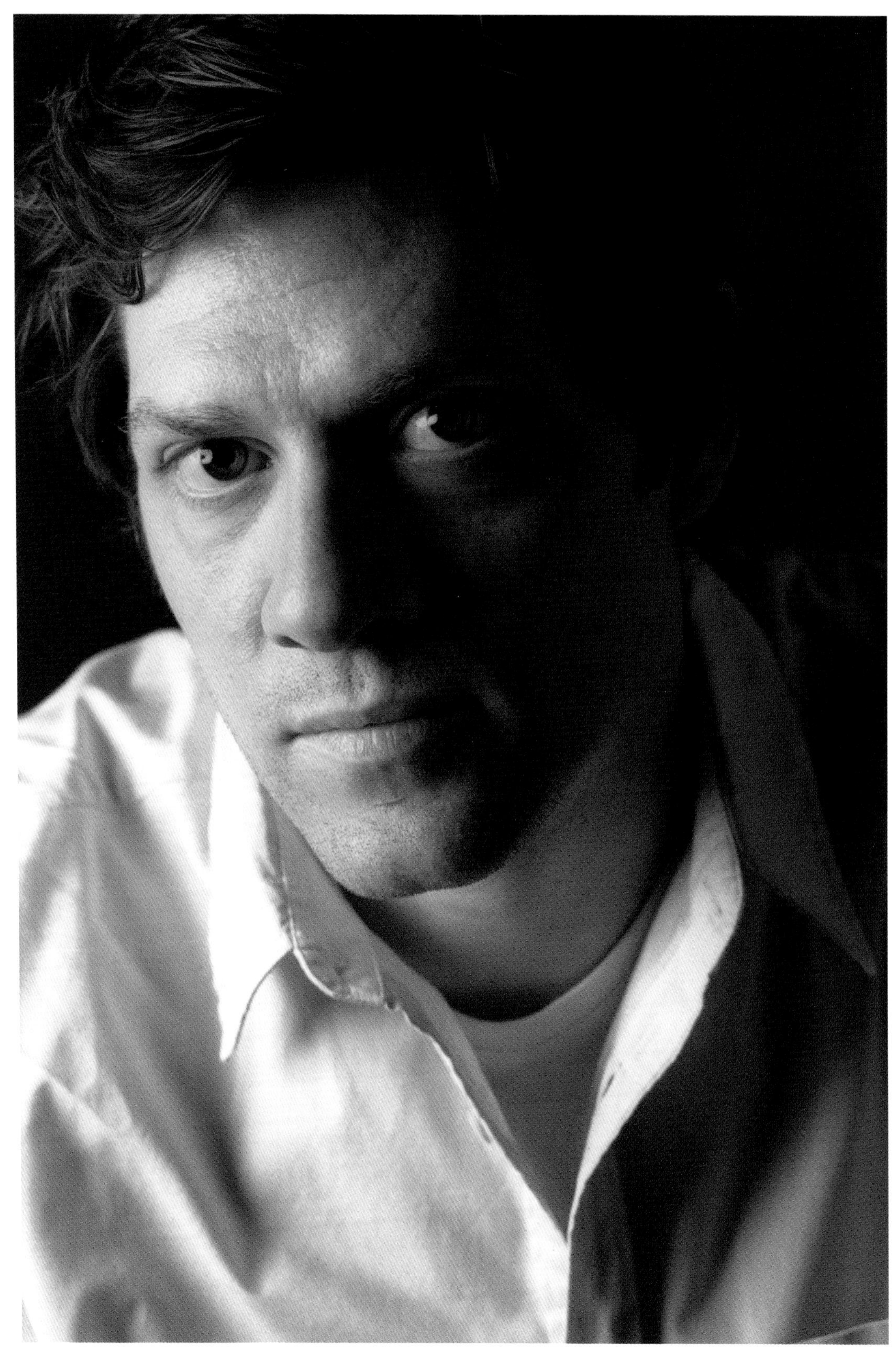

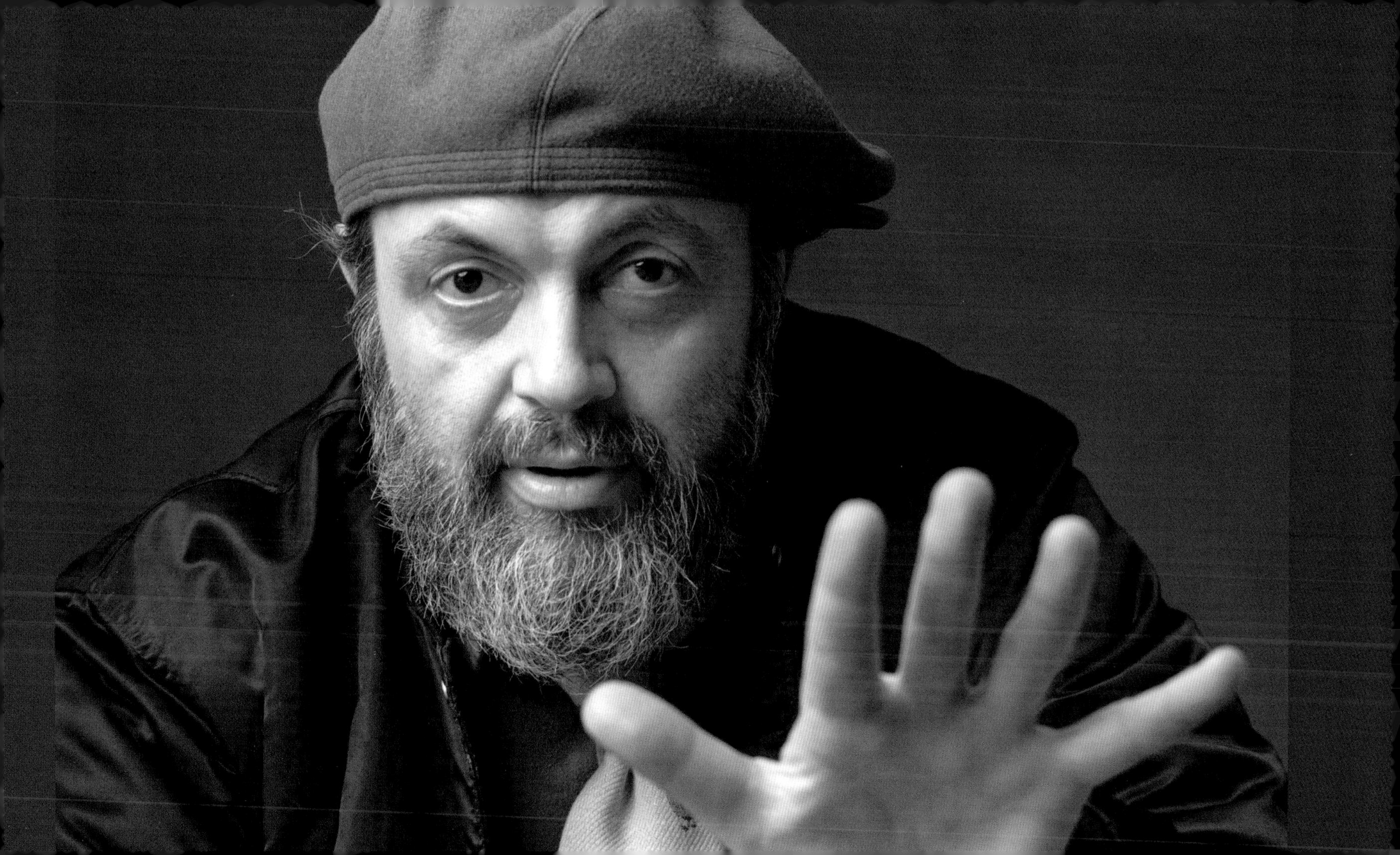

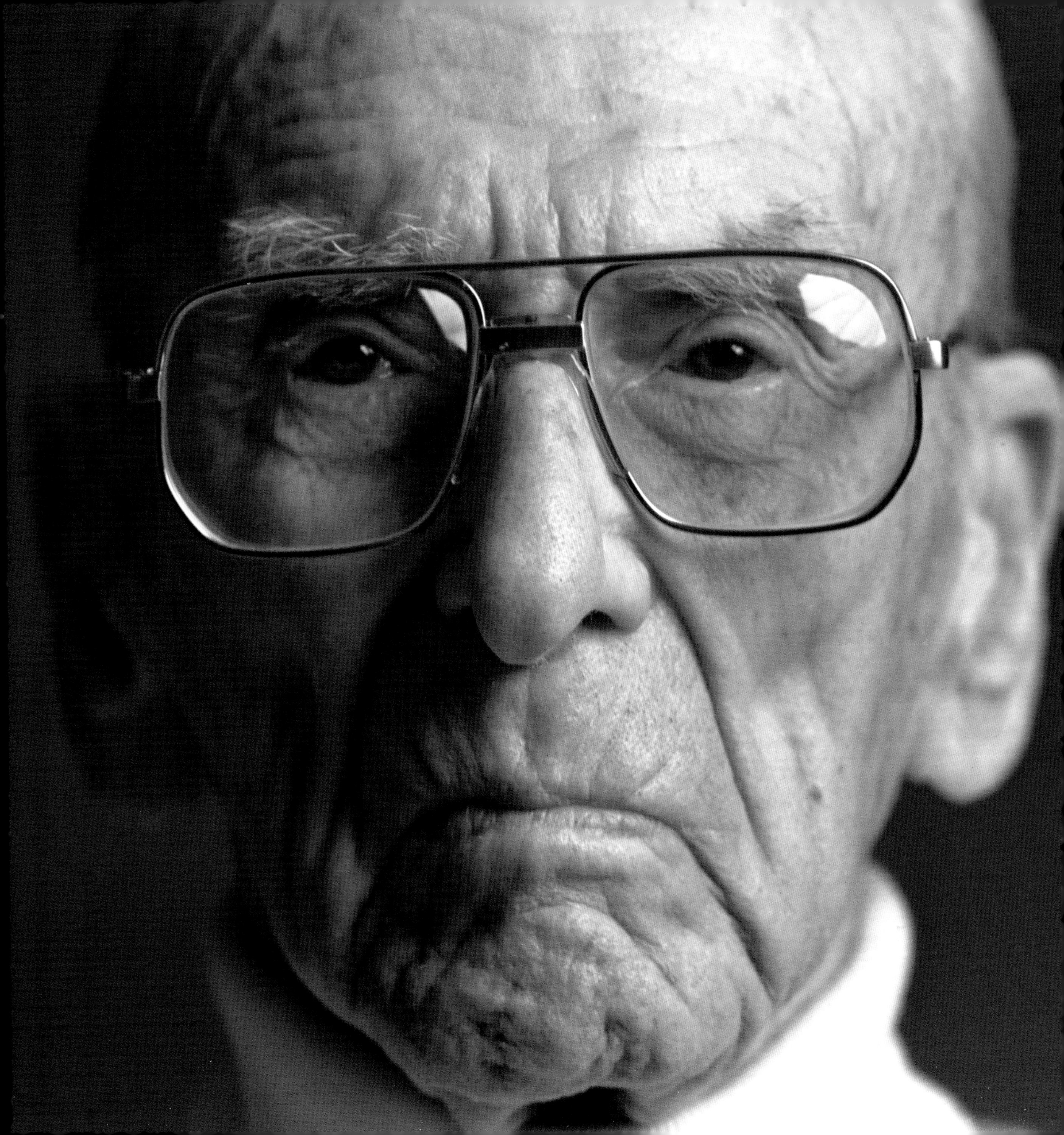

GEORGE ABBOTT

(1887–1995—American playwright, producer, director, screenwriter awarded the Pulitzer Prize and numerous Tony Awards, best known for Damn Yankees *and* The Pajama Game.*)*

Given that George Abbott was 104 years old in 1991 when I got the opportunity to photograph him and do an informal interview, I understood that I should go to the mountain. I drove upstate to his summer house in Merriewold, near Monticello, New York. He had been summering there for at least thirty years. George Abbott was already old—and still formidable—when I first met him in 1974, through my husband, Dallas Johann, who was working with him as assistant choreographer and lead dancer in the first mixed-race revival of one of Abbott's hits, *Pajama Game*, starring Cab Calloway, Barbara McNair, and Hal Linden.

Mr. Abbott, who was always called "Mister" Abbott by all but his closest friends, was napping on the screened porch when I arrived but was immediately alert when I was brought in to meet him. We chatted a few minutes and then moved inside and found a place in the living room to set the backdrop, lights, and cameras. We never stopped talking.

He was still writing daily but, like most writers, he didn't want to talk about his current work except to say it was a play about a woman taking her revenge after a gang rape. He worried about finishing it.

I wanted to know how he felt about his mortality. I told him, "I have every intention of living to 105 or maybe even 110. What do you think?"

"I don't think I'll live that long. I can see signs of weakness growing all the time, and my memory gets worse. I'd hate to get so bad with my eyes that I couldn't read. I'm reading but they tire."

There was talk of the coming millennium and a time capsule planted at Merriewold the summer before. Mr. Abbott put in a picture of himself that said, "This is me at 103."

He said, "It is not unthinkable that this earth could become uninhabitable. We know there could be another Ice Age. The atmosphere could change and create a hothouse. Maybe by that time we'll have discovered another place to live. A select few can take off and inhabit another world."

"Where would we go?"

"Well, they're still not sure about Mars. The only thing we know is . . . life *is* and almost always has been."

"And where do we go from here as individual souls? Do you think we go on, Mr. Abbott?"

"No. No, I think we have our eternal life in the fact that we leave the seed which will produce other humans, other trees, other things so that life goes on. But I don't think there is any heaven where we stand around and talk to the angels. It was easy to think that when we didn't know what was up there, when that was all a mystery from the tops of the mountains. It was easy to think there was another world up there. That was the basis of our present religious idea that heaven's up and hell is down. Evolution seems so easy to prove when you get a cliff where every strata shows different animals lived and changed and grew. I just think we become part of the whole of nature again." Mr. Abbott has always been a practical Yankee, with the soul of a witty theatrical alchemist. Some things don't change.

I wanted some pictures with Joy, his lovely and very much younger wife. When they posed together, the proximity of his wife, her presence in the frame, changed the tone of his conversation. "Nature is inevitable. You're born. You mature. You die. It's as simple as that." I kept taking pictures.

Joy said, "I just found out butterflies only live twenty-four hours."

I couldn't resist. "They say only the good die young. That's what they say, Mr. Abbott."

He knew I was teasing him. He was better at it. "That's what *somebody said*," emphasizing the singular and the past tense, "not *they say*."

Joy told us a story about Mr. Abbott on the golf course at ninety-three. He leaned down to pick up a tee and fainted. When he came to, he was lying on the grass with his head in Joy's lap. "George, just lay there," she said. "Someone's gone for help."

"It's *lie* there, Joy, not *lay* there."

According to his doctor, Mister Abbott needed a pacemaker. "How long do they last?' Mr. Abbott asked.

"George, I don't think you need worry. They last about ten years," the doctor told him.

Mr. Abbott had his pacemaker replaced exactly ten years later, when he was 103. I found him feisty and charming at 104. And he could be intimidating. I could not stop thinking of him as one of the great forces in musical theatre history—*Pal Joey* (1940), *Call Me Madam* (1950), *The Pajama Game* (1954), *Damn Yankees* (1955), *A Funny Thing Happened on the Way to the Forum* (1962). The list of shows with the Abbott stamp is now a century long. He won the Pulitzer Prize for the book of *Fiorello* and was known throughout the industry for his long career as a "show doctor"—the guy who comes in at the end of rehearsals and is a fixer, usually without credit except in the business itself.

In 1987, when he was 100 years old, he was in New York City (staying, appropriately enough, at the Algonquin Hotel) for the opening of a revival he had directed of his 1926 play, *Broadway*. He told a reporter from *People Magazine*, "I think I'm as excited as I was in 1926. It's the same play, but you never lose that anxiety. I'll still be in the audience watching—to see if people are reading their programs."

I was invited to come back to Merriewold the following week for lunch. I didn't tape that next visit. And now I'm sorry. He left us in 1995, at the age of 107. A visit with Mr. Abbott should be remembered in every detail. As Mr. Abbott, playwright, director, play-doctor, and theatrical wizard, knew, it's all in the details.

His 1995 *New York Times* obituary reads, "Mrs. Abbott said that a week and a half before his death he was dictating revisions to the second act of *Pajama Game* with a revival in mind. Last year, at a mere 106 years old, he walked down the aisle on opening night of the *Damn Yankees* revival and received a standing ovation. He was heard saying to his companion, 'There must be somebody important here.'"

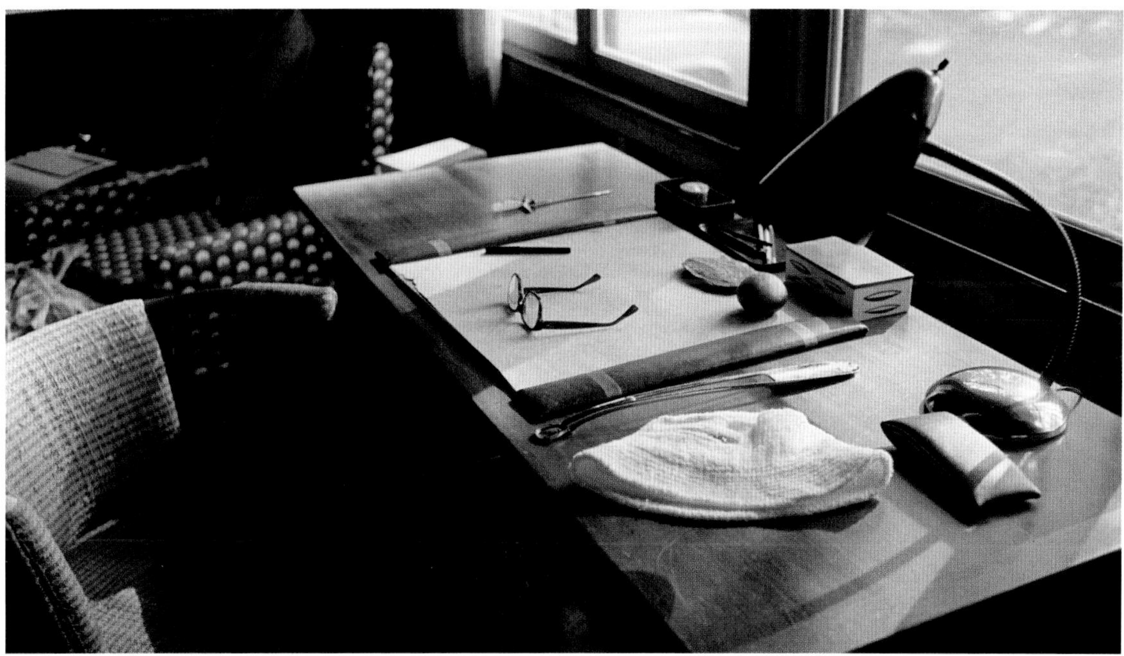

Abbott's desk

ROMULUS LINNEY

(1930–2011—American playwright and professor, member of the American Academy of Arts and Letters, winner of the Obie Award for Sustained Achievement in Playwriting, founding playwright of Signature Theatre Company.)

One of the playwrights I sought out initially was Romulus Linney. At the time of the interview, he had gone to Los Angeles to see his daughter, actress Laura Linney, perform at the La Jolla Playhouse, so we spoke by phone. We talked about his start in theatre and how he evolved as a playwright, a playwright whom Mel Gussow, then drama critic of the *New York Times*, praised as the "Poet of the American Heartland."

* * *

"Playwrights are connoisseurs of conflict. It starts as a child, as little kids, or maybe even infants. We look up and see giants on the verge of conflict. We remember those things and later reproduce them in our plays. Basically, plays are the looming of conflict and then suddenly the happening of some big conflict. That comes from very early memories. Katherine Anne Porter said that by age ten, a writer has learned everything he uses later on. She's right.

"As a child, most of the time what I did was read. There were rather meager library facilities in the little town where I lived so I grew up reading, as many American kids did, things off the drugstore rack—*Amazing Stories,* and Ellery Queen, and *Bomba, the Jungle Boy,* and *Tarzan,* and all that I'm not sure is such bad, early reading for a young person at all.

"I relished finding my own material so that later, when I studied Homer and Dante and Shakespeare, I wasn't afraid to say, 'Well, I like this and I don't like that and this.' It wasn't bad training.

"I was an actor first. I grew up in a suburb of Nashville called Madison. I used to watch my mother act in an amateur theater in Nashville. I would go to the rehearsals and I was in some children's plays. When I went to college, I just acted all the time and had a wonderful time. I loved it.

"I went to Oberlin College where there was a wonderful man who directed the plays. We didn't get a credit or anything like that, and we just did four plays a year, but we did Ibsen, and we did Shakespeare, and we did Shaw, and I loved being in those plays. I also did summer stock. Those were the dramatic influences.

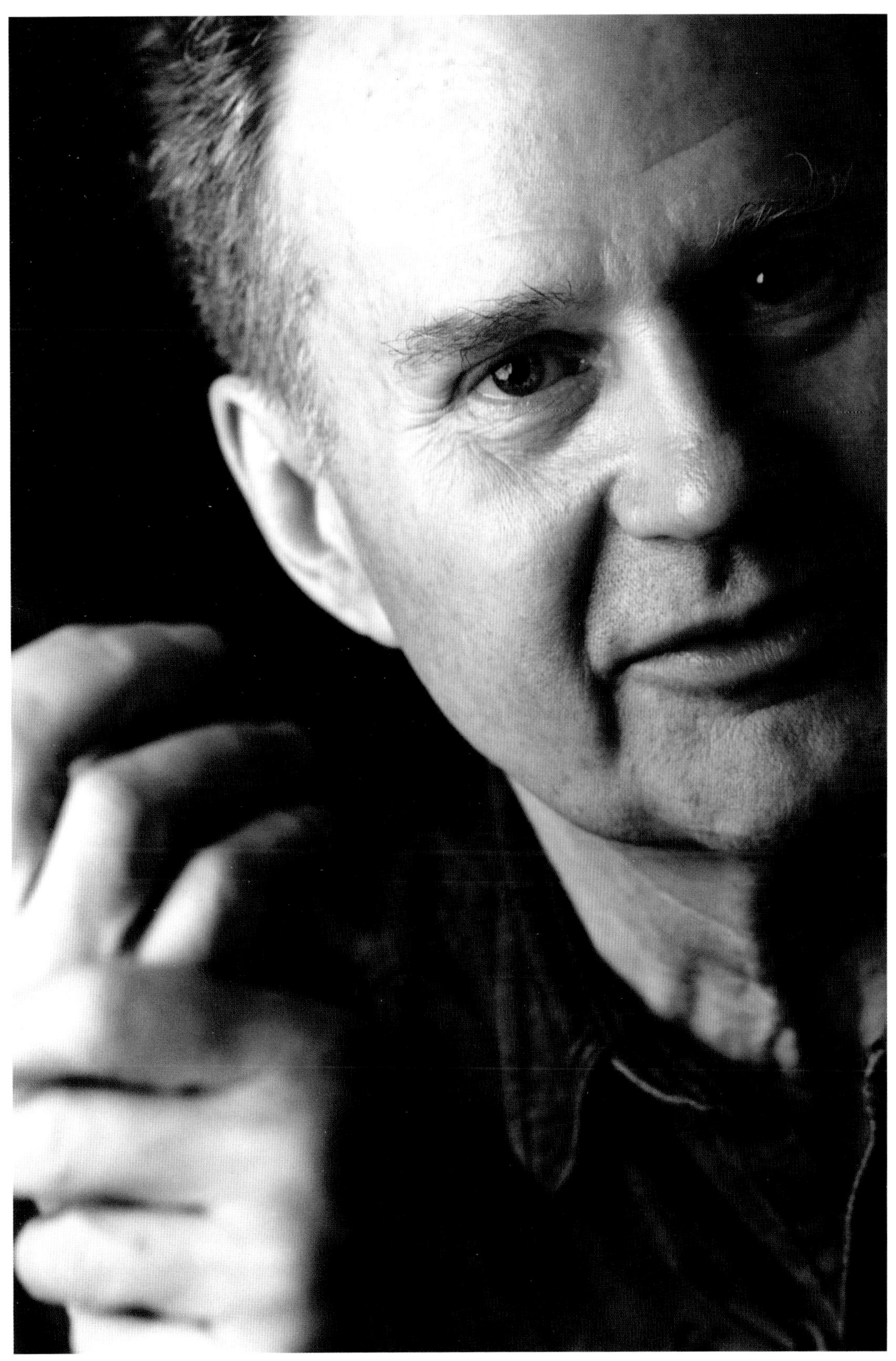

"I went to Yale Drama School to study acting for two years. After a year, I changed and became a director. Something was changing inside me.

"Then I left the theatre completely and said, 'Phooey,' and very painfully learned how to write. I published two novels not critically well-received and then wrote a play. From then on, I've been writing mostly plays.

"One of them is an historical play—about Frederick the Great. There's one about Byron. The play *Two* is about Goering at the Nuremberg trials. There's a one-act play about an Indian King—King Phillip. Another part of my work, equally important and maybe a little bit bigger now, is devoted to characters and situations from my Southern childhood. In those plays, my dialogue is at its best, my ear at its sharpest. These are the people who were my father's family and my mother's family so I relate to them very directly. The historical plays are equally emotional in their conception. I don't know if I could write a play that was not.

"Whenever I try to write a play that's a good idea, you know, like, 'This is a great theatre idea,' it never works out. I throw it away after a while. There is some kind of deep inner spring that psychologically feeds the idea, the dramatic conception, and when that's in operation, a play almost writes itself. When that's not in operation, it will never work. It will never work because it's not connected to the deepest part of oneself, making the characters real, the situation believable, and so on.

"The historical plays are entered into in a certain way. What happens is that I get involved in some particular incident in a great life. With Frederick the Great, it was his relationship with his small dog. The relationship of man to dog was an emotional entrance into the life of an eighteenth-century Prussian king. It is a peculiar way to go about it, but it was emotionally truthful. I felt I understood this one thing about Frederick the Great, so it was an emotional way of entering his life. It wasn't intellectual at all.

"It was the same way with *Childe Byron*, my play about Byron and his legitimate daughter, Ada. She was Countess of Lovelace and was estranged from Byron. He never really saw her except for a moment when she was a baby. What a relationship that was. It's based on my daughter by my first marriage, who is now twenty-six and a wonderful actress.

"My interest in these great lives was a very directly personal and emotional one. In the Appalachian plays, *Holy Ghosts* and *Sand Mountain,* and in those plays that take place in the mountains of the South, the connection is more direct and obvious.

"There are playwrights who, in the struggle to get their plays produced, undergo a lot of emotional wear and tear. There is a lot of competition. I think that way down underneath, everyone really respects another playwright who writes a play that works.

"I also think that once people go to the theater and they take to it and they like it, they realize it is important for them. It gives them the same kind of unusual and irreplaceable sensation that walking through a great museum does. When you go through a great museum and you see a great number of paintings by great painters, you come out a different person. It's the same thing in the theatre. When you see a really great play that addresses such tremendously, deeply personal and political issues, including your own life, you just come out a different person, and you realize that you're not going to get that watching television."

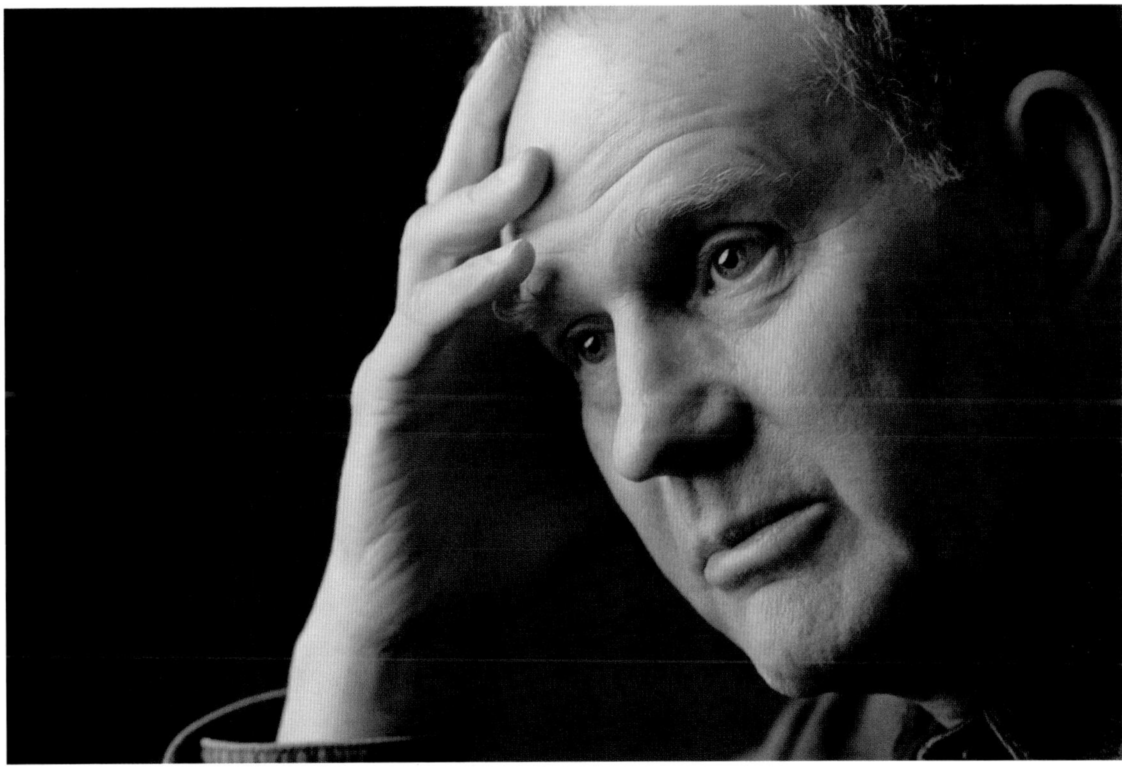

Romulus Linney

NICKY SILVER

(Born 1961—American playwright known for dark comedies from his 1993 Pterodactyls *to* The Lyons, *his first Broadway play in 2012.)*

At the time of our interview, it had been two and a half years since the opening of *Pterodactyls* put Nicky Silvers in the vanguard of American playwrights. It would be another seventeen years before he made his triumphant arrival on Broadway with *The Lyons*. When we talked, he was living in the same tiny apartment in Chelsea he had lived in since before *Pterodactyls*. He kept his sweaters in the cupboards in the kitchen because he never cooked and storage was at a premium. He went out every morning for a Snickers bar, which he refused to buy in bulk. He needed a reason to emerge from the apartment in the morning.

It is 1995, a summer afternoon at Man Ray Restaurant in Chelsea. It is cool and dark. Nicky Silver drinks Diet Coke and smokes. In September, his new play *Fit to Be Tied* is to open at Playwrights Horizons—a play that includes the usual mix of love, fear, death, obsession, the family, plus an angel from the Radio City Christmas pageant.

* * *

SJ: Tell me a little about your life before *Pterodactyls*. How did you balance your writing, rehearsing for the Vortex Theater, and working full time at Barney's?

NS: I did plays at the Vortex for a number of years with my friends, whether they were right for the parts or not. We painted the sets, we hung the lights, no one got paid. I did seven plays there.

SJ: So you were moonlighting?

NS: Yes. My Barney's money paid for the Harlequin Rehearsal Studio, which is very glamorous. It's right next to the gay male burlesque, and you can hear the disco throb coming through the walls, so all my plays had this rhythmic cadence—because it was the strippers' music.

SJ: And then you'd go into the pristine world of Barney's where everything is very *sotto voce*.

NS: I was never like that. I was so un-Barney's. But I quit Barney's before, long before *Pterodactyls* opened. I was upset and depressed and I thought, "You can't go on like this. If you quit, something will happen." And I quit and lived off my credit card and

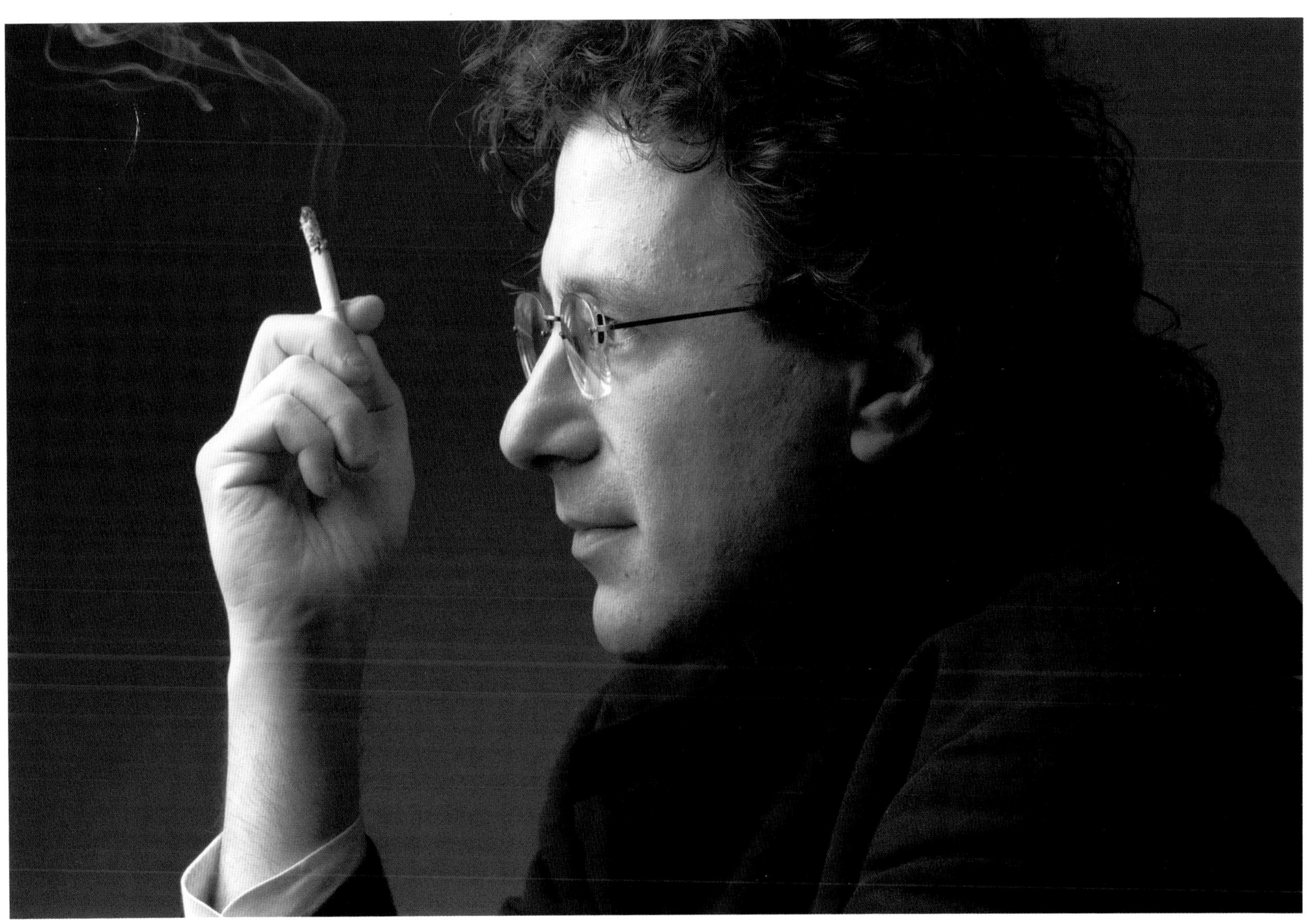

something happened. *Pterodactyls* was the next play I wrote.

SJ: And here you sit in a three-piece suit.

NS: Well, I do wear a jacket and tie every day, yes. I started overdressing for life because I realized that my personality does not lend itself to be taken altogether seriously. So in rehearsals, I would make sure I wore a suit and tie. Maybe if I can't act like an adult, at least I can look like an adult.

SJ: Do you go to rehearsals?

NS: Every single one of them. I missed one for *Pterodactyls* and I missed one for *Food Chain*. While I'm in rehearsal I don't like to work on anything else. I just like to be in the world of the play. The reason to work in the theatre, for me, is the community, working on a play and being there every day.

SJ: Where are you going from here?

NS: Literally, I'm going to Atlantic City the day after *Food Chain* closes. I'm taking the bus. By myself. I'm staying at one of the cheaper casino hotels. That's my big splurge. You know I have the tastes of a peasant, it's so sad. I don't go to the big rooms. I go to the lounges. There is something in *Fit to Be Tied* that's straight out of Atlantic City. Boyd's adoptive parents [Boyd is the angel from Radio City] were lounge performers from Asbury Park. And the name of their act was "The Salt and Pepper Review." I actually walked into a lounge and there was "The Salt and Pepper Review"—two white people. Whenever you want your ego boosted and you want to feel thin and glamorous and sophisticated, you must go to Atlantic City.

SJ: This new play is being mounted at Playwrights Horizons. Would you write differently if you were writing for a Broadway house?

NS: No. I don't write for any "market" anyway. You're lucky if you get a good idea for a play. You're so happy to have something that seems to work a little bit. I'm sure people think *Food Chain* was written for a commercial audience. It wasn't.

SJ: How was the writing for that different from your other work?

NS: *Food Chain* was written for me just to have a good time. I was working on *Raised in Captivity*. I had to put that aside—because I was dealing with things in it that were sort of disturbing to me personally. I just wanted to write for fun, and I wrote *Food Chain* very quickly during a break. As soon as I finished it, I said, "Well, I had fun, and I think other people will."

SJ: What is your writing process? Do you write every day?

NS: No. No, I don't believe in that. I don't write until something is really on my mind to write. And then, I have a little tiny roll-top desk with a Powerbook on it. If I'm in the middle of a first draft, I will sit basically without getting up—except to get a Diet Coke or go to the bathroom—sometimes twenty hours. I have terrible insomnia, and I have learned not to bother to try to sleep. Just keep going, and rewrite the next day.

SJ: And then you get up, you put on your three-piece suit, and you go out and get a Snickers.

NS: Yes. Exactly right. I have to tell you I'm not sitting naked at the typewriter.

SJ: The next play, *Fit to Be Tied*?

NS: It's a touching little fable.

SJ: About Arloc. And his mother.

NS: Nessa. And Boyd.

SJ: The Radio City angel. A family. Is the theatre for you like a family?

NS: Far superior to my own, but like one, yes. When they read my plays, people ask me all the time what horrible things must have happened in my childhood. Nothing horrible happened. Just mundane things that I perceived as horrible tragedies. *Fit to Be Tied* is a play about the cross-generational burden of fear that Arloc and his mother are living under and how they learn to get past it by realizing that they are not alone.

SJ: Is it a continuation of your other work?

NS: It's like a marriage of *Food Chain* and *Raised in Captivity* in terms of its aesthetic. I hope they're sort of mushing together, like Strindberg with songs.

SJ: You use direct address often in your plays. What about in this play?

NS: I use direct address for a couple of things. Often it's just the quickest way to get to the peak experience. There is a lot of direct address in this play. All actors, no matter what they say, very much want to be liked on stage. They want their characters to be liked. And I really write that into the plays now.

SJ: What about other devices and influences?

NS: It's always really pleasing to me when people review a play and refer to some classic piece I'm supposed to be aping. I never read the classics. I don't approach writing from any literary or academic place. I didn't study writing. I never read the classics.

SJ: Are you a child of television?

NS: Oh, absolutely.

SJ: And how is that mirrored in your work?

NS: It honed my comedic ear. 'Cause when I was a child, I think, it was a great era for television.

SJ: Your plays are more abstract than anything we see on TV.

NS: All mediums have an abstract language, and I think *Fit to Be Tied* does use some theatrical abstract language, where all of a sudden you're lifted out of reality. My plays walk a very narrow line between too broad and too serious. One of the things I've learned is to find actors who can fight to win and not be revolting. Because my characters are all fighting for things vehemently—with huge passions and violent natures. So you find someone you can send onstage and say, "Kill them. Get what you need." And yet there's something vulnerable or soft or comic about them.

SJ: About the angel. All of us in New York have been to Radio City Music Hall, and we all remember those angels. But angels have been omnipresent recently—they are on television, Tony Kushner's play—

NS: Which is referenced in *Fit to Be Tied.* Boyd is complaining about the quality of his Radio City Music Hall costume and comparing it to the quality used in *Angels in America.* He wishes it were a little spiffier. That's what it comes down to. The idea of angels being winged figures, of course, is silly. Any psychiatrist will tell you that believing someone is with you or looking down on you or protecting you is really your mind creating some comfort. So angels for me are things that, I guess, come when you need them. That's what they are.

SJ: Is there another play after *Fit to Be Tied*?

NS: I'll have another play almost finished before *Fit to Be Tied* opens. It makes me too scared not to have another finished. You never want to put out your last piece of goods.

SJ: Do you think most of us live under some sort of fear?

NS: Yes. Absolutely.

SJ: So this play may be a way of gathering together and finding out we're not alone.

NS: I think we're all very much afraid and I think there is a lot to be afraid of. But it oughtn't to immobilize you, and it has immobilized these people to one degree or another.

SJ: What scares you?

NS: What scares me? Poverty terrifies me. Limblessness. Nudity frightens me. Not in others, but I haven't been naked in front of anyone in many, many years. I haven't been to a doctor in eighteen years, so I guess they scare me. If I had a motivating fear, it would probably be poverty more than anything else, homelessness and poverty—because I don't have any marketable skills beyond, you know, I can generally pick out a good tie, if called upon.

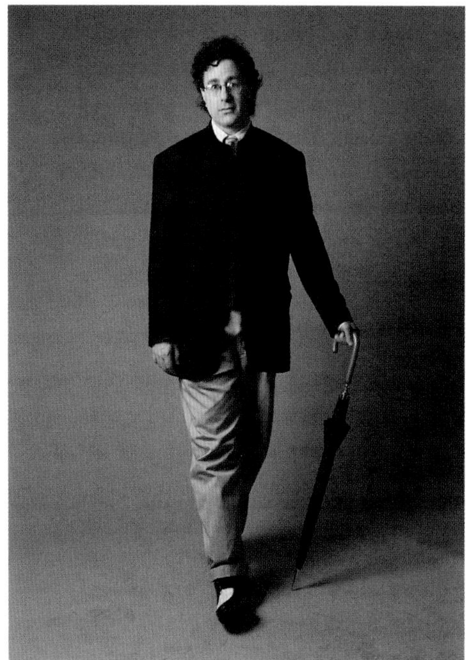

Nicky Silver — Jeffrey Hatcher (opposite)

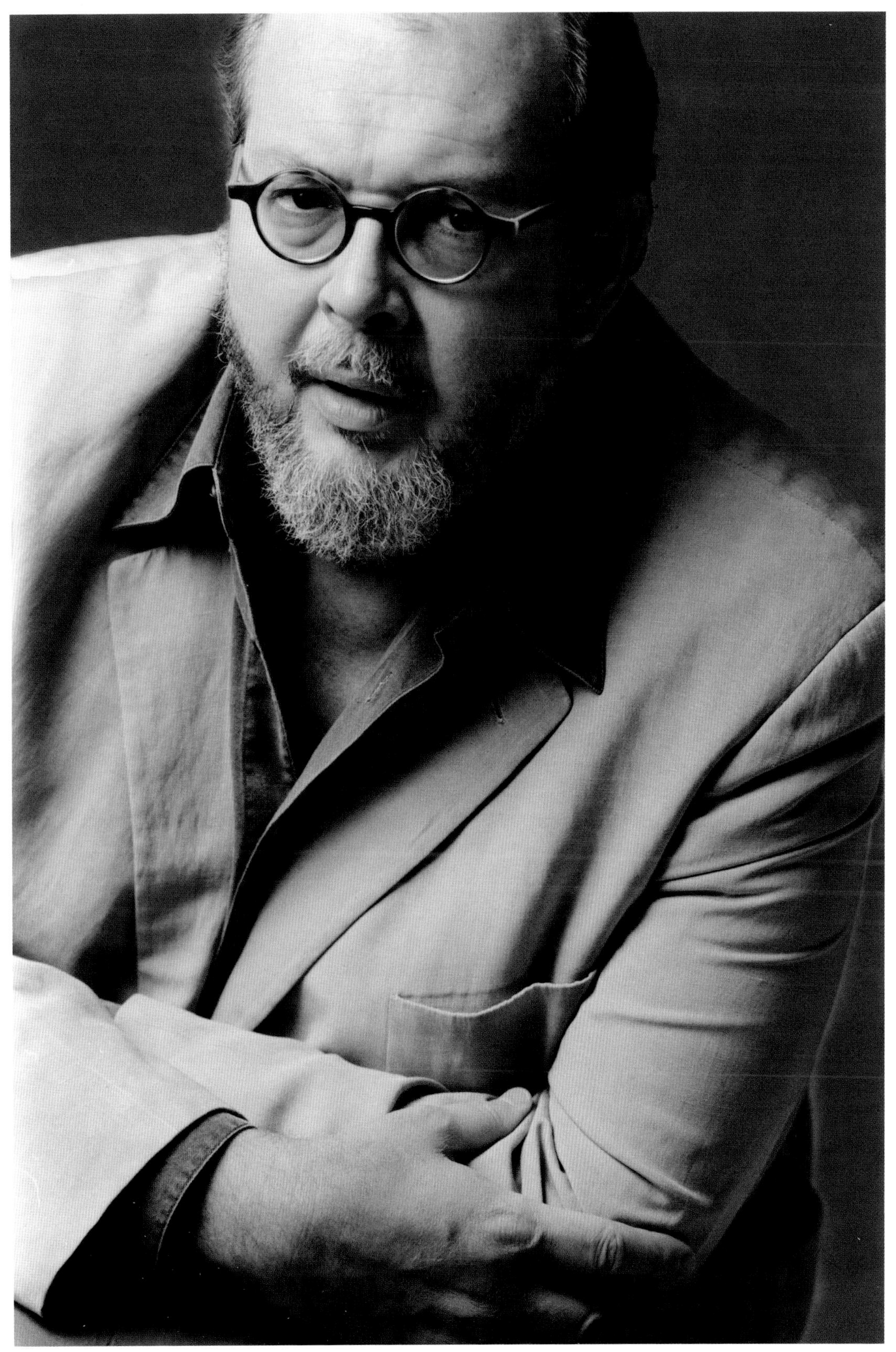

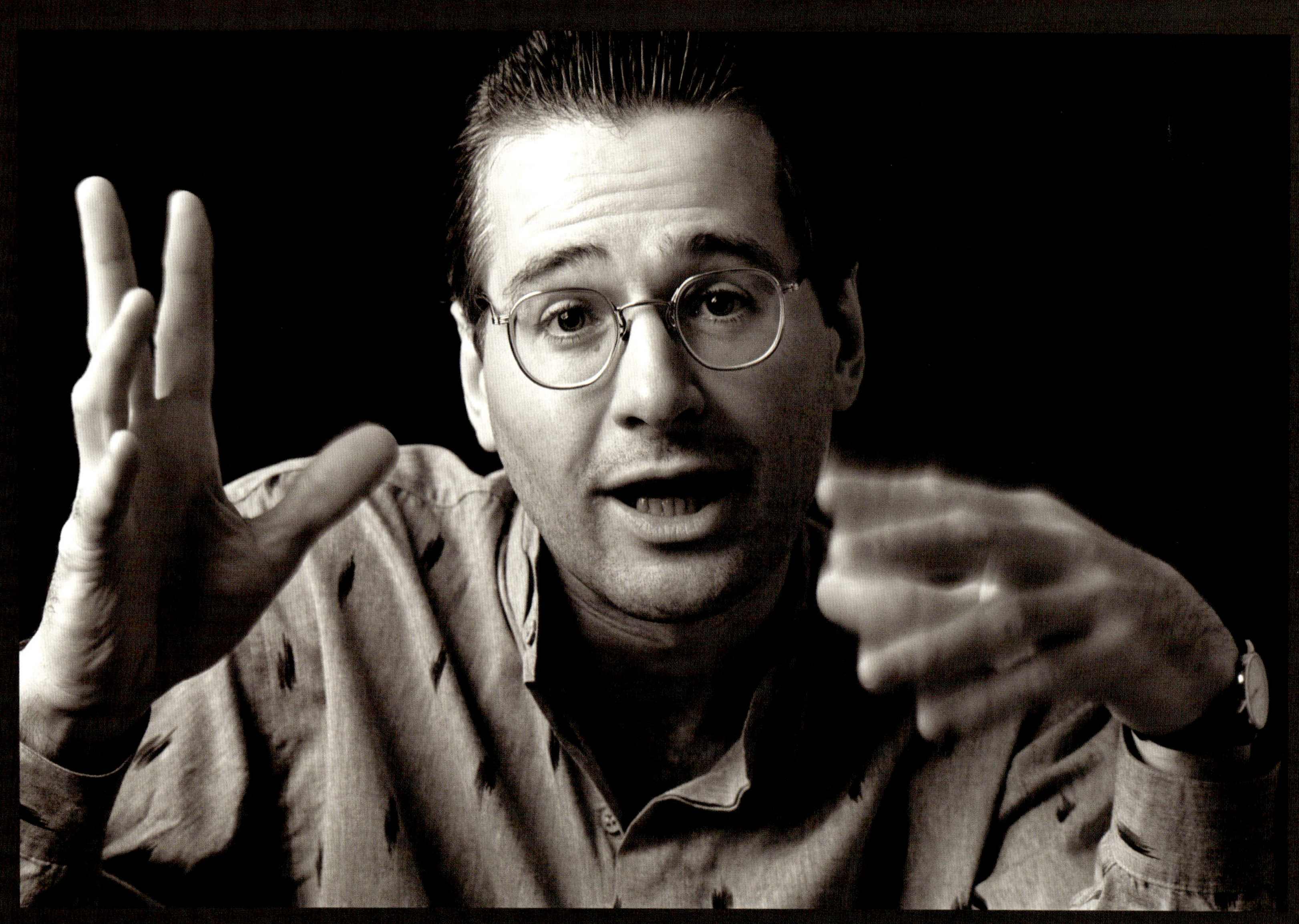

John Patrick Shanley

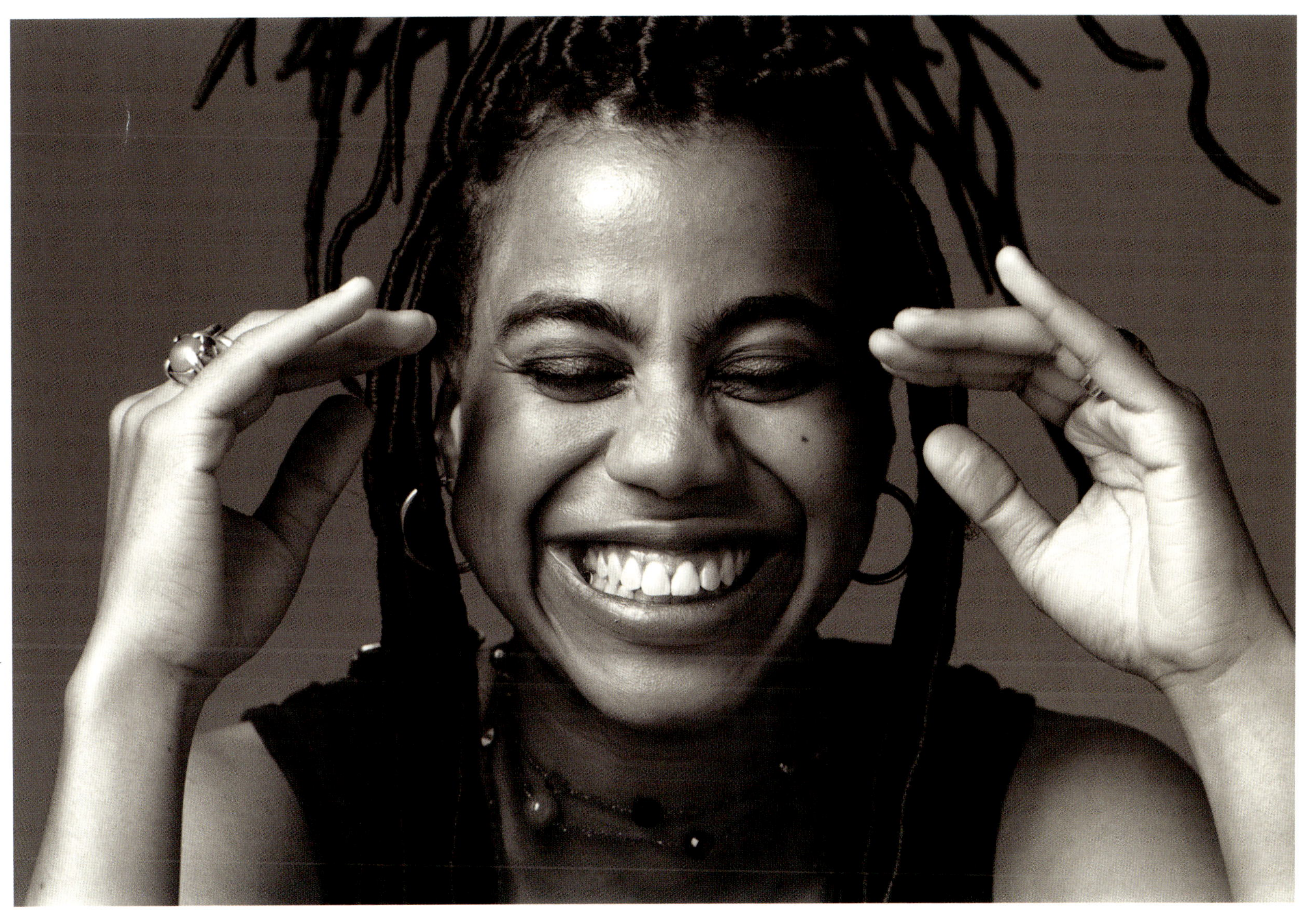

Suzan-Lori Parks

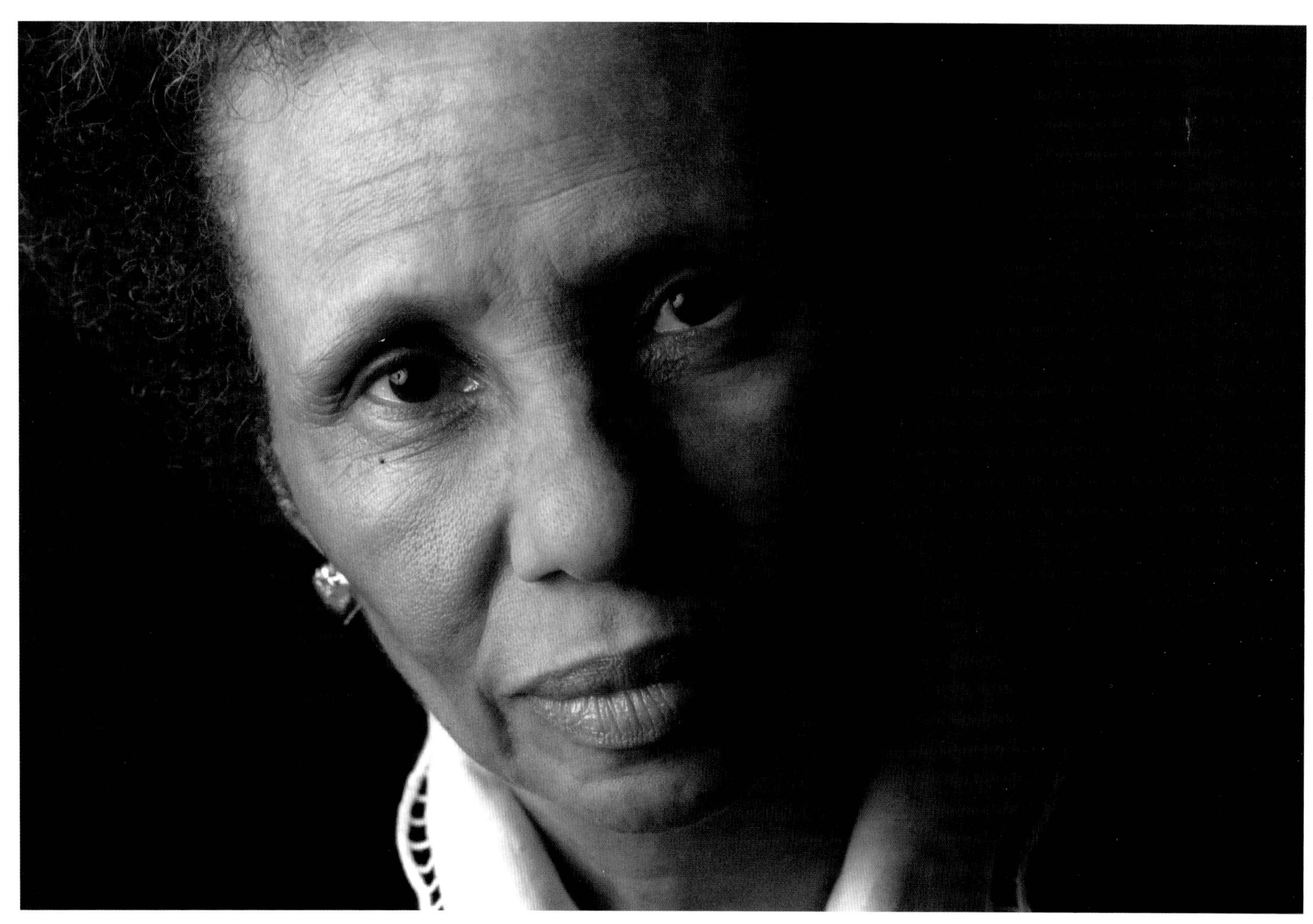

 Adrienne Kennedy — Reinaldo Povod (opposite)

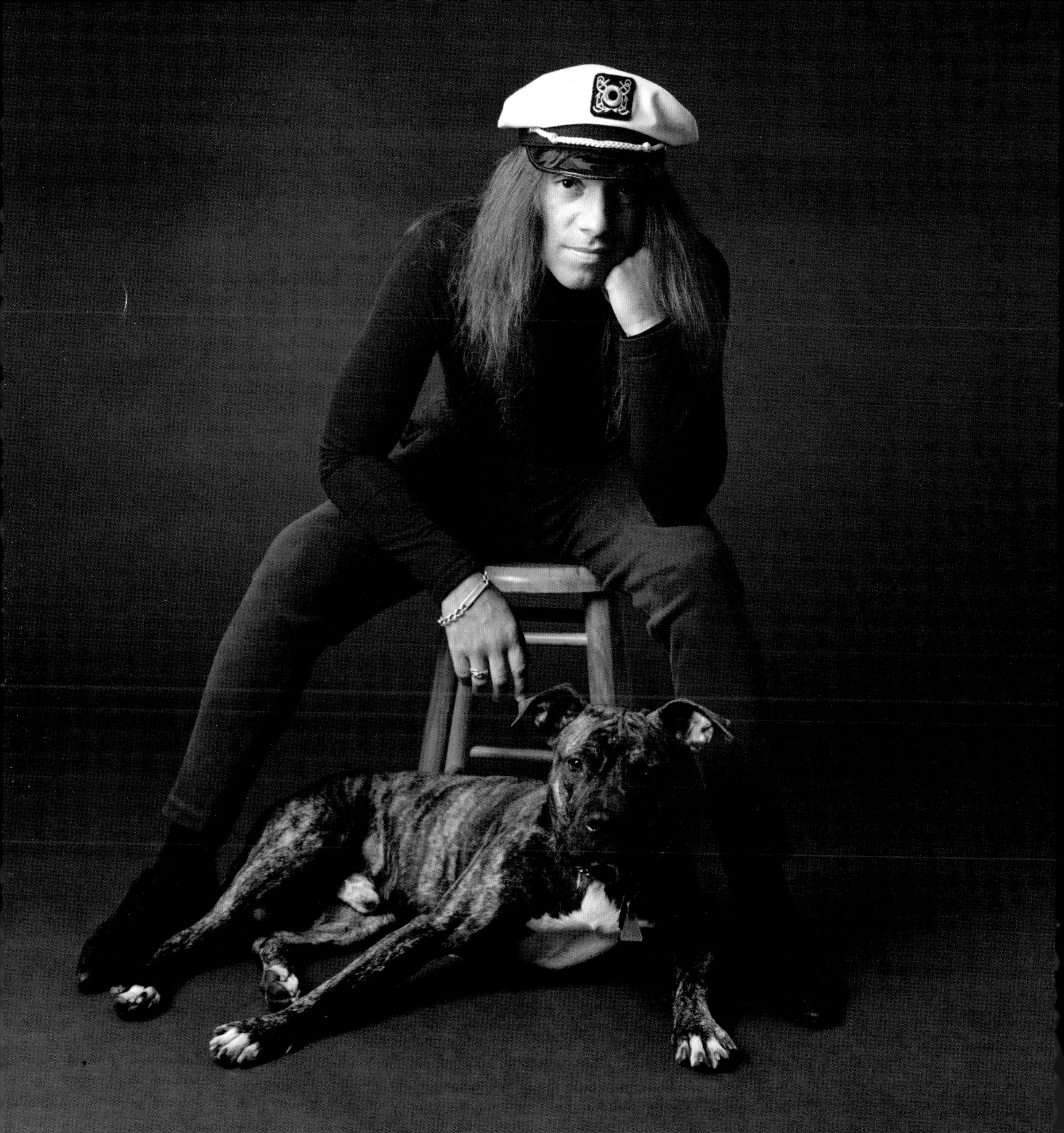

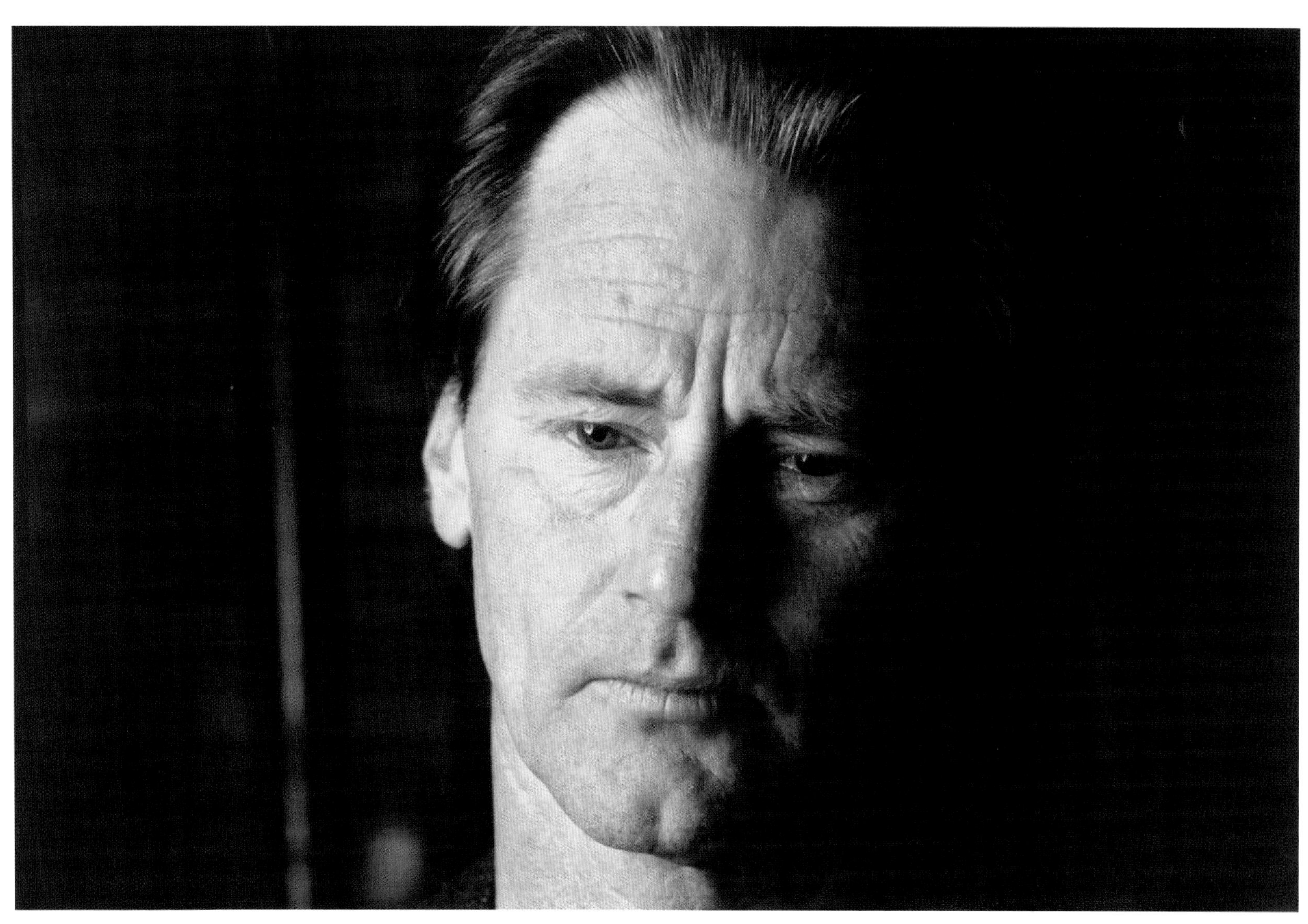

Sam Shepard — Keith Glover (opposite)

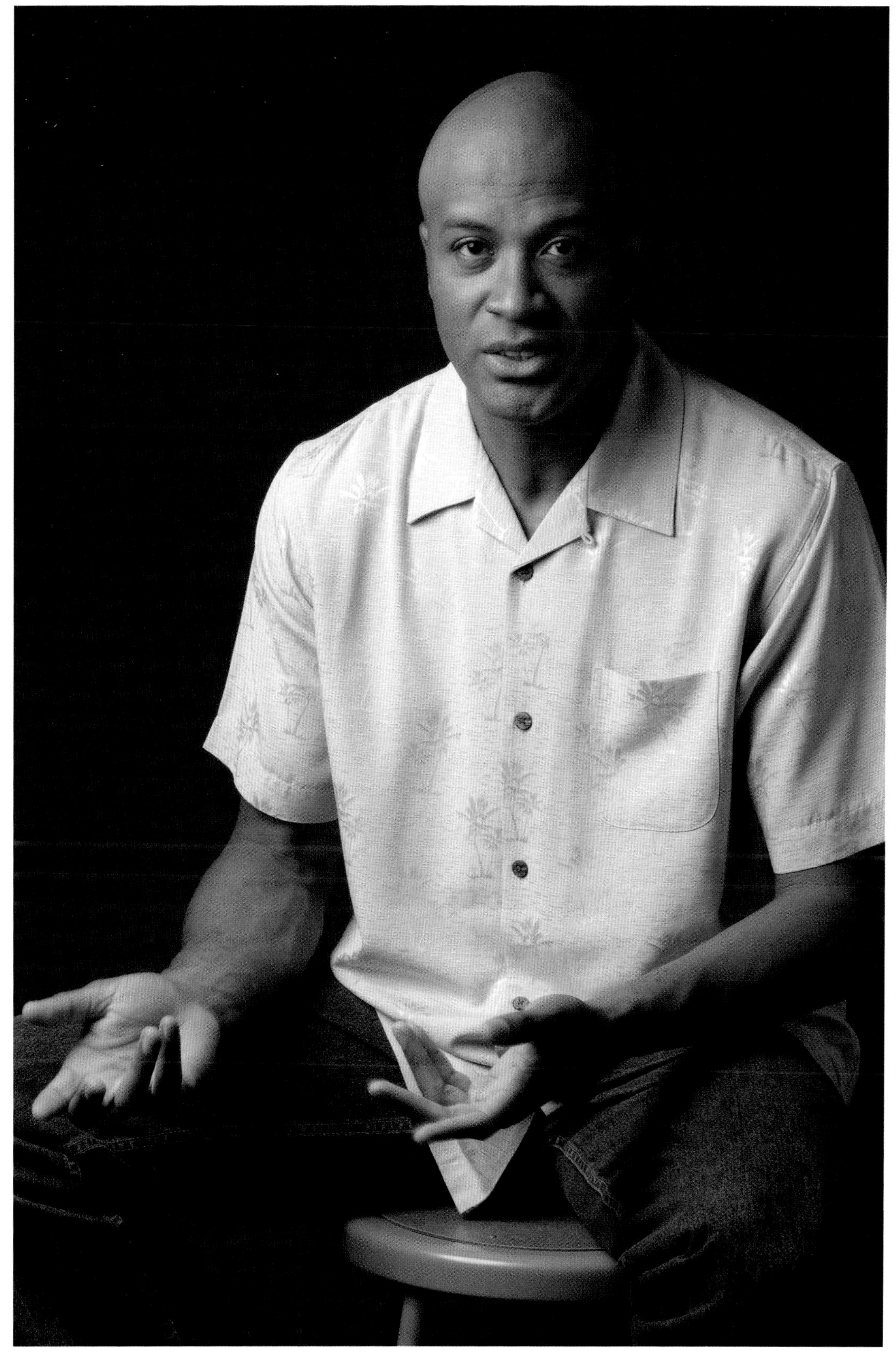

WENDY WASSERSTEIN

(1950–2006—American playwright who received the Tony Award for Best Play and the Pulitzer Prize for Drama for The Heidi Chronicles.*)*

She is breathless as she sweeps through the Soho restaurant for our breakfast meeting, "I'm so sorry, but my mother kept me on the phone." Wendy Wasserstein seems to balance continually between apology and assertion. Even her speaking voice bounces between a schoolgirl airiness and the resonant octave below. "It's funny. The other day I had a drink with my sister. We were talking about our lives and why you end up doing what you're doing. I thought, 'I'm not actually a very aggressive person. I'm just this nice Jewish girl.' I used to make plays when I was young, in the living room. I used to dream in terms of musicals. I remember that."

Her life now may seem like a dream and very far from her early, Brooklyn, middle-class upbringing with "Yeshiva and all." Her mother was a dancer, "or a want-to-be dancer, very theatrical." As a kid, Wendy went to the June Taylor School of the Dance. (She tap danced for me during our photo session.) "I knew chorus girls growing up and a life like that was amazing to me. I went to this stuffy, rich-girls' high school in New York. It wasn't one of the fancy ones. I was rejected from the fancy ones. I used to write something called The Mother-Daughter Fashion Show because they'd let me out of gym if I wrote these shows."

Wendy's entire education from high school through Mount Holyoke College was all female. "That's why I'm the damaged person I am." She is laughing when she says it. What this gives her is a very strong understanding of female bonding. "I'm a really good shopper because of my high school."

At the Yale Drama School, she made fast friends with other playwrights. To make ends meet after her graduation from Yale, she was a go-fer for the O'Neill Playwrights Conference. "I was Lloyd Richards' go-fer. I used to bring the scripts for the O'Neill on the subway to the readers. I'd torture Lloyd and tell him they were judging the plays by their covers. And I used to get lunch for them." She was also stenographer for the Society of Stage Directors and Choreographers. "I just pretended I was like Thelma Ritter in her B-movies. I had these two odd jobs. The deadline was December 31 for the O'Neill Competition and so all through Christmas I worked taking these mailbags in. I loved it. It was a great time actually. You get to observe, be part of the theatre.

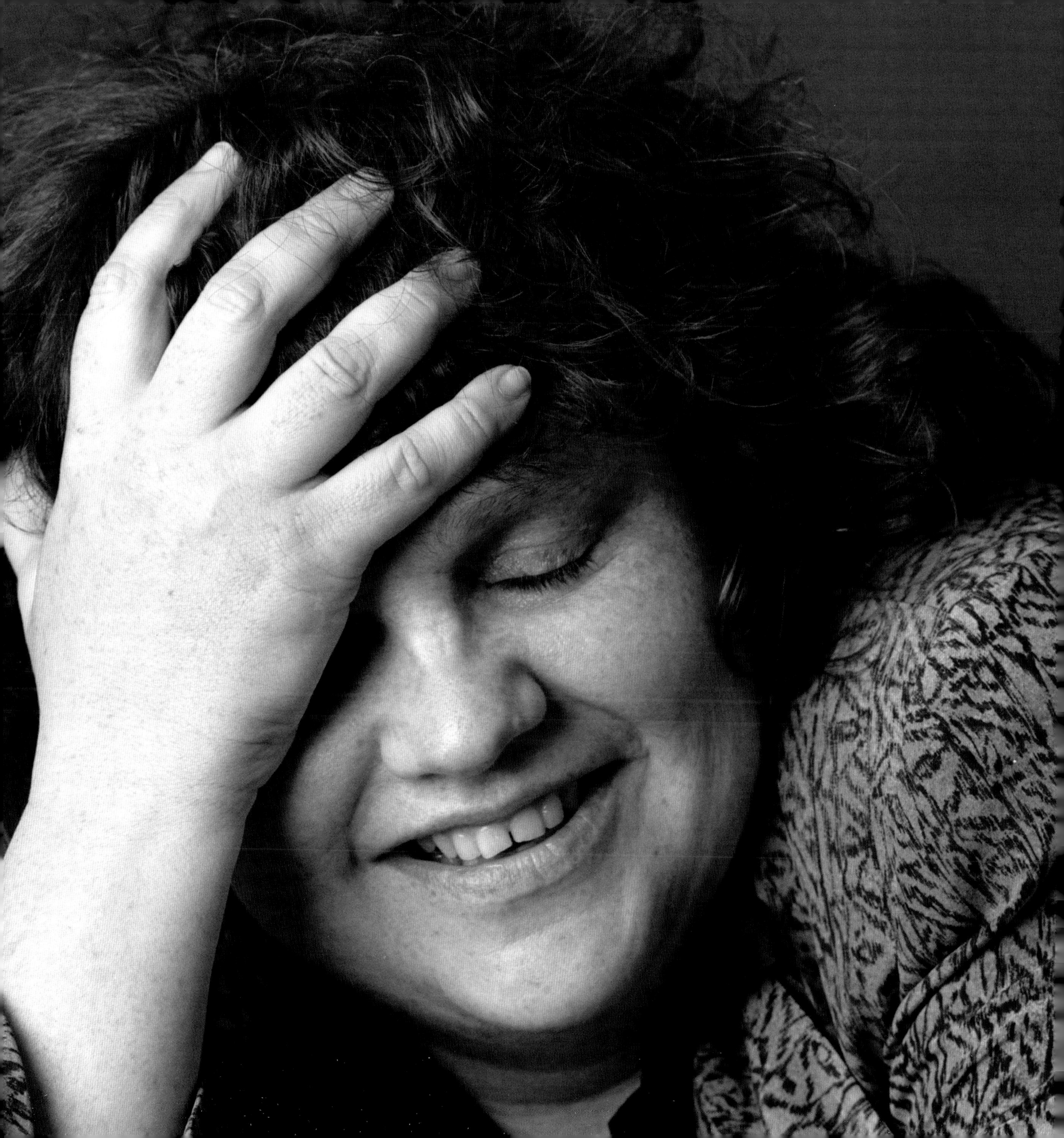

"I like the rehearsal process. There are some playwrights who don't and some who do. I do. It's why I like it if my friends show me their plays." Wendy's skill in talking with her friends about their new plays is legendary. Throughout these interviews, when I have asked playwrights who reads their initial efforts, Wendy Wasserstein's name has come up—with Terrance McNally, Christopher Durang, and A. R. Gurney. Christopher Durang said she helped by being "delicately frank."

She tells me that she and Pete Gurney have joked for years about doing a play together called *The Wasp and the Jewess.* It is obvious in her descriptions of collaborations with directors and actors that the communal life of the theatre is a great part of the draw.

"It also can be some form of hell, too, if you've got the wrong actors and things aren't going well. Playwrights are so vulnerable all the time. I'm this great believer that plays have lives of their own. And sometimes it's great and sometimes it's not. I remember when we were doing *Miami.* One night, Phyllis Newman wasn't able to go on. I went on for Phyllis. And the night I went on for Phyllis I thought, 'This is going nowhere fast.'" Wendy laughs heartily.

"My sister was asking the other day about my writing and whether I feel it's important. I do think it's important. If I didn't write, those particular characters would be missing from the stage. You remember little things about different people. I'm not that much of a talker. But there is nothing I like better than sitting around watching people. If one of these sort of overwhelming people sits down and starts talking to me, I find it just fascinating. I could sit for hours."

The way she nods her head, leans in, and listens, makes one eager to confide. "Sometimes there is someone you remember from meeting once. In the play I'm writing now, one of the characters is based on someone I met once in a panel discussion. But that somebody just resonates. I once was seeing a man who said, 'If you write about this, I'll be so angry.' And I think, 'Well, tough luck.'" Her laughter billows. "'That's your problem!' Right now I'm writing a play about my three sisters. It's getting a little close. Two sisters and me. The hardest character to ever write is me.

"And the Wendy characters like Heidi and Holly are more recessive in a world of brighter colors. Maybe it's because it's more fun to write characters who have brighter colors. It's much more fun to write about this woman who's screaming, 'You little shit!' Or the part Swoozie played in *Uncommon Women*, Rita—the one who tastes her menstrual blood. That's much brighter. In fact, the autobiographical characters are not only the hardest to write, they're somehow the least interesting, too. There's a reason why Heidi sits back and observes. It's the eye, the writer, the observer, that the audience identifies with. Heidi is an art historian because she watches."

Wendy was a history major at Mount Holyoke, and her studies honed her observational skills and sense of social movements. But there are always surprises. "I was on a plane coming back from East Hampton. I visited my brother out there. I was staring at this woman. She had red fingernails and a little yellow suit and a big diamond, holding hands with her husband and children. She was one of those unbelievably perfectly groomed sort of wealthy, Upper East Side women. I was looking at her and thinking how different our lives were, and that I felt like a UFO around her. I thought how interesting it would be if we exchanged lives. After the plane landed, she came up to me as we were getting off the plane, and she said, 'Are you Wendy?' I said, 'Yes.' And she said, 'I have to tell you. I am you. I read everything you write.' I thought, 'You are what?!'" Wendy's laugh is contagious, and we laugh together. "It still seems so bizarre to me. I think it has to do with if you're honest. If it's real, it will strike a chord. If it's not, it won't."

Women and their lives in the late twentieth century are the province of Wendy's plays. Often they are women facing the world alone as the heroines do in *Isn't It Romantic?* and *The Heidi Chronicles,* or women banding together, as in *Uncommon Women and Others.* Wendy tells me, "There are Heidi's in Portland, there are Heidi's in the Bronx, there are Heidi's in Chicago; they're all there. I always thought the best *The Heidi Chronicles* ever got was the first reading at Playwrights Horizons. But simultaneously, you can sit there and it can be horrible. That's the fear—that there's a reading and it's terrible. And that can happen just as well. It's read and it's awful.

"I'll never forget during the run of *The Heidi Chronicles*, there was a Christmas party in the basement of the Plymouth Theatre. There were the crew and the actors. There must have been a hundred people there. And I thought, 'I wrote a play in a boarding house in London and all of these people are working.' That is great and so, sure, you go on TV and say, 'Come see my play,' because it's about you, but it's also about all of them. It's about the producers. It's about the directors. It's about the life of the theatre. It's about the excitement."

Wendy spent most of 1990 traveling and doing lectures around the United States. In Portland she was thrilled when at a lecture hall "there were maybe five hundred people or more to hear a playwright speak. The woman introducing me said, 'This is Wendy Wasserstein, and next week we're having Richard Ford and Tobias Wolfe.' And five hundred to a thousand people stood up and said, 'Yay!!!' And I thought, 'This is unbelievable.' What was so interesting about *The Heidi Chronicles* on the road was, there are whole audiences [for it] across the country, across America.

"You look at playwrights as opposed to screenwriters. The theatre is the domain of the playwright. It's our play. It's our voice. When you see a movie, god knows. You go to Hollywood. All these people know how much everybody else makes. They will tell you, 'Oh well, so-and-so made a deal for four point five blah blah blah, and he's got this and he's got that. And I fuckin' want to kill him, and he's only twenty.' I have no idea how much money other playwrights make. We don't know how much money we all make. I know that you don't assume when you write a play that you are going to make a living from this play. Plays have become more and more vehicles of personal expression. Plays are now more like journeys or something. They are acts of the imagination and also of a voice."

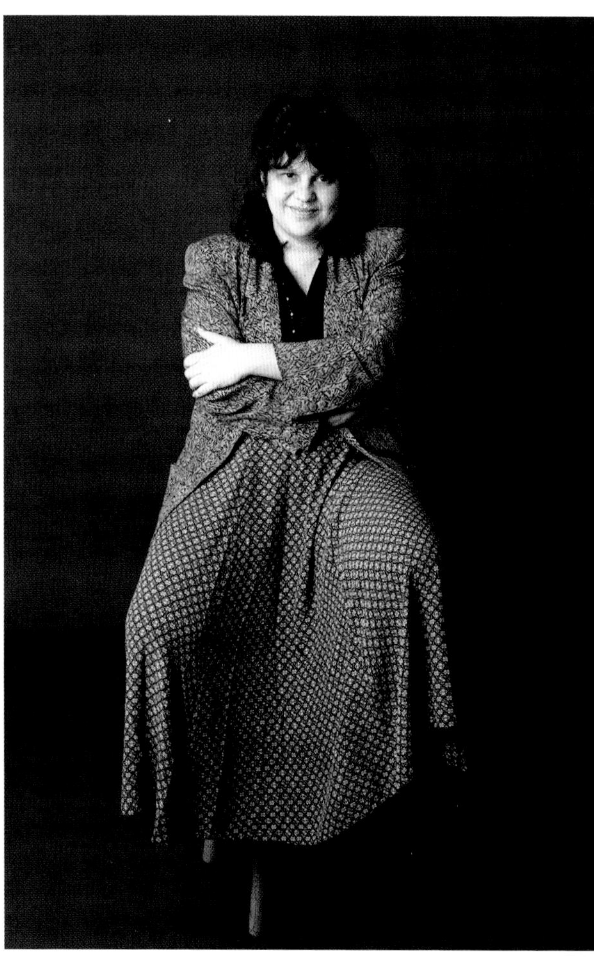

She has a strong sense of the importance of theatre and also how unpredictable it is. "A play—about one woman's journey, the feminist movement, and the gay movement—played on Broadway for a year and a half, so we have to redefine. What is commercial theatre? And who is the audience? That is very important to look at in terms of playwrights making a living. I don't know of anyone. It's one thing that's very, very hard to do. Most of the people I know write television, write film. In the late fifties you could be a playwright and that was it.

"Everybody always talks about the critics and I say, in a sense, it's part of a process. It takes two years to write a play. Some people can write them in three weeks. It takes me a year, basically." She talks about the exhausting schedule from rewrites to casting, then to production two years later. "So to make the whole thing about one night when the theatre critics come is insane.

"*Heidi* on the road didn't actually get very good reviews. That play sold out on the road; we did great. It had good word of mouth, people liked it and I went on 'Hello, St. Paul.' If anyone wanted to say hello, I was there. I spent this year going on 'Good Morning, St. Paul' and 'Hello, Boston.' I was on 'Hello, Boston' between a woman whose daughter was married and a woman who had made up a new way to bake potatoes."

Wendy Wasserstein was someone who never thought she would win a Pulitzer Prize. "All in one year, I think my life sort of exploded. I was on the David Letterman show. A part of me thought I should be a talk show host; I had this unseen gift. It's also very nice to have turned forty with that. I think it made a difference to me, a big difference being a single woman and all of that. Marsha Norman called me when I won it and said it was like having a rock. It was there, no matter what. They can't take that away. Then I won the Tony. It was the first time a woman alone had won the Tony. Isn't that odd? I'd never won anything before; I'd won a babke at a bakery in New Haven. So it changes everything . . . and it doesn't.

"People will continue to write plays. Because a play is yours. No matter what, that's your baby. It's really scary. I'm writing a new play right now and I find it terrifying. I mean really terrifying. I sit there and I think, 'Is this honest? Is this not honest?' I'm not even thinking about the reviews. I'm sitting there with a piece of paper—thinking. Which is the horror, the complete horror of what's going on in my house, writing that play . . . and it's great.

"The thing about playwrights is they have an innate theatricality to them, so you have people who alternate between observance and looking back. But they have this innate sense of 'Whoopee!' I think that's why I can go on those talk shows."

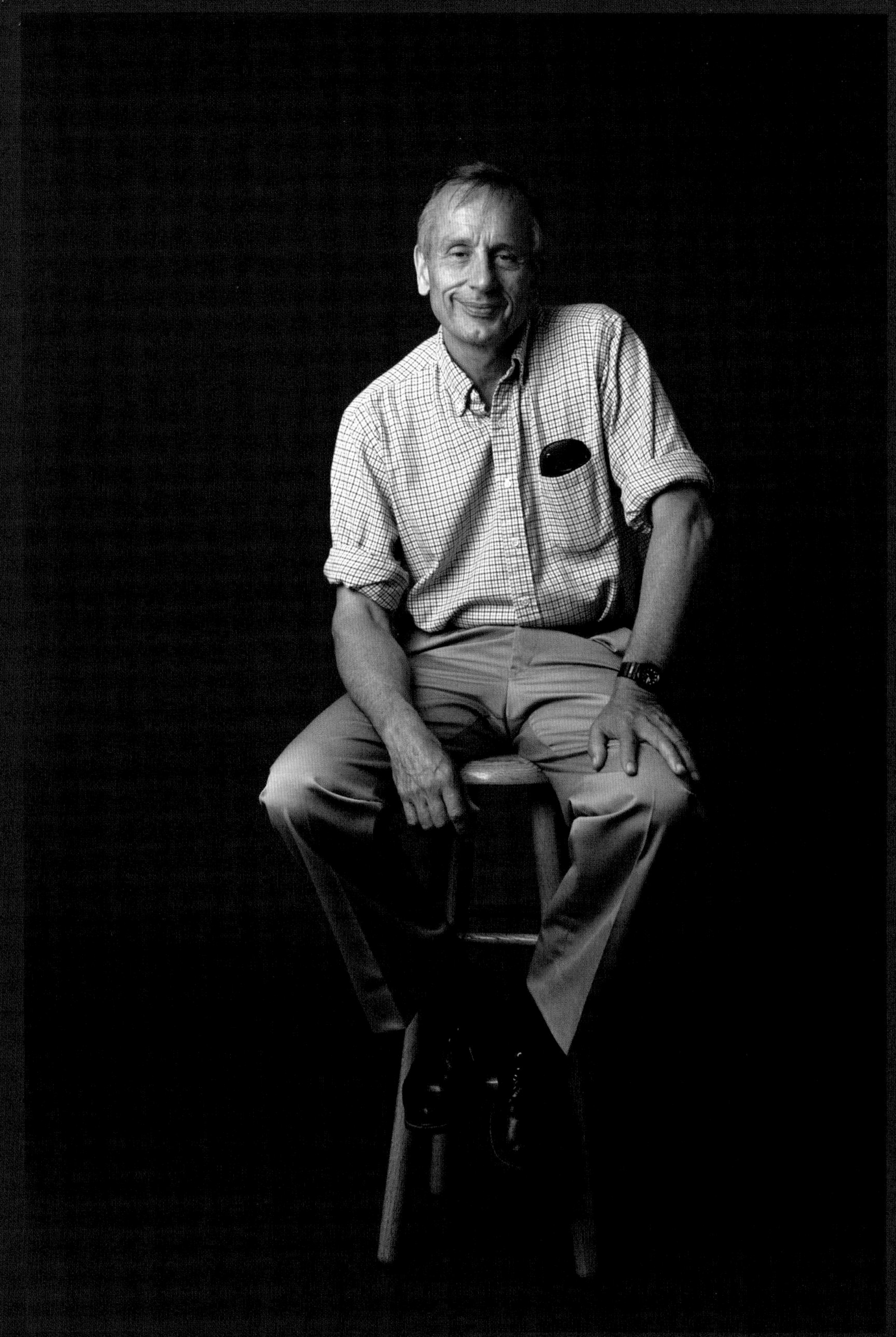

A. R. GURNEY

(Born 1930—member of the American Academy of Arts and Letters, American playwright known for The Dining Room, *was awarded PEN/Laura Pels International Foundation for Theater Award as a Master American Dramatist.)*

SJ: For a time I called this series, *Chroniclers of Their Time*, and I was thinking today about the *Dining Room* and *Love Letters*, two of your plays that seem to be vivid pictures of a specific real place and time.

ARG: The critics tend to describe me as a chronicler of WASP mores, and I think in some ways it's very accurate. Since the world I grew up in has so much disappeared and seems so remote now, part of me simply wants to record what happened. I found myself almost compelled to explain it to myself and to the world in a rather public way in the theatre.

SJ: Why the theatre?

ARG: The theatre is a very public statement, more than a book, and I've written books. It says, "Look. I'm here, listen to me." I see that world so lost, so gone, and many things about it should have been lost, should have been gone, but. . . . I just think it should be remembered in some way, and the theatre leaves a more indelible stamp on the mind. So many of my characters are playing roles in life, forced to wear masks, acting. The theatre seemed a natural form because the theatre is so much about masks and roles and acting.

SJ: You have actors playing multiple characters going through a lifetime and a day in the *Dining Room*. By having one actor play five characters, there is a cumulative effect.

ARG: You do get the sense that the maid is a role, the grandmother is a role, and what kind of mask you have to wear. Through this form, you get the sense the grandfather might be played by the same actor that plays the grandson. You get the sense of connection—the grandfather is really a young man at heart, or the young man is forced to be an old man before his time. All those resonances you can get with this doubling of actors.

SJ: In other plays, like *Middle Ages,* you have done a conceptual thing where you jump back and forth in time. During our photo session, you said something interesting about how *Middle Ages* was a premonition about something that happened to you and your family later in your life.

ARG: Yes, I wrote that four years before it happened. My father was still alive when I wrote *Middle Ages*. And my wife's mother was still alive, so what seemed like a rather amusing turn in a play became an ultimate fact in life. Since I was talking about a closed, rather hermetic society, people who don't look far beyond the walls of that metaphorical club, it was almost natural that my mother [*He laughs.*] would marry my wife's father just as it had seemed organic in the play.

SJ: Wow. What authors have affected you?

ARG: Cheever, obviously as a prose writer; Philip Barry, to some degree. Thornton Wilder, in his experiments with form to give the audience a detached and involved perspective simultaneously, was very influential. Brecht, to the degree that he also was impatient with straight realism. Brecht did anything he could to break up what he felt was an unhealthy, willful suspension of disbelief. I'm not happy with just straight realism. I do anything I can to remind the audience constantly that they're watching a play.

SJ: Your family and friends, how do they feel about finding themselves "on the stage"?

ARG: I've had difficulty with my family over the years with these plays. Particularly my father was unhappy with what I'd written. He felt it was a kind of intrusion on the family's privacy. My mother has always been rather quietly and skeptically encouraging about my plays. As I've gotten older and learned my craft more, I think my mother has appreciated my plays more. So it's always been kind of a mixed bag. I've discovered that in certain areas, people are more upset when they're not in your work than if they are. I wrote a novel about academia, about MIT, and I think some people thought I trod on a few toes. Others were really quite offended they weren't included.

SJ: Isn't that odd?

ARG: You know, as a photographer, you show a group picture and everybody goes, 'Where am I?'

SJ: Definitely. In the postlude to one of your plays, you say something about a choral tone, as though everyone in the play were of equal importance.

ARG: I cannot stand to write plays with minor roles. I really believe in the democratic form that everyone is equal on the stage. The idea of having one actor play a walk-on or asking an actor just to come out in the third act, I can't do that. I've tried. I just can't do it. Once I introduce a character, that character has to be a strong part of the play. In the *Cocktail Hour,* the sister who probably has the fewest lines is constantly arguing and insisting that she's not going to play a minor role. And she gets more lines because she's constantly making this point.

SJ: When there are siblings, one realizes there's a certain "thing" going on. It often seems to be in the subtext.

ARG: You can get a lot of power in the theatre with what you don't say as well as what you do. I don't believe in spelling it all out. I like it as a strong bass clef. It's good to ask the audience to work. I think the audience likes to collaborate.

SJ: Do you think you are revealing more of yourself in your plays now than you were early on?

ARG: I've been on the outside moving in for quite a while. It was very significant in my writing career that I happened to have a sabbatical in 1981. We happened to come to New York, I happened to have *The Dining Room* produced, and it happened to give me enough money so I didn't have to teach. As I explored the city and my responses to it, in my own time, I did become more personal in my writing. Now, my instinct in the next phase of my life is to stretch in other directions rather than to look in the mirror.

SJ: Does TV keep people from the theater?

ARG: Oh, I'm sure it does. Some television is horrible, but some of it's delightful. I have just finished a meeting with some television people about a possible project. If you write for the networks, they own what you write, and every executive wants to change a line or two to earn his keep. By the time it comes out, it can be a parody or bastardization of what you wrote. And that is really irritating.

SJ: So in the theatre the author is king?

ARG: The author is very much king. There, I hear a human voice in a particular way. In the theatre, you own your material. They can't change a line without your permission. You fight it through. Sometimes the actor or the director has a good point, sometimes they don't, but it's a fair fight. That's why I've stayed with the theatre—because of that integrity you maintain. Doesn't mean you win every time. You can get caught in bad productions. You can write a bad play. At least you go down on your own steam.

SJ: If you were to caption one picture of A. R. Gurney with a line from his play, what would it be?

ARG: At Juilliard last night, some young actors ran through the first act of the *Dining Room*. At the end of the first act, after the crazy old grandmother is taken off, the women are sitting there alone. Nancy says, "It's as if we didn't exist. As if we were all just . . . ghosts, or something." I thought that was very close to the way I feel sometimes.

I was reading a review of a new book by George F. Kennan, and there's a line where he says, "A man's life is too long a span today for the pace of change. If he lives more than a half century, his familiar world, the world of his youth, fails him like a horse dying under its rider, and he finds himself dealing with a new one which is not really his."

The world is changing so fast that the familiar values, the values you grew up with, the assumptions you were given as a child, are like a horse dying out from under you as you are cantering along. And everything you were riding on and counting on and they told you was true is suddenly not there any more. It's collapsing underneath you. That's what my themes were in my plays. What so many of them have been about. I've tried to celebrate that horse, and I also try to talk about how it is sick and dying.

ROBERT PATRICK

(Born 1937—American playwright and author of more than sixty published plays, best known for his work in Greenwich Village at Caffe Cino in the sixties and for his Broadway play, Kennedy's Children.*)*

My favorite moment in my photo session with Robert Patrick came when we started reciting Edna St. Vincent Millay's "Recuerdo." We finished together out loud, "And she wept, 'God bless you!' for the apples and the pears, / And we gave her all our money but our subway fares." It is the moment of the finishing of the poem that we see registered on Robert's face, the expression that to me shows his deep love of language, spoken language in space. Theatre.

Later I interviewed him over tea in his downtown apartment in New York on a gray January day in 1990. It was a long, generous, wide-ranging conversation, beginning with the Caffe Cino scene in Greenwich Village in the sixties—with Lanford Wilson, Marshall Mason, and Sam Shepard. We spoke of his peripatetic childhood moving from the Depression into the fifties, his coming of age in the sixties, politics and, always, playwriting, its process and purposes, whether done in a little cleared space in a café or on Broadway.

Caffe Cino may well have been the beginning of the Off-Off Broadway movement. It was begun in 1958 by a retired dancer, Joe Cino, who wanted a place where he and his friends and fellow artists could hang out. "It's a storefront. There's no stage, just a coffee house with tables, and we cleared some tables away and did the play in the middle. So we didn't write plays that needed any scenery and all of us wrote primarily verbal plays because that was all we had. Everybody—actors, directors, writers, musicians—all shared a common outlook socially, politically, emotionally, and aesthetically, so rehearsal was very much a part of that process. We were all aiming toward such a common goal, it was a joy."

Much of the theatre that came out of the Caffe Cino scene was considered avant-garde, political, certainly gay-friendly in a time where almost nothing else was. "I was never consciously very political. We were American kids, and in the fifties we had been carefully guarded from learning anything about political reality. Great forces were at work to keep us from rocking the boat. Before we discovered, say, specific racial issues, political issues, economic issues, life in the fifties was so horrible that one just kept saying people cannot have been meant to be this unhappy.

"So we broke out. We broke out in all directions and did not know that was political. We weren't like European students who have always been a political force. We had all been told as we grew up in the forties

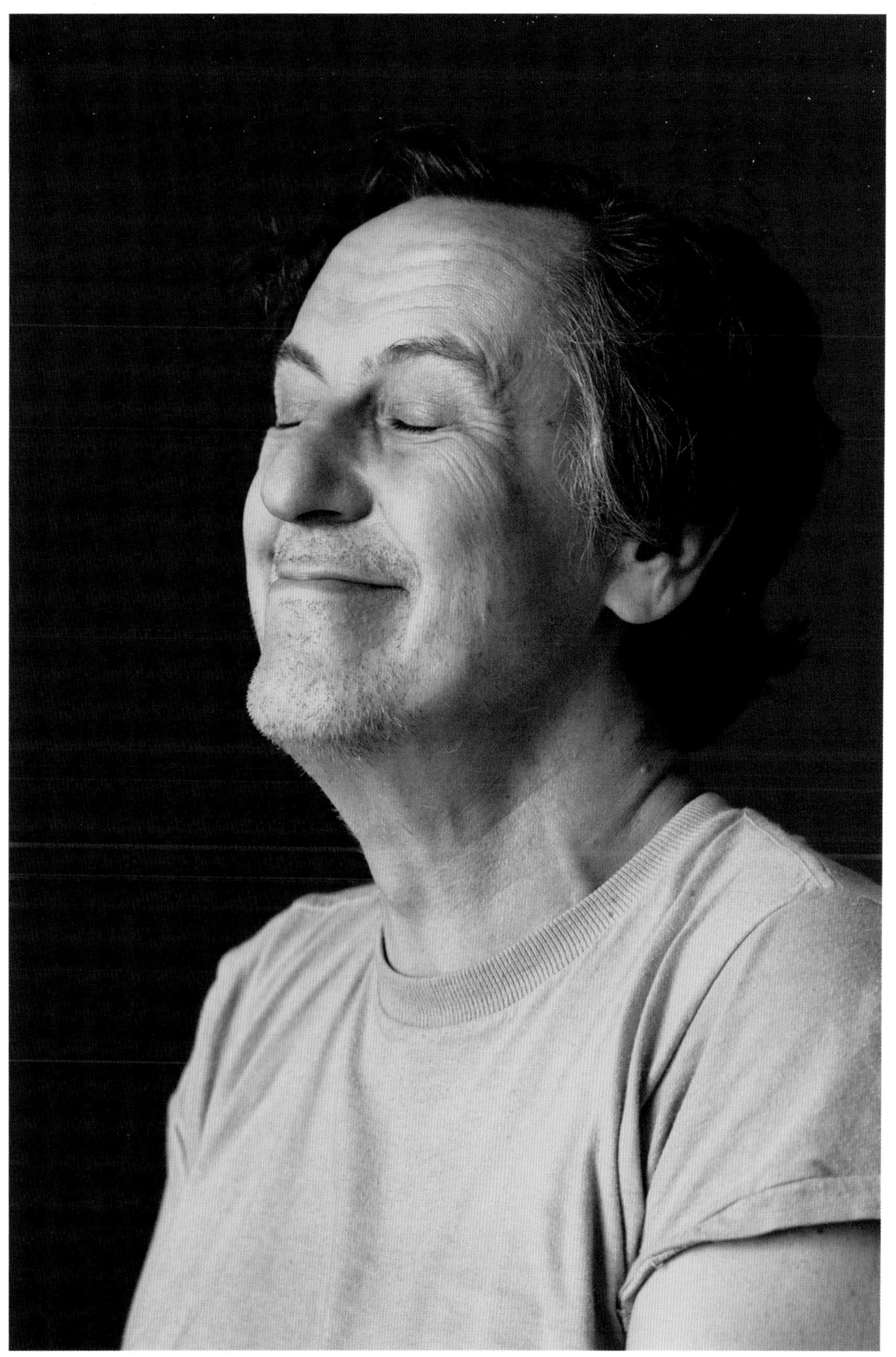

and fifties that this was the country of equal rights for all. We believed that. So when we got to the big cities and ran into starving Blacks, enslaved Hispanics, alienated Orientals, we were shocked. We said, 'Oh, our parents must not have known about this.' The whole revolution was based, not on being a revolution, but just straightening out what we thought were a few little pockets of error."

Before he moved to New York, Robert Patrick spent a lot of time thinking he was crazy. In New Mexico, during a stint in a job whose sole purpose was to pull files for Native Americans who had died that day of alcoholism, he thought, "This is insane. I mean, everyone else seemed to accept that there should be enough Indians dying of alcoholism for there to be an eight-hour-a-day job pulling their files. I thought this was horrible and it seemed to me that everything in my life was like that. Everything seemed vastly unthinkable and it could not be that everybody in the world was crazy except me. I'd read enough psychology to know that was one of the surer signs of insanity."

He even tried checking himself into an asylum. "And they said, 'There is nothing wrong with you; you should move to a big city.' When I came to New York, I encountered a group of people who had the same intuition: yes, the world was mad. And it was such a relief. 'Oh, well maybe I'm not.'" But he still didn't think of himself as a political writer out to change the world.

"When I wrote *The Haunted Host*—which is, after all, a funny love story with a gimmick and a lot of wise cracks—the very idea of gay liberation had never even been broached. It was not consciously written as a gay lib play and wasn't—until one evening when I was playing it at the Cino, leaning on a customer's table. At one point, I heard a little boy who was sitting there with a man and woman say, 'You see, Mom, Dad. I'm like that. I'm a homosexual.' I'd never thought of the effect of my plays on the audience. Not really. So that was the first and very startling realization—'This has an effect on people'—aside from making them laugh and making them love me. Until then my only concerns were to please people and get attention.

"Then I began to notice what I was doing. I started looking at other people's plays differently, you see. Not just as an audience. You start noticing, 'Hmm, that's a very interesting thing that Shakespeare or Shaw did there. How did he do that?' And you go home and you do that and say, 'Oh,' and you add another little tool.

"The moment you plug it into a real theater, and real actors, and real costumes, variables start coming in. You discover your particular actor does not have the booming voice you heard, and as a director you have to find compromises as to what they can do, reaching toward the same affecting vision. Or you rewrite. If you had John Gielgud, that speech would work as you wanted it. You don't have John Gielgud, and you may need to make the speech much stronger so *that* actor can achieve the strength and effect you wanted.

"You never know what instruments you're writing for when you're writing a play. Nobody expects a composer to write a concerto without knowing what instrument it's going to be played on. A composer would think you were crazy if you asked him. And yet that's what playwrights are asked to do. It's only the last hundred and fifty years or so that playwrights were expected to write as we do now, not knowing who's going to play it, not knowing what shape stage it's going to be on. Moliere and Shakespeare had companies they wrote for. Or else there was an approved, official style of acting so that you pretty much knew how it was going to be acted and mounted. Even up into the thirties and forties or even into the fifties in this country, what difference did it really make if George C. Scott or Jason Robards or Ben Gazzara or Pat Hingle played the role? They were going to play it the same way, and it was probably going to be on a Broadway proscenium stage. So the writers had some idea. Nowadays, we write in a void."

When I asked about *Kennedy's Children*, his only play to be produced on Broadway, and wondered whether he had visualized it there, he responded with gentle sarcasm. "Oh, sure. Oh, sure. In 1969, I was sure the next big Broadway demand was going to be for the hopes of the failed generation. No. I started writing it the day Bobby Kennedy died. Did another draft of it in '73 for friends to hear. The people next door in my building on First Avenue came over every night to hear what I'd written that day.

"It lay in the drawer for quite a while, and then a boy I knew who wanted to be a director came over to see me. He said, 'Bob, I'm sleeping with a guy who runs a theater and he says he'll let me direct a play. Have you got a play that hasn't been done?'

"I said, 'Look in the drawer.' He pulled out *Kennedy's Children* and it was put on, not because the man that ran the theater thought it had any value, but just to please his boyfriend.

"One of the actors in it thought that Sparger was a juicy role, optioned the play from me, and for two years went all over America, then all over the world, trying to get someone to put it on. And finally, he found a bankrupt pub in a slum in London that did plays in its back room. They decided they loved the play, thought it had no chance, but figured since they were bankrupt anyway, they might as well go out with a play they liked. On that basis they put it on.

"The day after opening, I signed a contract for translations to sixty languages. Now, you would have thought an intelligent person would have stayed in England to work. But no. I said, 'Ah, now I'm famous. Now I can go back and do some good in America.' That was fifteen years ago. I have learned a great deal. I've learned things I didn't want to know, but then, ninety percent of the things you learn are things you don't want to know."

He looked at me—world-weary, toughened, yet deeply vulnerable. He had been talking, flat out, for a long time and he asked, half-smiling, "Is this of any value?"

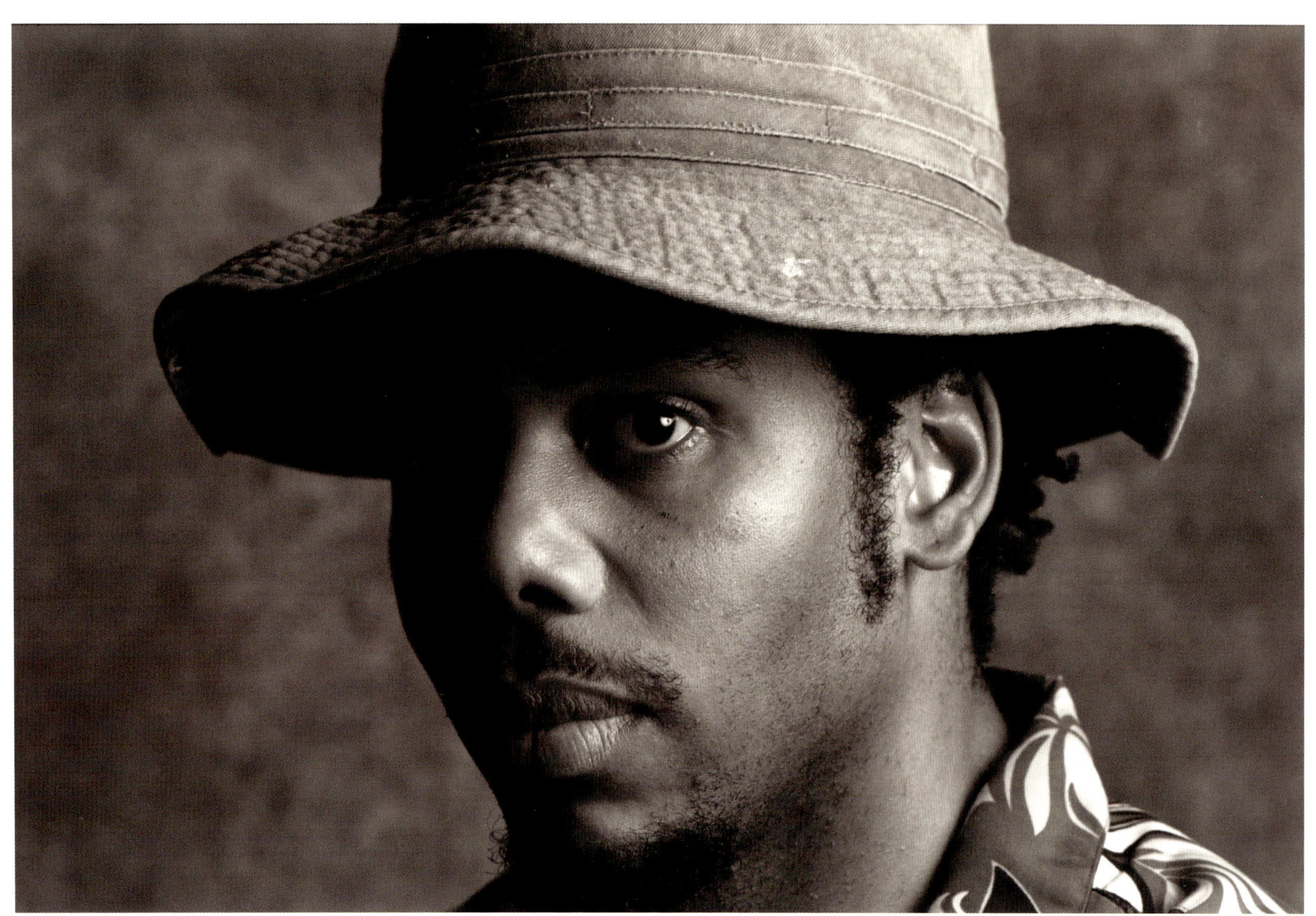

Carl Hancock Rux — Naomi Wallace (opposite)

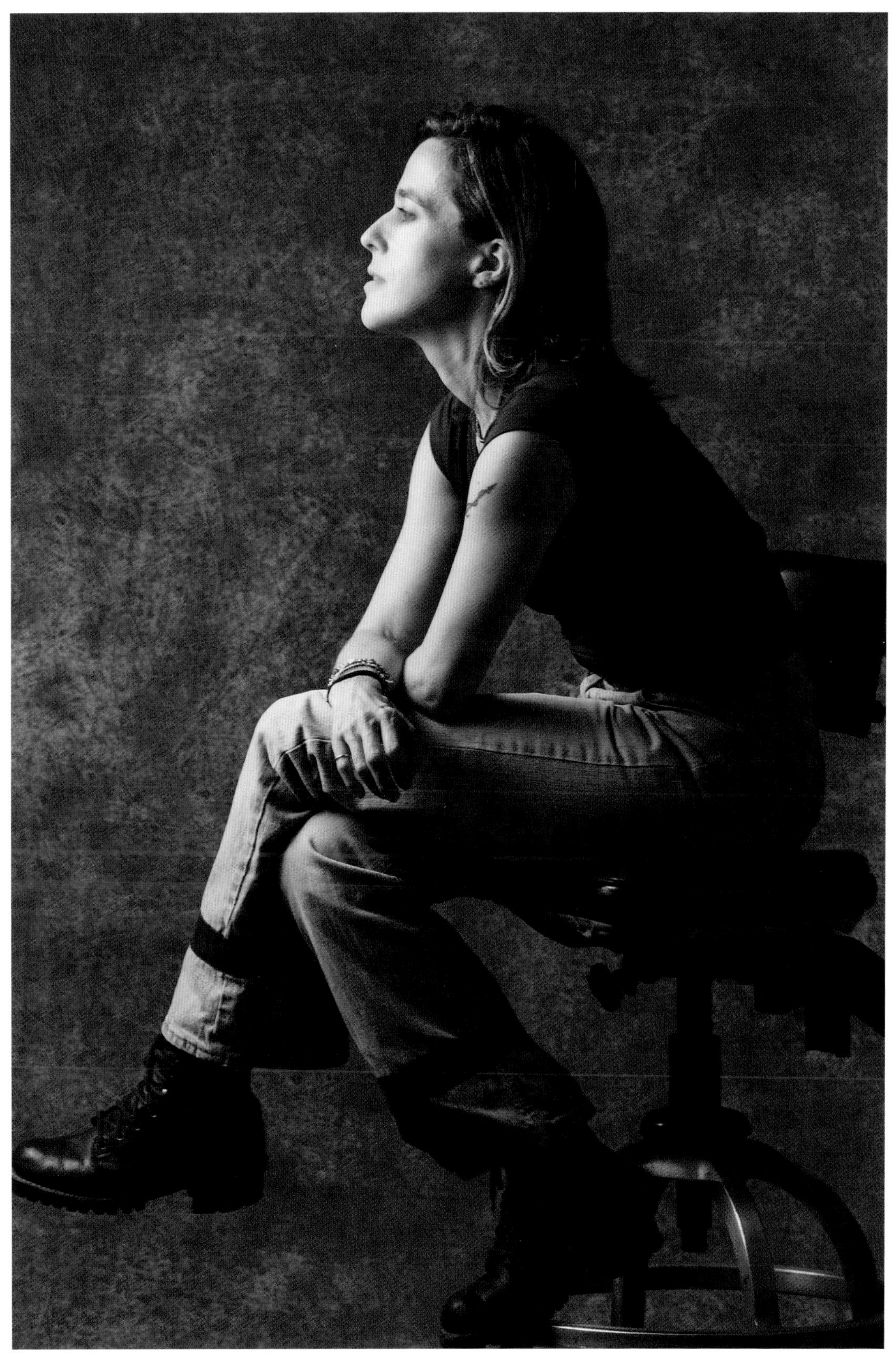

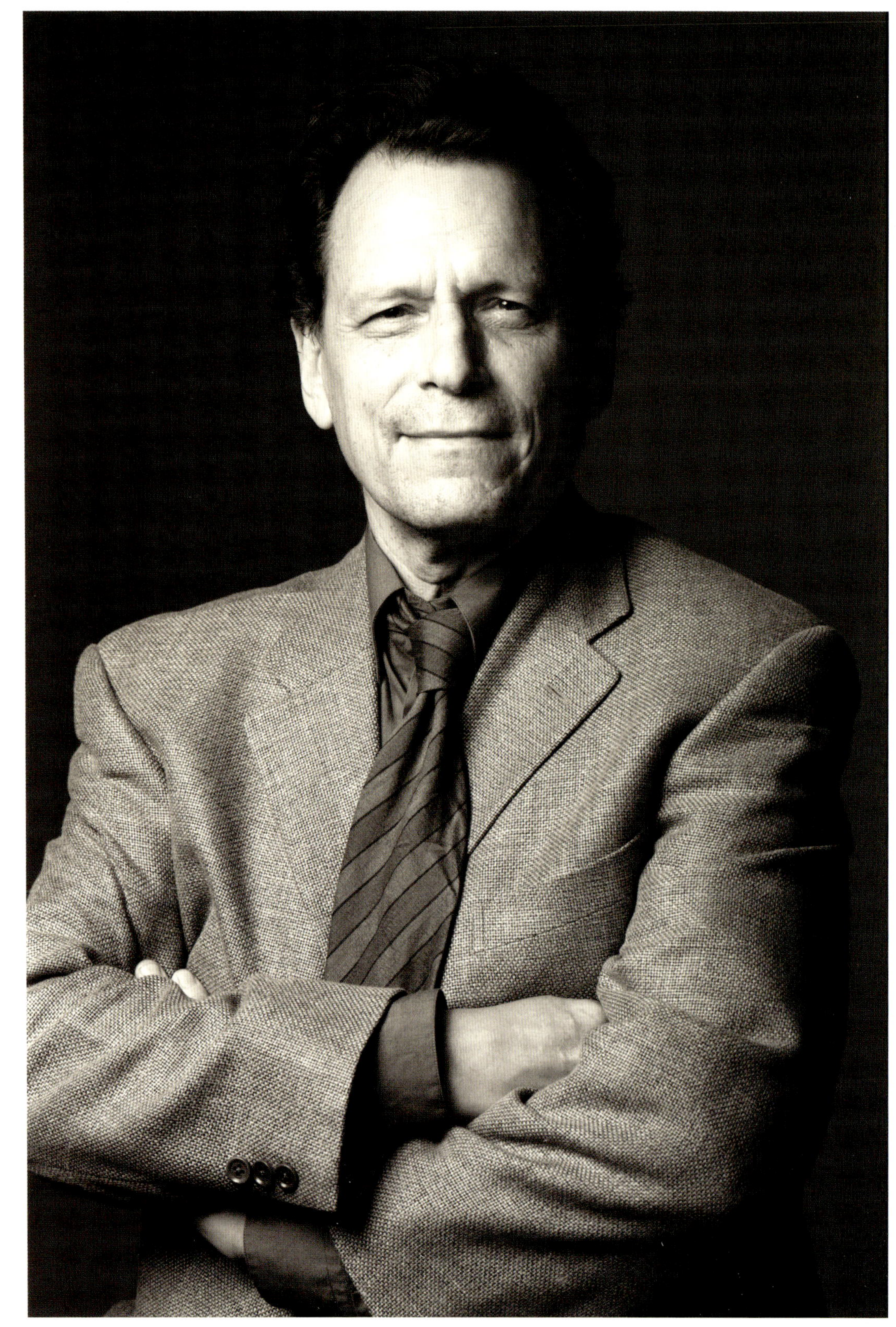

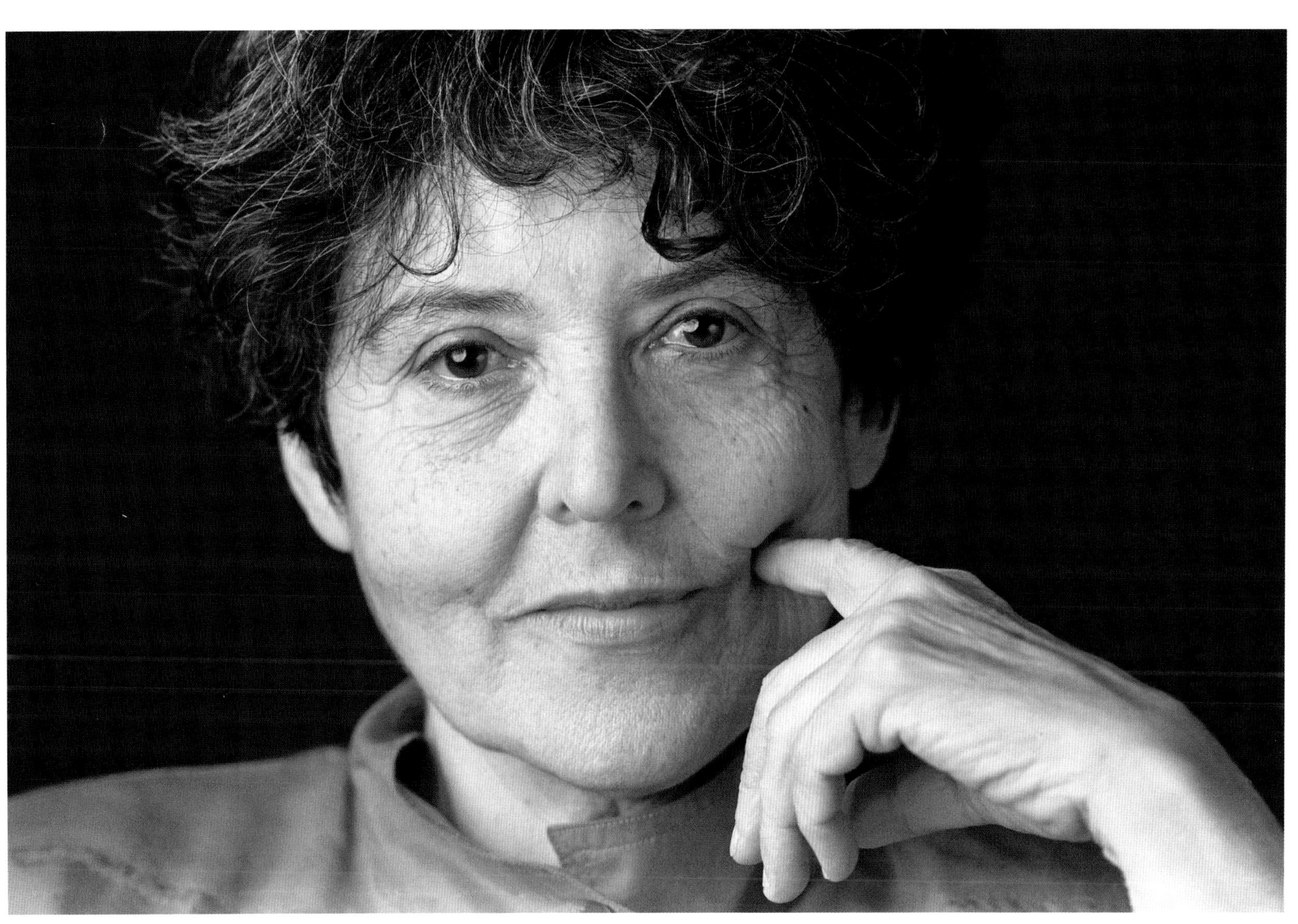

Michael Weller (opposite) — Maria Irene Fornes

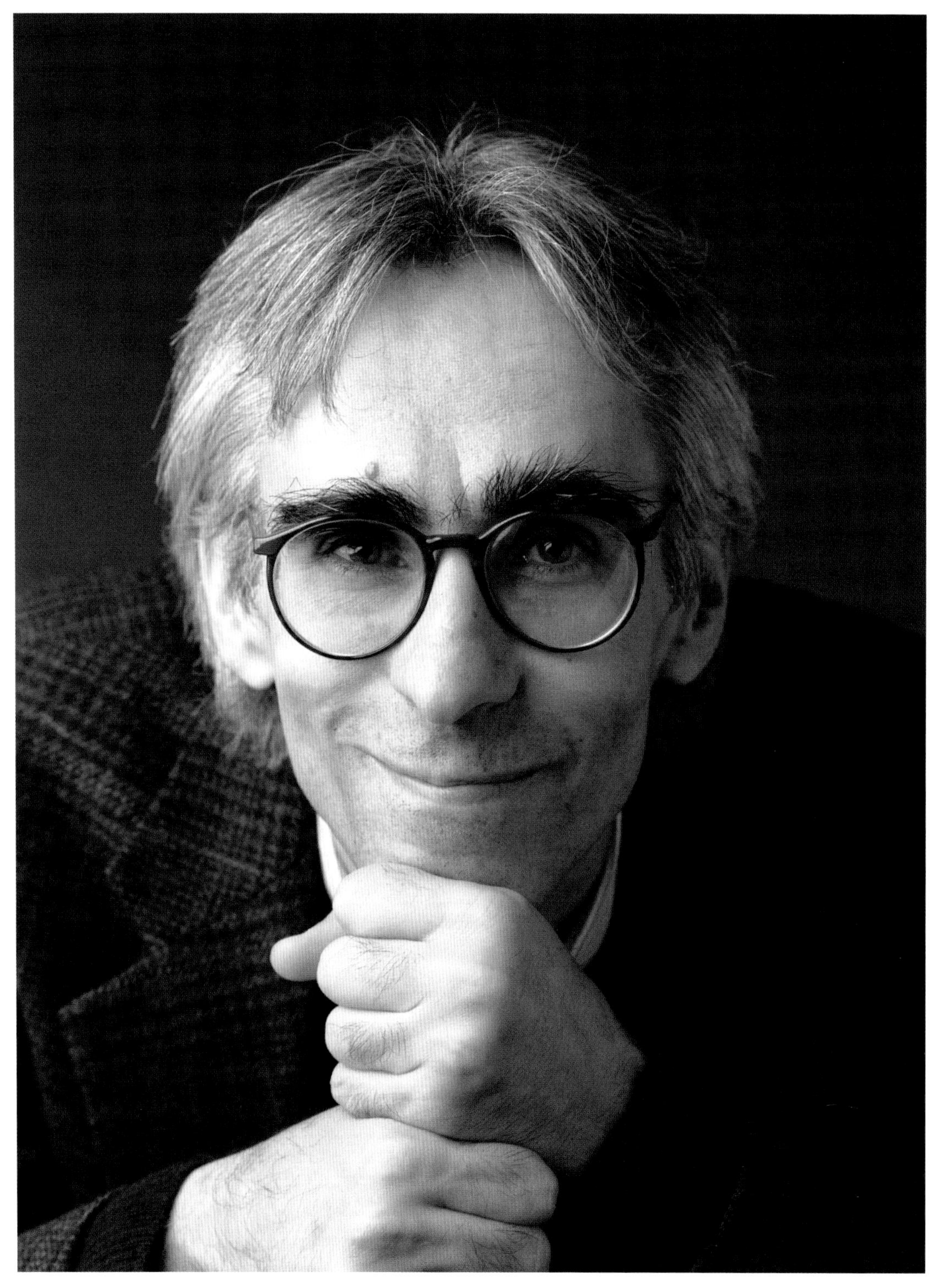

David Ives — Al Carmines (opposite)

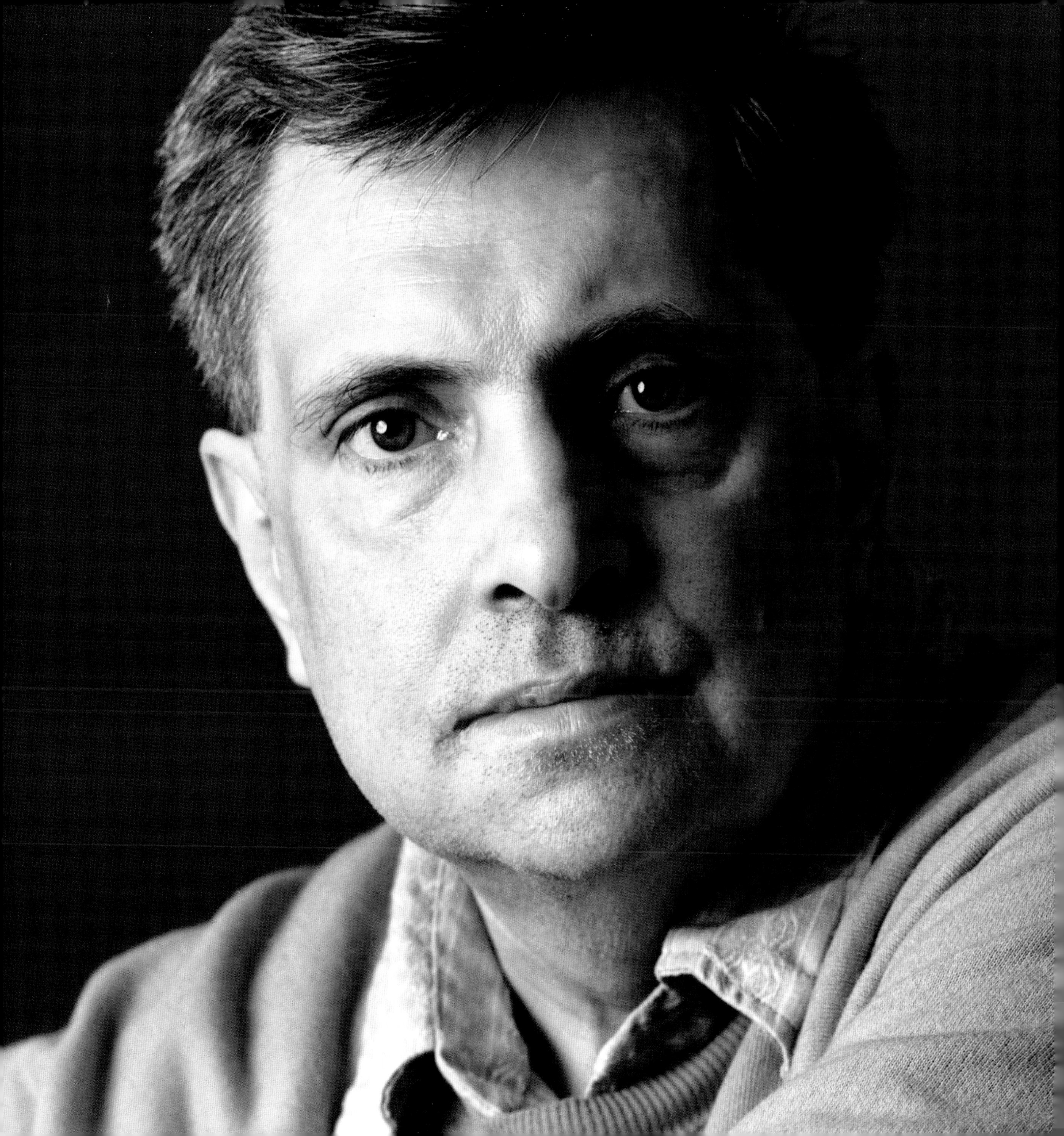

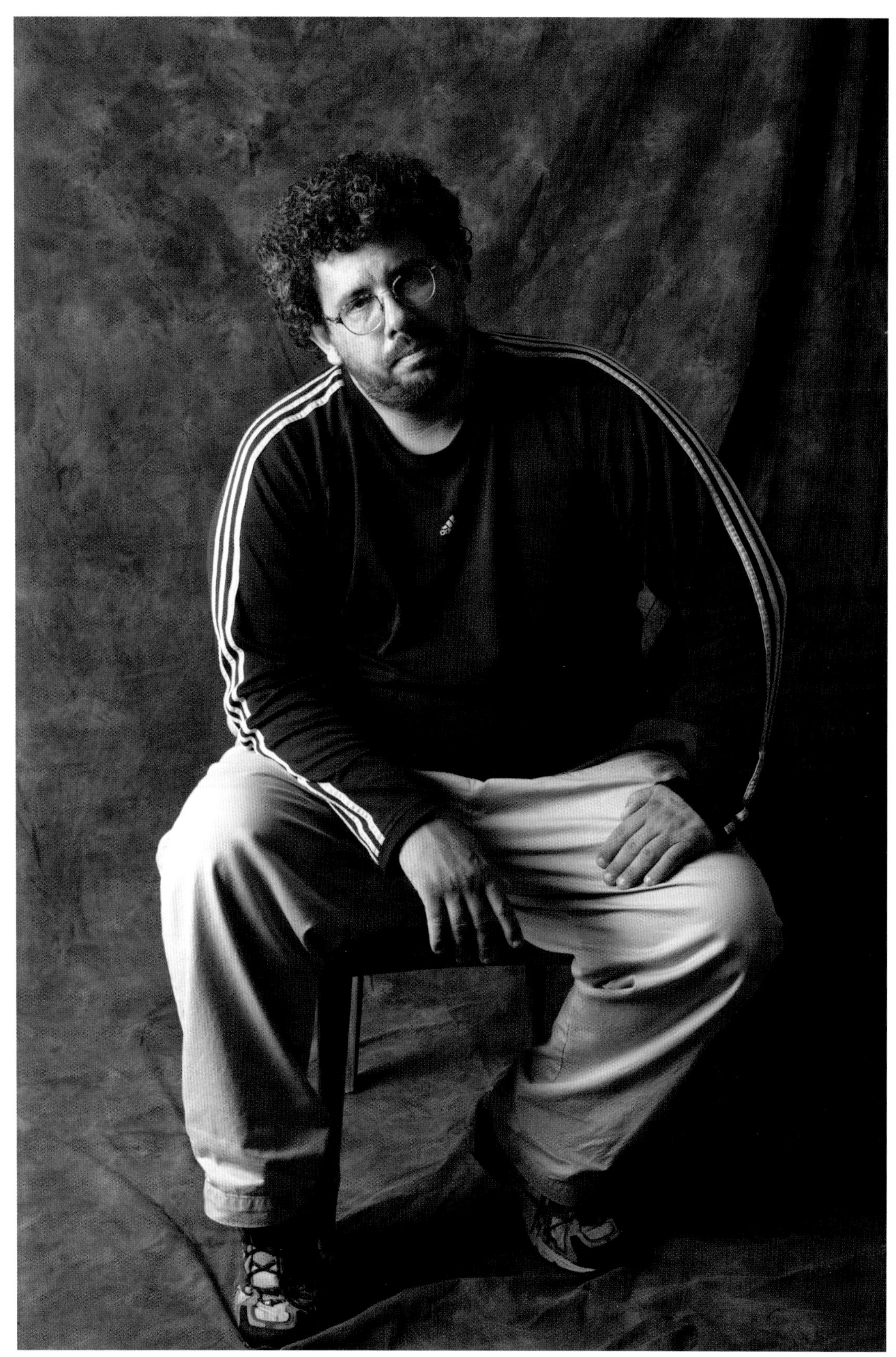

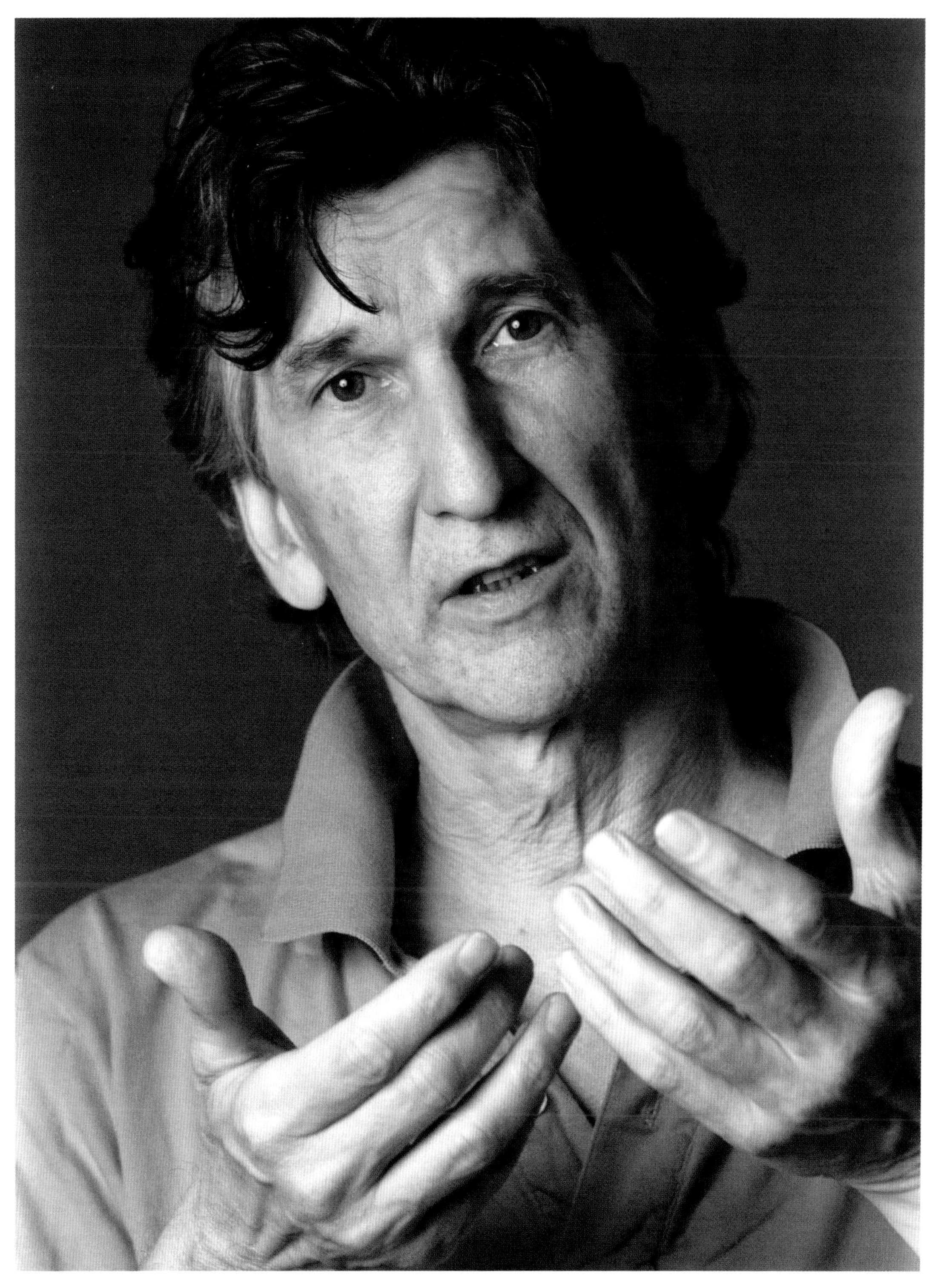

Neil LaBute (opposite) — Charles Mee

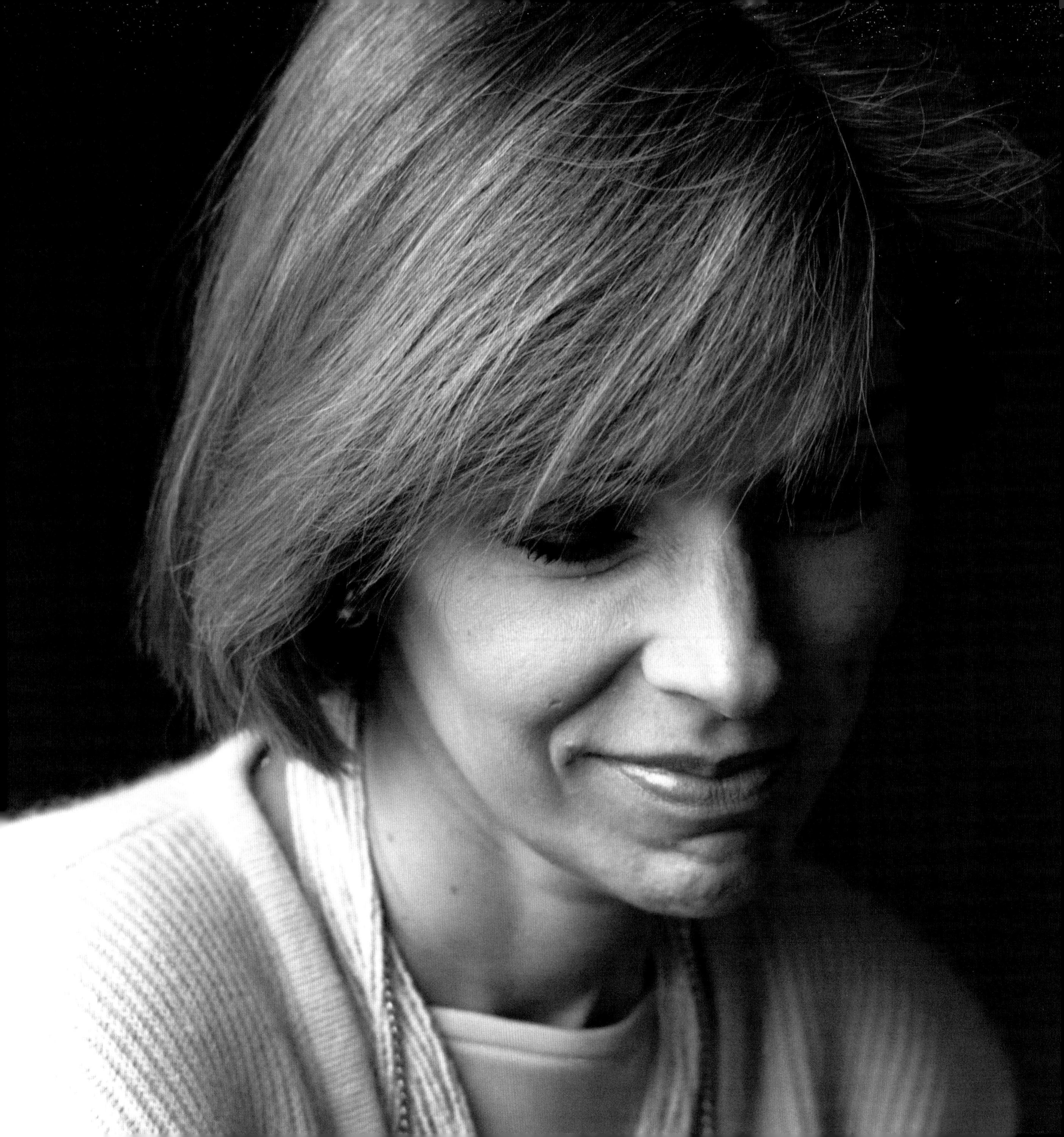

MARSHA NORMAN

(Born 1947—American playwright, screenwriter, and novelist, on the faculty at the Juilliard School, winner of the Pulitzer Prize for 'night, Mother.*)*

[The following is Marsha Norman, in her own words.]

*   *   *

My grandfather was a master storyteller, and he lived with us, so I grew up listening to his tales of adventures in the Wild West. What was thrilling about Granddaddy's tales . . . they had this theatricality to them all of us kids were aware of. Oral tradition is quite important. You grow up hearing a story, hearing it over and over and over again, and you come to love the story, and you love the storyteller.

Aside from Granddaddy's stories, the house was a place of enforced fear so that I was not allowed to speak up, or rant, rave, or rebel in any kind of outward way. As a result, I did that all internally, living a life of internal monologues. I was thinking of what I would say if I didn't have to stand there and smile. Repression of that talk ultimately explodes. I think that's certainly the case for me—all that silence for all those years is what allows me to do all this talking now.

Actors Theatre opened up in Louisville when I was a kid. They were operating in a small theater up a very narrow staircase using peach tree baskets for lights. It was a very shoestring operation in everything except acting, and, of course, the choice of plays. As a ten-year-old, I walked up the stairs to see *Glass Menagerie.* That was pretty much it for me. I thought, "Well, this is where I belong."

On into college, when I was in the theater I felt at home, and I felt I understood things. I knew I could do this. Lots of times I would walk out of shows with adolescent contempt and say, "I can do that. I can do *better* than that." This is exactly where a career comes from—finding a place where you seem to already speak the language and know what's going on there and are just waiting for the moment when it's your turn. This was all covert. These were all my little dreams.

What actually happened is that I went to college, and I was a philosophy major, and I came back home to Louisville and got a job. I did not believe for a moment that I could make a living writing, so I worked in the world. I worked in a state mental hospital. I worked in a program for gifted kids, and finally, I worked for the Kentucky Arts Commission.

When I was twenty-nine, I arrived at a moment of despair and boredom and realized that if I ever wanted to find out if I could write, I should do it. At the Actors Theatre, I had just seen a play called *Female Transport*, with Susan Kingsley in it. I was so moved, so shaken by Susan's performance that I decided, "Not only do I want to write, I want to write for her." So I had gathered up enough money from working three jobs to quit work for a year.

I went to talk to John Jory [Actors Theatre of Louisville founder and director]. He wanted to know if he could commission a play about busing in Louisville. I would go and gather people's thoughts on a tape recorder, and then I would come back, and we would all put them together into a play. He offered to pay me five thousand dollars. I was mightily impressed by this, but I knew almost instantly that I couldn't do it. I hadn't worked three jobs for the past year to take another job now. I wanted to write something I knew about.

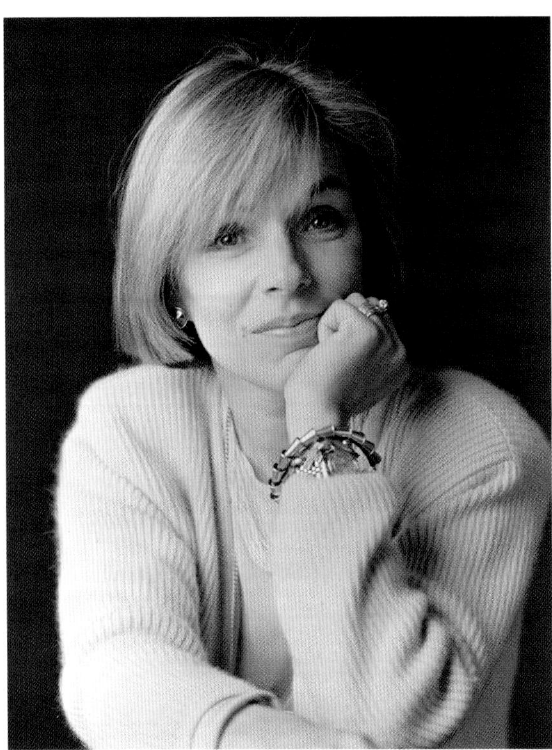

So I went back to John and said, "I can't believe I'm turning you down, but I just don't want to write about busing."

And he said, "What do you want to write about?"

I said to John, "I don't know."

He said, "Why don't you think back to a time when you were frightened, when you were actually afraid for your physical safety, and write about that."

I didn't get three steps out of the building when I realized there had been such a time, and it was when I was working at the mental hospital. A girl there was very dangerous. She was thirteen at the time, and we all lived in mortal fear of her. This thought occurred to me, "What happens to a girl like that if she's ever locked up and she can't run off, run away?" That was the beginning of *Getting Out*. My life changed in one moment—the moment when the curtain came down on the opening night performance.

I regularly advise young writers that if they can find any way to communicate what they have to say other than writing, then go do anything other than write it as a play, because it's only that court of last appeal that the theatre is. It has that urgency only then, that intimacy you really need. A piece of theatre needs to be driven by the overcoming of some obstacle. You must be writing this because you don't have any other way to talk about it.

Novels deal much better with the scenery of one's life. The theatre can really only deal with the life itself. In that way, theatre deals with the same kinds of things that have been dealt with around tribal campfires since the beginning of time—what is required to survive.

When I wrote *'night, Mother*, I did not think anyone would ever want to see that play but me. I was wrong about that. There are other plays I had thought, "Lots of people care about this" and in fact, they don't. You don't know at the time. What happens when a piece leaves the hands of the author and goes in front of the audience is that the audience decides if the piece belongs in this, the communal record, or not.

I don't write from a political consciousness of myself as a woman but from an emotional and intellectual consciousness of myself as a woman. I write stories of women because those are the stories I know and not because I want to make some point about women's lives. I am proud to be telling stories of women because that is basically an unwritten literature. The stories remain untold until people like me tell them. I'm doing it out of very personal reasons. The audience brings the politics of it.

I think we're in trouble in America because the critics here seem to have an attitude of consumer journalism, where they say, "Buy this, don't buy that." The consumer has to be warned about faulty products. The effect of the eighties on the theatre was that if it didn't make money, it wasn't valuable.

I will always write for the theatre because I like the interaction of the world of the theatre. I'm writing a play right now for John Jory's Actors Theatre because I know that means I get to have lots of conversations with John on the phone, and I'll get to go down to Louisville, get to watch rehearsals, I'll get to do the whole life of a play, which is really fun for me. This is that family I was always looking for and writing plays is how I get to go see them. In a sense, it's like if you want to see your own family for Thanksgiving, you make your carrot soufflé and you go see them. In the theatre, you do your part to get to be there.

What the electronic media has done is . . . appropriate most of the territory that used to belong to the theatre. What's left now for writers in the theatre are those things that must be seen live to be believed, and that's the province of musicals, the province of particularly theatrical plays such as those done by George Wolfe or Martha Clarke. My new play is certainly in that ilk. You have a guy running around in buckskins and another guy running around in jeans and a tee shirt. And they are carrying on an active, present-moment battle for the spirit of the same woman, and she is trying to figure out what there is to love in the contemporary world. That's an idea you can't make a movie about, you can't do TV about.

In the moment of writing, the characters themselves come from the characters themselves. I sit here and am aware of how this person speaks and what's funny to them, what their problem is. And my task, as I perceive it in the moment of writing, is simply to record as fairly as possible what it is they have to say. It's a kind of awareness of a pre-existing person whose story I'm recording. Later, when I see it on the stage, I am aware of the connection between myself and that person. I'm aware of what was happening in my life at the moment that caused me to choose this one of all the stories that were possible to record.

Writing for the theatre needs to be very transparent. You need *not* to see the writer at work. The audience doesn't want to even be aware that someone made it because they want in fact to have the journey themselves. I think the job of the playwright is to nominate for permanent memory a number of people who've acted nobly or courageously or bravely, or perhaps, in a cowardly fashion—people who have walked down the path of life and made some choices and have seen what happened.

In the South, the chronicling of life takes place on the porch. There's an acute awareness of the individual in the South. In the North, there is much more of an awareness of the dilemma of a group of people. In the South, you are talking about one person and only one person—that's the power of Southern material. It is still that way. Those are porch issues. This is not to diminish their size, but you talk about them on the porch because it just means the porch is where you can breathe. You can sit out there, and you can sip tea or that lemonade or that julep, and you can talk about that person all the way back or all the way forward. Any place where you retreat from the labors of the day—that's where the talk begins.

Conor McPherson (opposite)

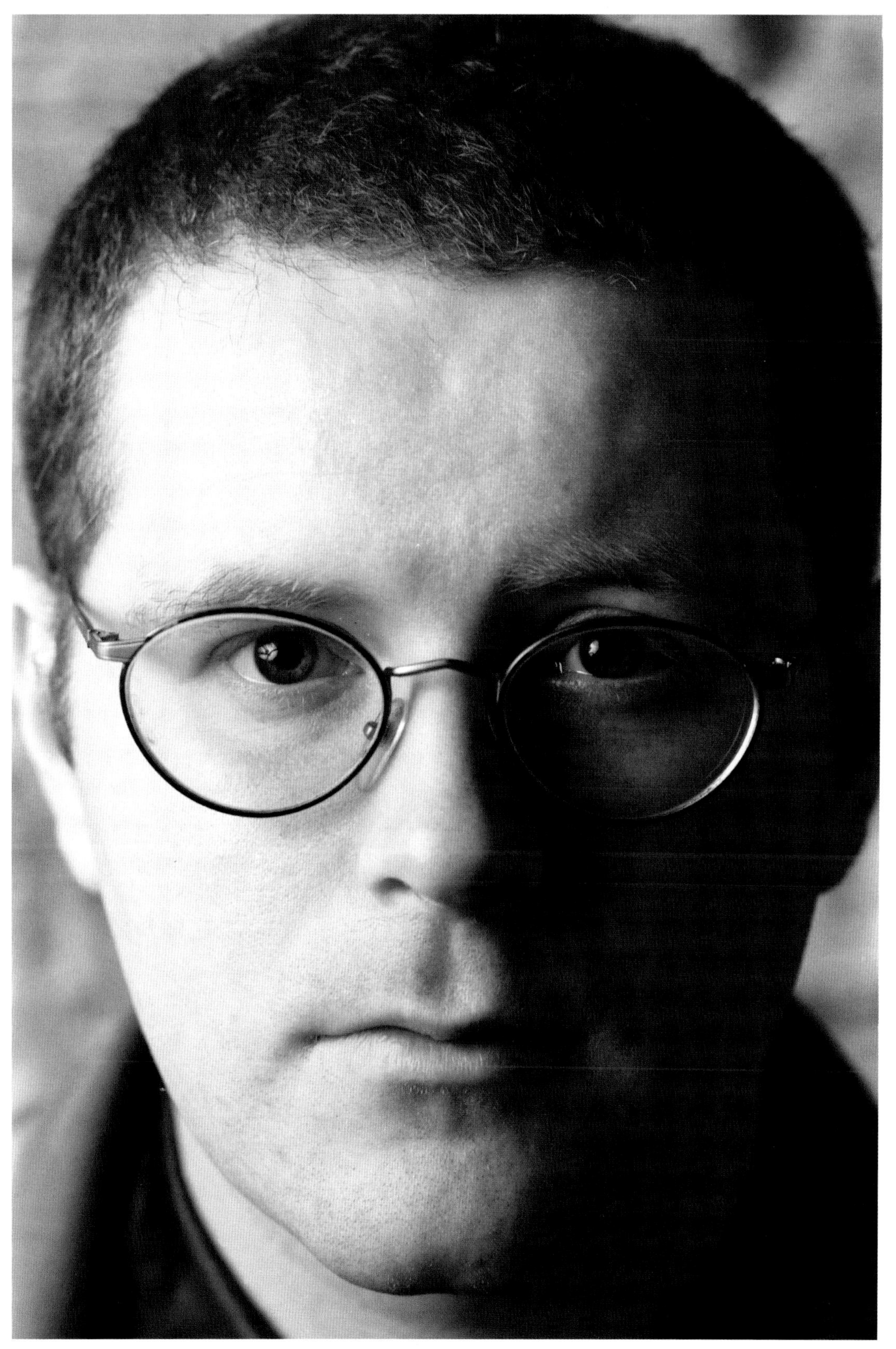

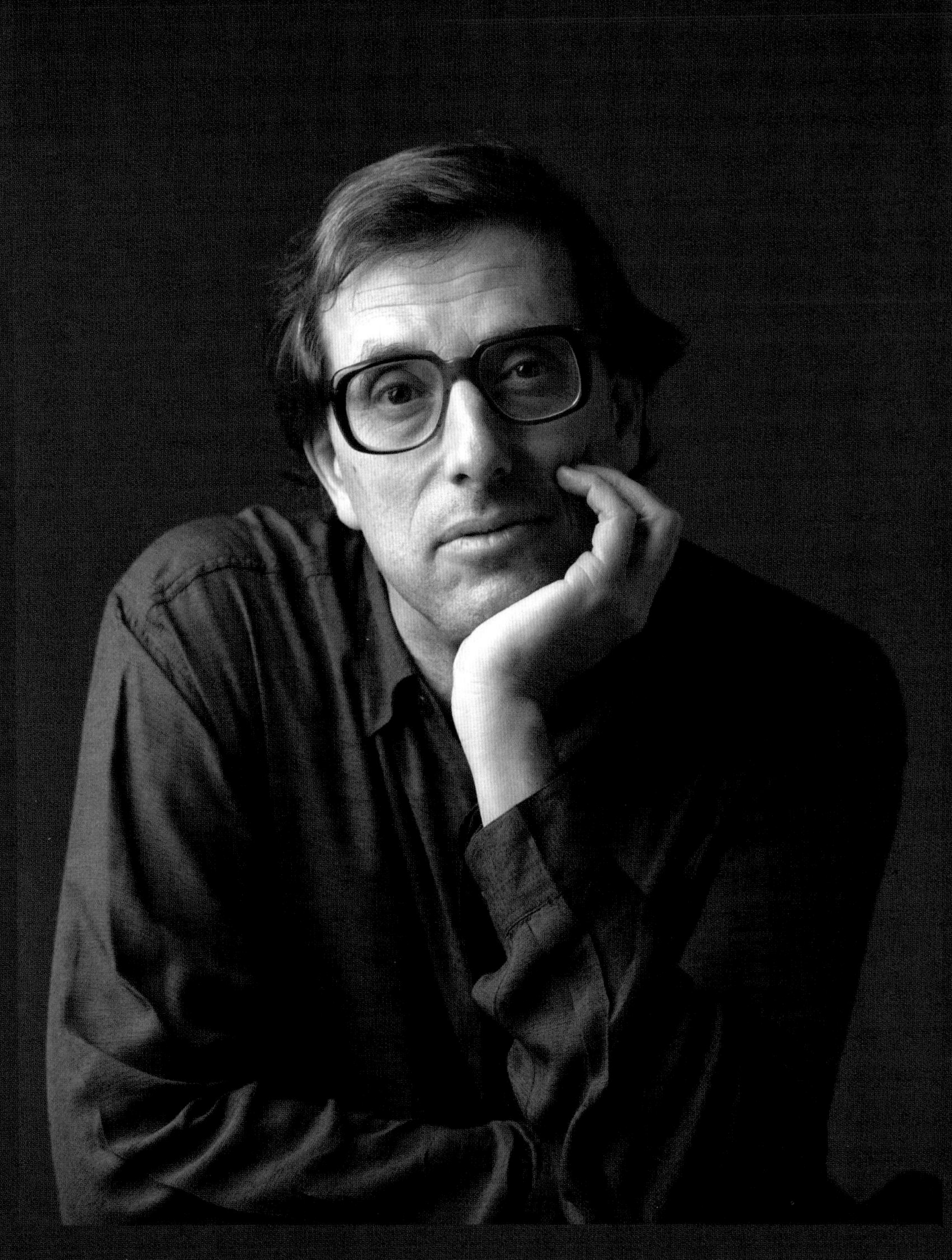

Ariel Dorfman — Horton Foote (opposite)

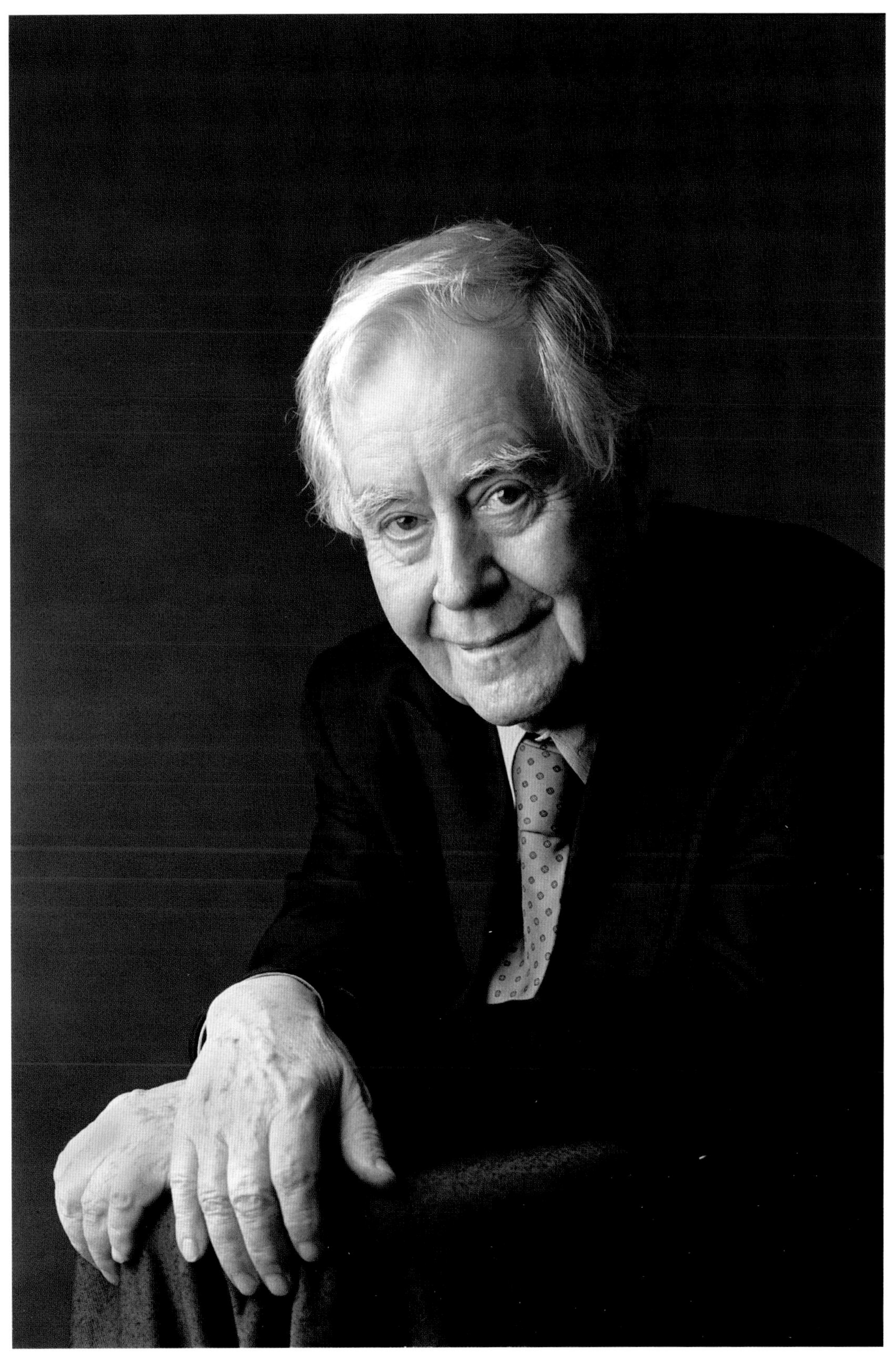

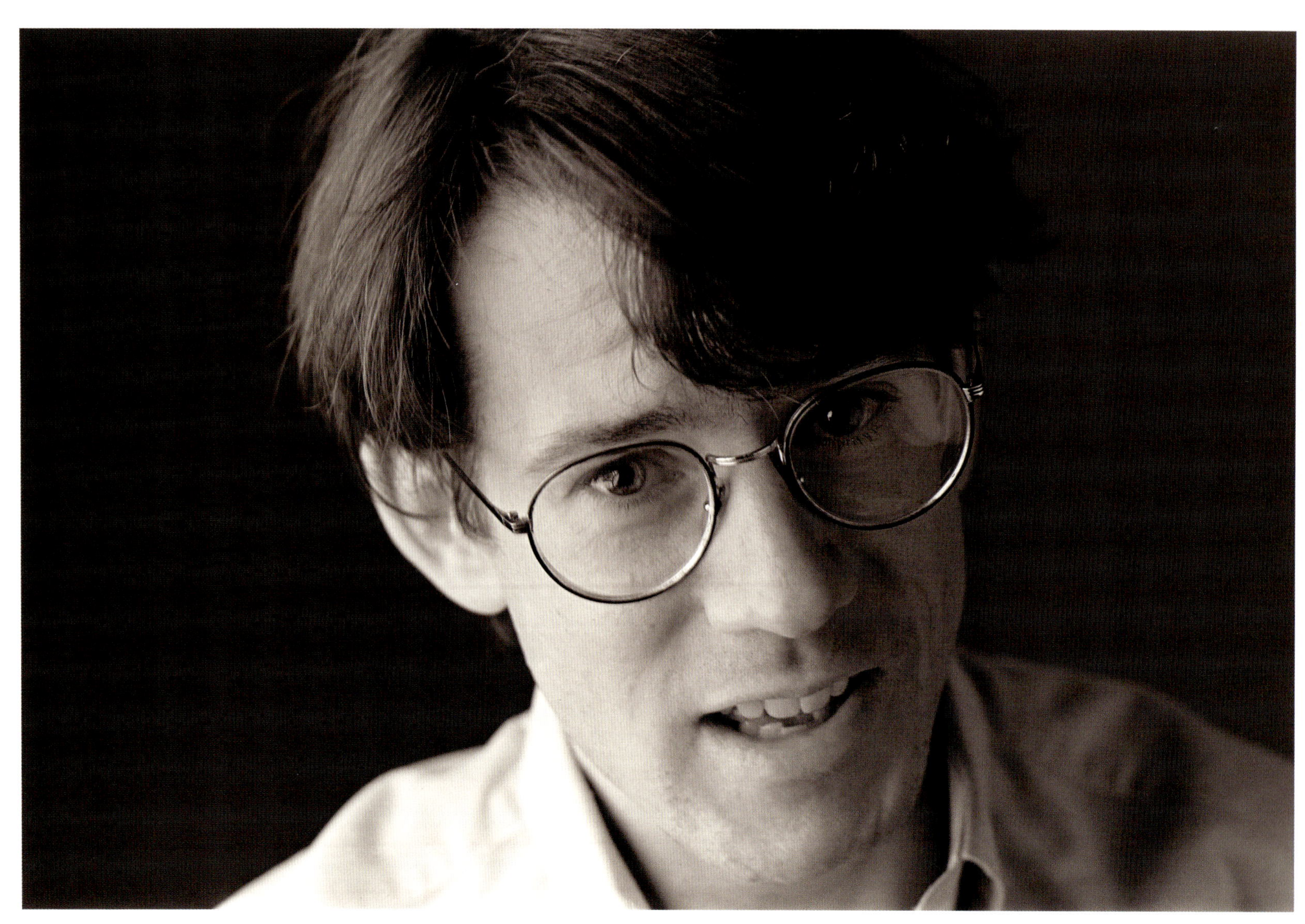

Keith Reddin — Dael Orlandersmith (opposite)

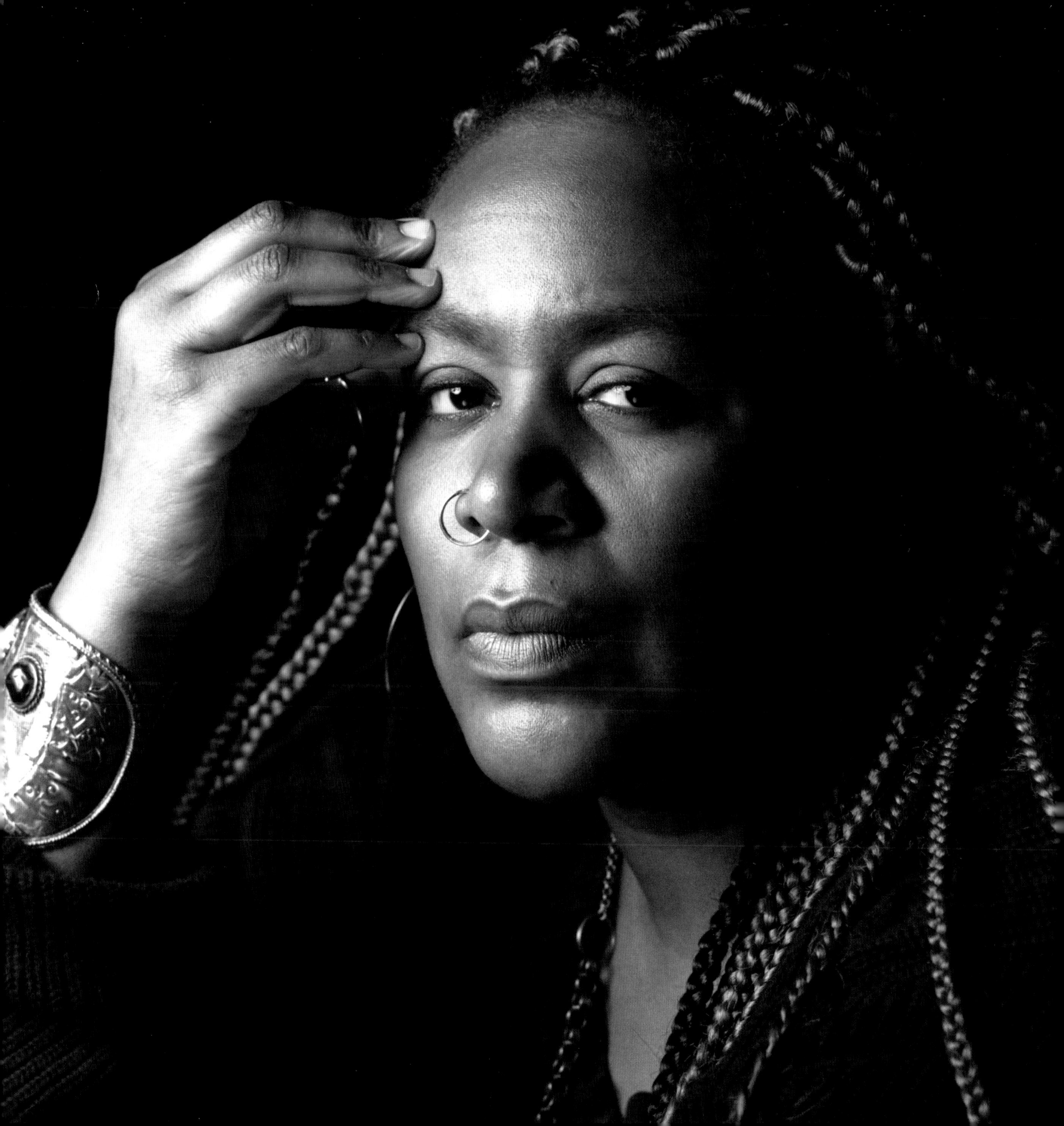

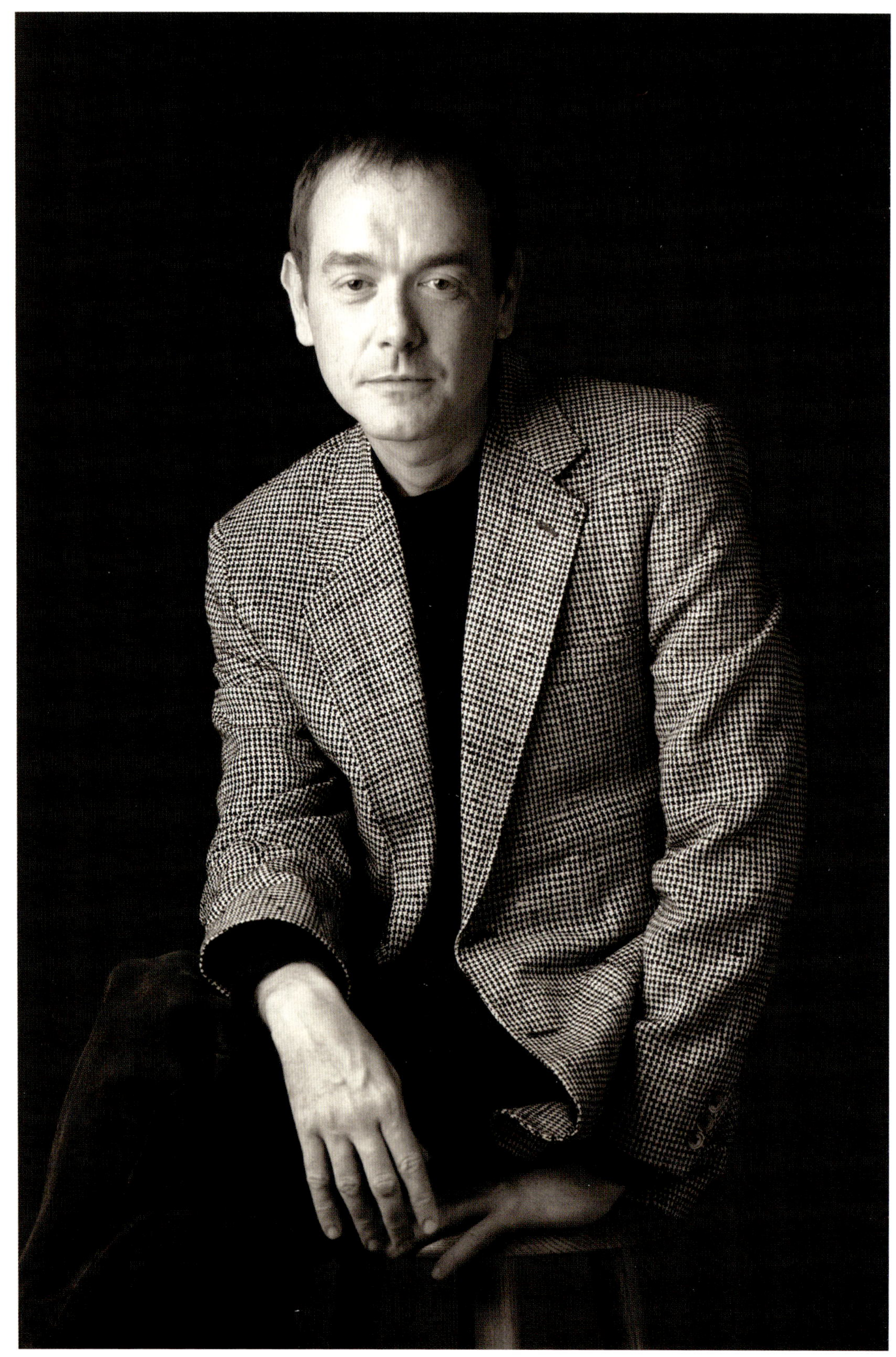

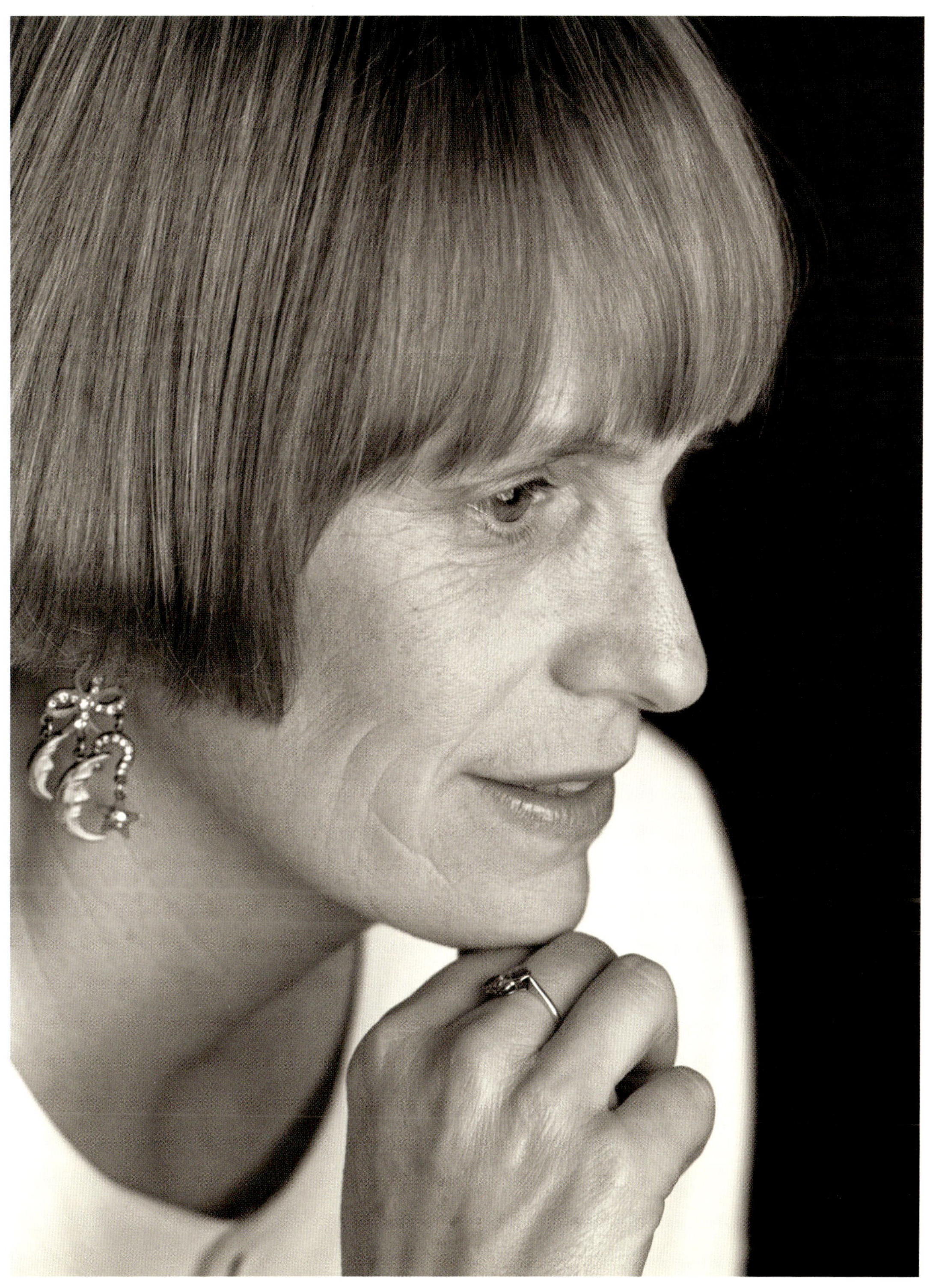

Jim Grimsley (opposite) — Tina Howe

CRAIG LUCAS

(Born 1951—American playwright, awarded Excellence in Literature Award from the American Academy of Arts and Letters and the PEN/Laura Pels International Foundation for Theater Award for a playwright in mid-career.)

Craig Lucas is someone who laughs easily. It was early 1990 when Craig and I met at his apartment and spoke—and laughed. I remember large windows in an informal, open-plan Tribeca apartment. Craig and I share a Broadway musical theatre performance background so we reminisced a bit. We discovered we also had the same iconic first theatre experience—seeing *Peter Pan* with Mary Martin. The magic of theatre made its mark on both of us.

Many children grow up putting on a show for family members. Craig was different. The kind of show he put on involved spending countless childhood hours meticulously writing plays for his collection of puppets.

"I was a playwright as a child, too. The stories had to accommodate the puppets I had, so I wrote. My father made me a puppet stage, a kind of elaborate stage, which collapsed so that we could travel with it and take it to people's houses, perform at birthday parties."

That image of his childhood seems to make sense for an only child. "I found that in a lot of writing friends: the 'only child' syndrome." He mentioned other writers who were only children: Lillian Hellman, Edward Albee. "You're making friends up with your mind."

That is where he is most comfortable—in the mind, daydreaming, spinning stories. As a puppeteer and during his twenties, he did a lot of performing, but then it changed. "I realized I wasn't very happy performing. The part I liked was staying home by myself and making up stories and getting to inhabit the characters and then handing it over to professional actors. I really like to be in the audience. Being a writer, being a playwright—it's like getting to act but nobody gets to see you act. You do it totally alone. Maybe it isn't true that we can be anything and become anything, but it's certainly an enchanting notion to follow. The theatre is especially suited to making anything seem possible. This is all pretend anyway."

Craig Lucas's playwriting path opened up like something out of fantasy. "The only thing I ever had to write without any sense of affirmation was the first act of my first play. And I gave that first act to Norman René and he said, 'If you finish this play by April first, I promise I will produce it.' That was *Reckless*. And then a year later

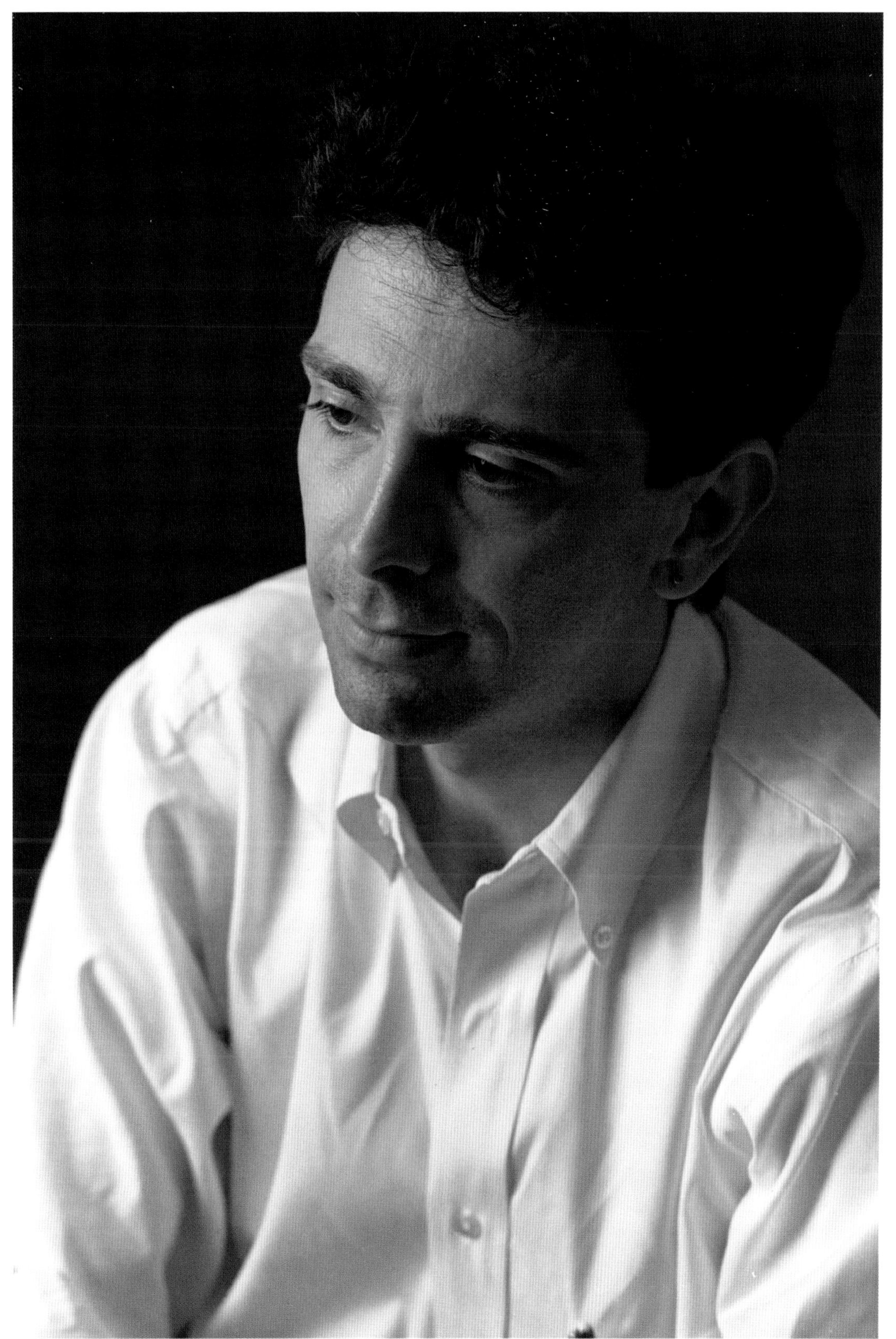

he said, 'What do you want to do? Let's put together a play for seven actors. Let's pick the best seven actors we know and let's write a play for them. Let's do it late night. How quickly can you write it?'

"And I said, 'Six weeks.'

"And he said, 'I'll do it.'

"So he gave me this gift and then after that I got a commission from South Coast Repertory to write *Prelude to a Kiss*. I really was very lucky in having a sense of family where I could work. For me, it's very important."

After the success of *Prelude to a Kiss* on Broadway, there were Hollywood opportunities—in a very different medium. "What's different and interesting about movies is that you can get in very close to the face and you can see things which in the theater—unless you're lucky enough to be in the front row—you won't catch. I build certain things into the dialogue, so the audience can glean as a whole where they are emotionally, including the person in the last row. In a movie, it's possible to do that without those words. They're both storytelling. The theatre does avail you a certain amount of artistic control. And in exchange, you make no money." He laughed.

"So, where do your germinal ideas come from?" I asked.

"For me it's like daydreaming. Most people think, 'Wouldn't it be nice if that man who's horrible to me at the office went outside and a cornice fell off of a building and hit him on the head?' I think all creative writers do is follow that lead. They say, 'So, if somebody does come out of the building and the cornice falls on his head, then what about the wives and kids? They ain't going to support themselves.' And then you begin to tell the story to yourself, which is a private process."

I asked him why the element of surprise seemed to come up so often in his work. "Actually life experience is hugely unpredictable, and disturbing, and chaotic. I think plays are lifelike when they can put the audience in the experience of the unpredictableness of living, the dangerousness of living."

"Is it sort of your job to wake us up? Do you ever feel that—?"

"I don't think there's one job. I think it's refreshing to go to the theatre and be woken up, as you say. I think it's refreshing and fun to go to the theatre and be lulled into a nice dream that isn't true and has nothing to do with reality. It really depends. I haven't ever done one project exactly like the other.

"Some parts I've written for particular actors; so I've gone through the process of asking them what they wanted to get out of the project and tailored what I wrote to them and to their needs. I find technical challenges are very freeing, sort of like writing a sonnet."

He talked about his years at Yale, studying poetry. "I remember when finally—after three years of studying with Anne Sexton—I sent her a little play I had written. She read it and called my roommate, I wasn't home, and said, 'Good news, good news, you're a playwright!' And I could tell in her voice when I finally got her on the phone that she was relieved I could do better than write poetry. She was very encouraging and told me not to go to graduate school and not to bother studying writing; that I should just teach myself, which I think was very good advice."

"Do you have a routine you do every day?"

"When I'm writing I try to make as much free time in the early part of the day to write, and when I'm rewriting I try to make as much free time in the morning and night."

"Do you get obsessive?"

"Oh sure, and I like that. Especially rewriting, and there's almost nothing I'd rather be doing. Though it can be painful, and confusing, and certainly in the middle of the process you think, '*What* was I thinking?' I remember throwing a script down on a desk and just screaming to the characters, 'Get yourselves out of this mess! I don't know how you got in there and I can't help you people!' It seems so real."

"Do they answer you?"

"No. It's frightening sometimes because you have this illusive feeling there is a right, correct, real play there. And I don't think that's true."

"It isn't like Michelangelo chipping away the marble to find the statue in the middle?"

"It feels that way but I think it's an illusion. It does feel that way, though, and then it becomes so real. You talk to other writers about their plays and you say, 'What do you think happens to the character afterwards?' You feel you're talking about real people.

"I find it personally difficult to write a character where there is some aspect of their behavior I can't identify with or inhabit. I don't believe in the concept of 'villain.' I would love to write a character that is really morally reprehensible and find some way to bring you inside them. That would be amazing.

"I go around and around about what I think art is for. I have a collaborator who I've worked with many years who feels people go to the theater just to learn how to live their lives better. I think it's something more primitive than that. It's about going through an experience like inhabiting another person's dream. You enter this dark place and everybody sits down and agrees to be quiet, or relatively quiet, and face one direction and look through a tunnel. It's like entering other people's dreams.

"It's like communion with other human beings inside one of those dreams and what I like about it is, it's not just the writer. When I go to see *'night, Mother*, I'm not just inhabiting Marsha Norman's nightmare. I'm inhabiting Kathy Bates's nightmare and Anne Pitoniak's nightmare—it's communal. These people all collaborated to bring you this experience, which is not real, and it's more real than what you would see on the street. Maybe that's my own pathology that I think theatre is more real than life."

I asked about the major influences on his writing. "I had a lot of hero worship relationships—not so much playwrights as love affairs with writers, fiction writers—in my teens and twenties. Isherwood and J. D. Salinger were important in my teens, Cheever and Virginia Woolf in my twenties. And I really was infatuated with Stephen Sondheim as a teenager and in my twenties. I managed to finagle an introduction to him. At one point we got some songs directly from him. I was in the chorus of *Sweeney Todd*, where I got to know him a little bit better. He's been very important, kind of a mentor. He's very, very helpful. He read my first play and told me what was good about it and what was not good.

"What you do with your ideas, and how you transform them into your own aesthetic, what you see in people's work, is taste. They're telling you, 'If I were to go to the theater, this is what I would like to see.' Taste is an ephemeral, non-quantifiable thing. Two people sitting next to each other at the theater and one goes, 'Why is that set so ugly?'

"And the person next to him is going, 'Why is that set so beautiful?'"

Laughter.

Everett Quinton (opposite)

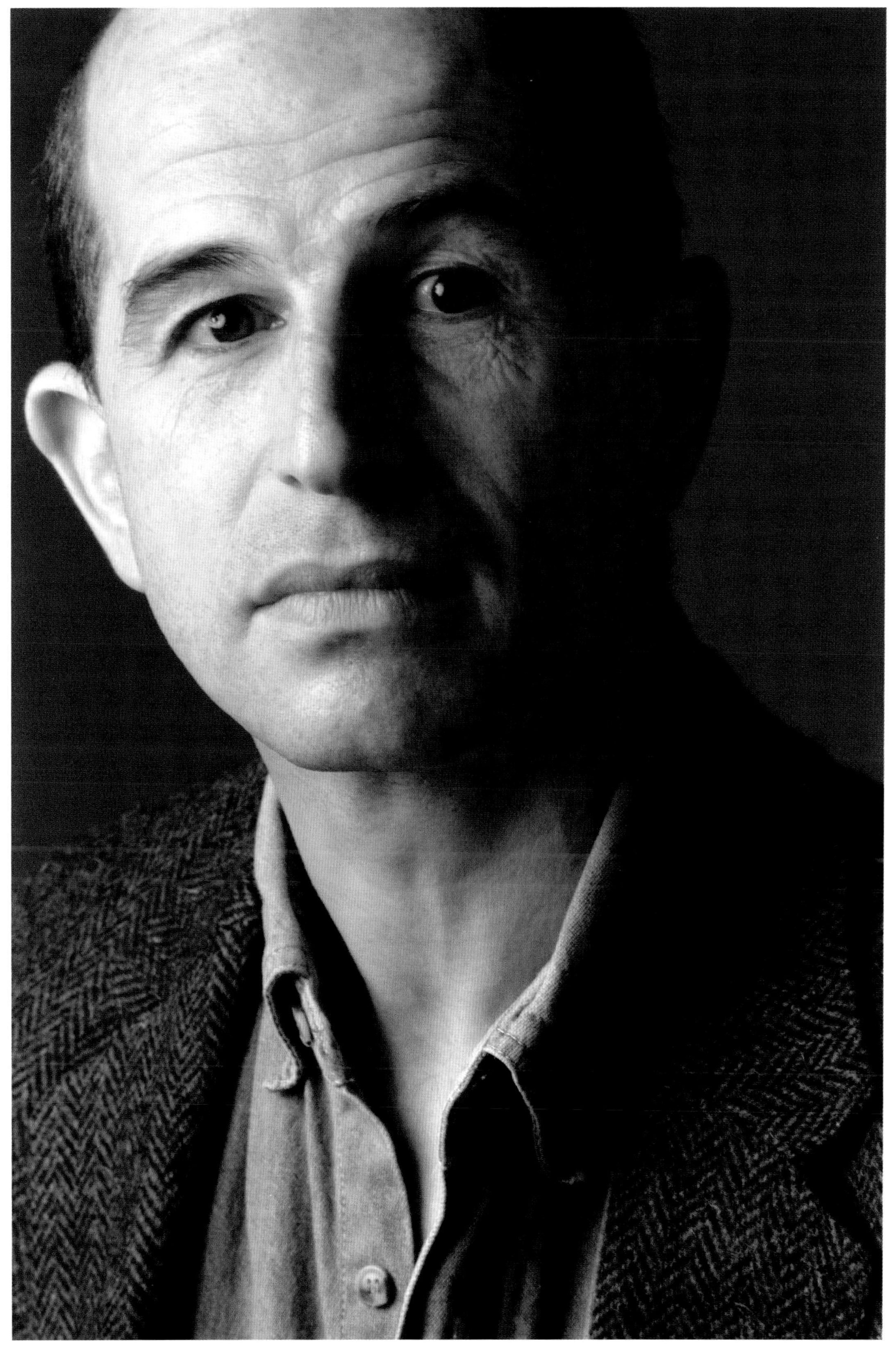

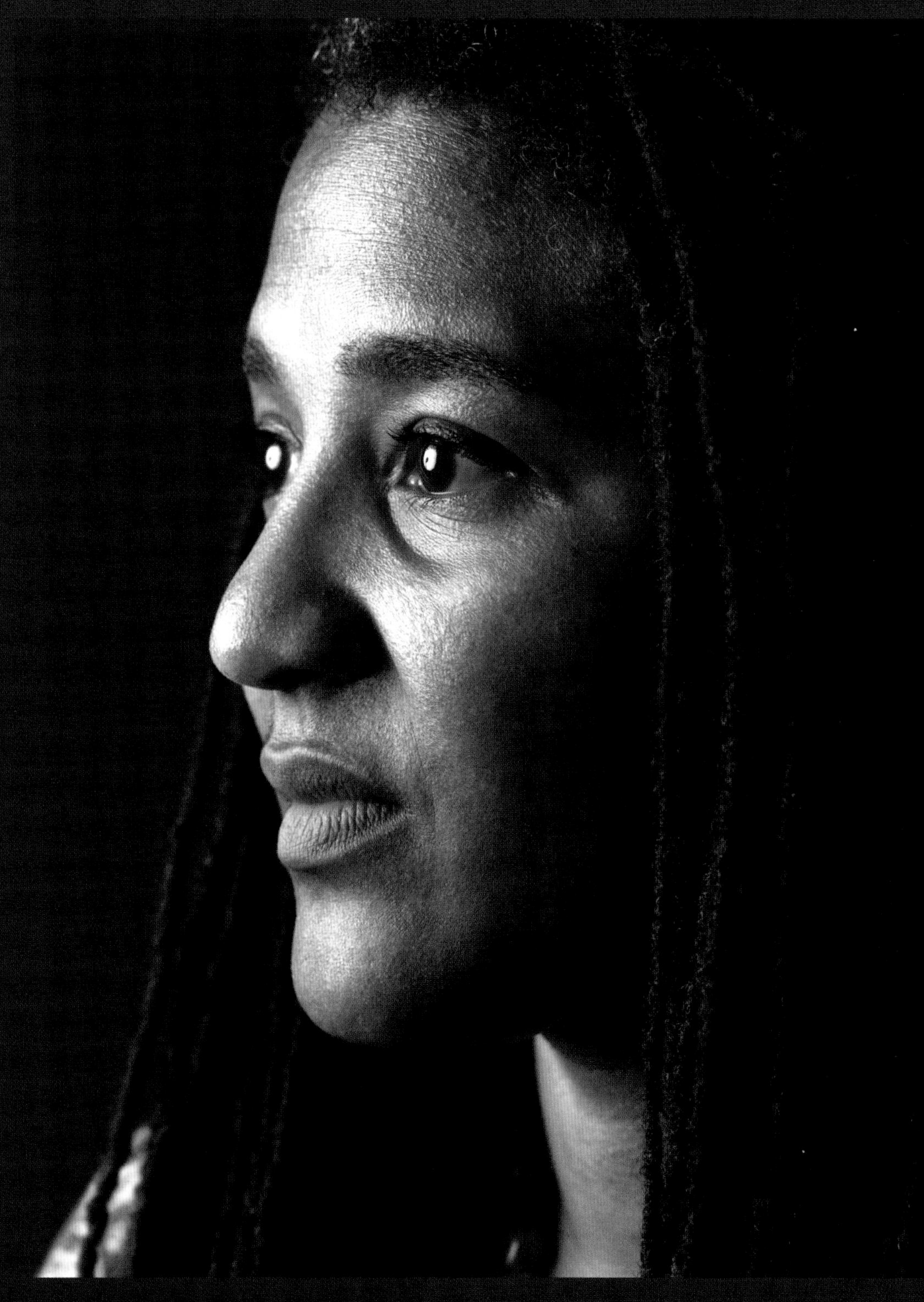

Lynn Nottage — David Henry Hwang (opposite)

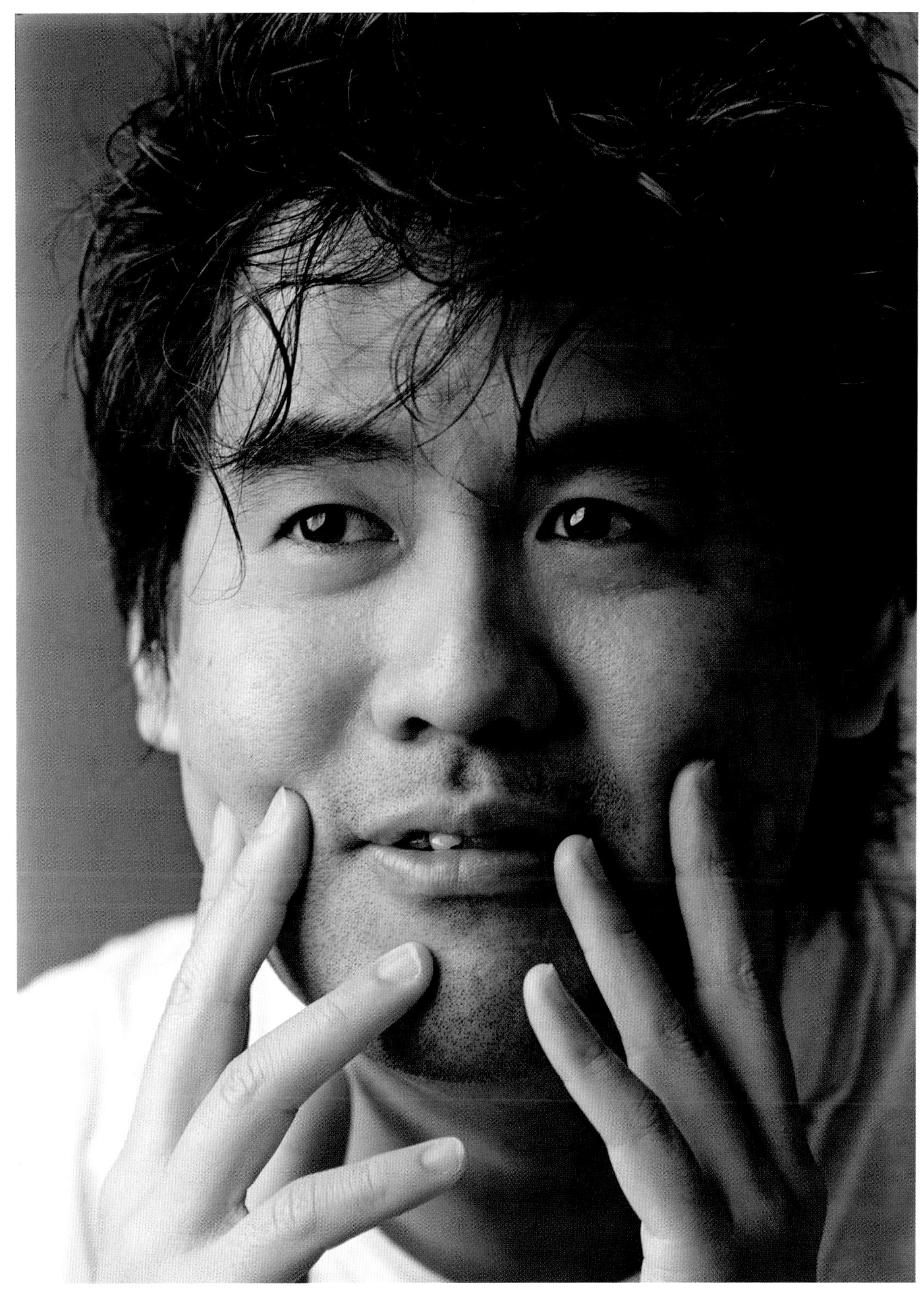

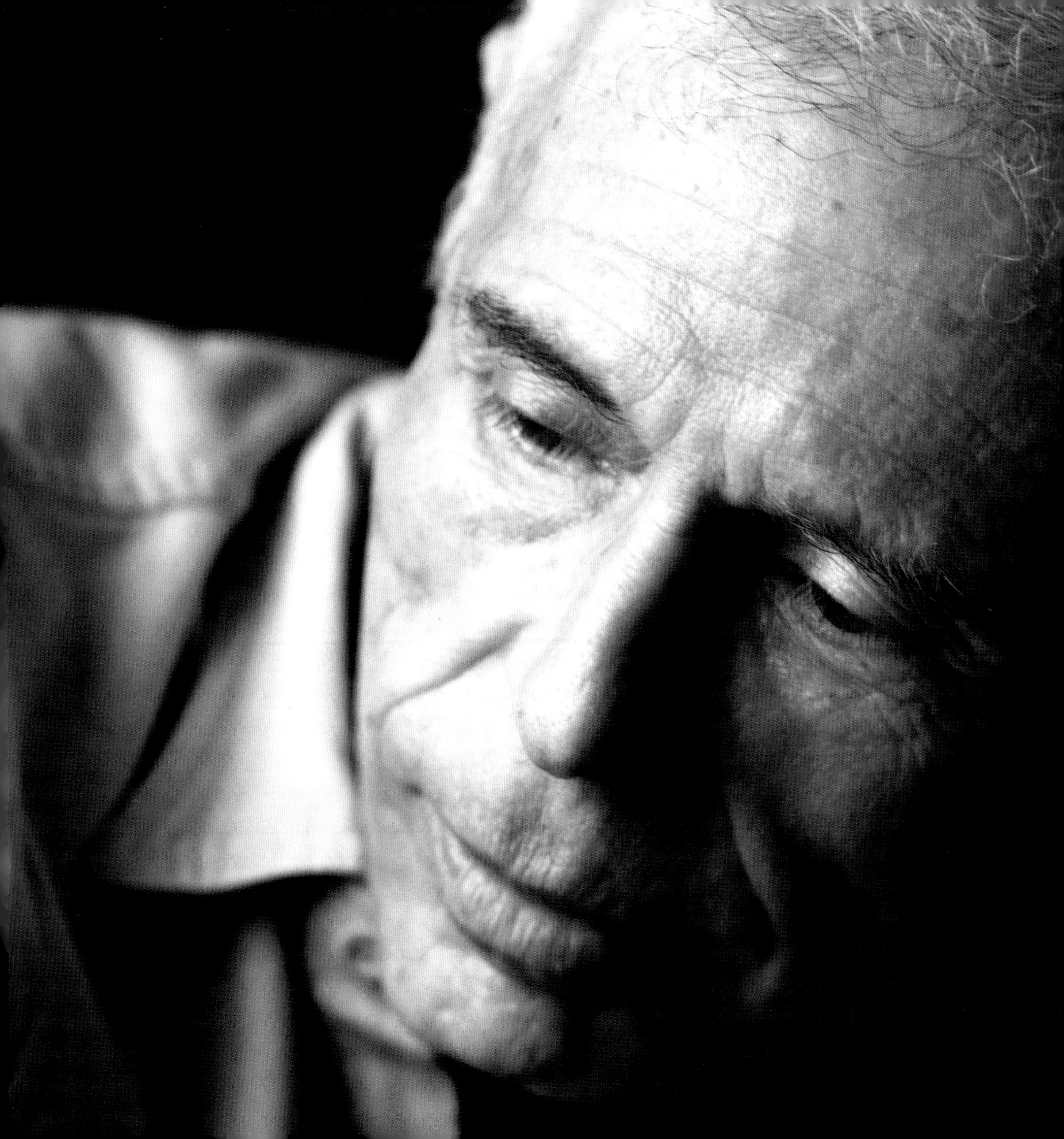

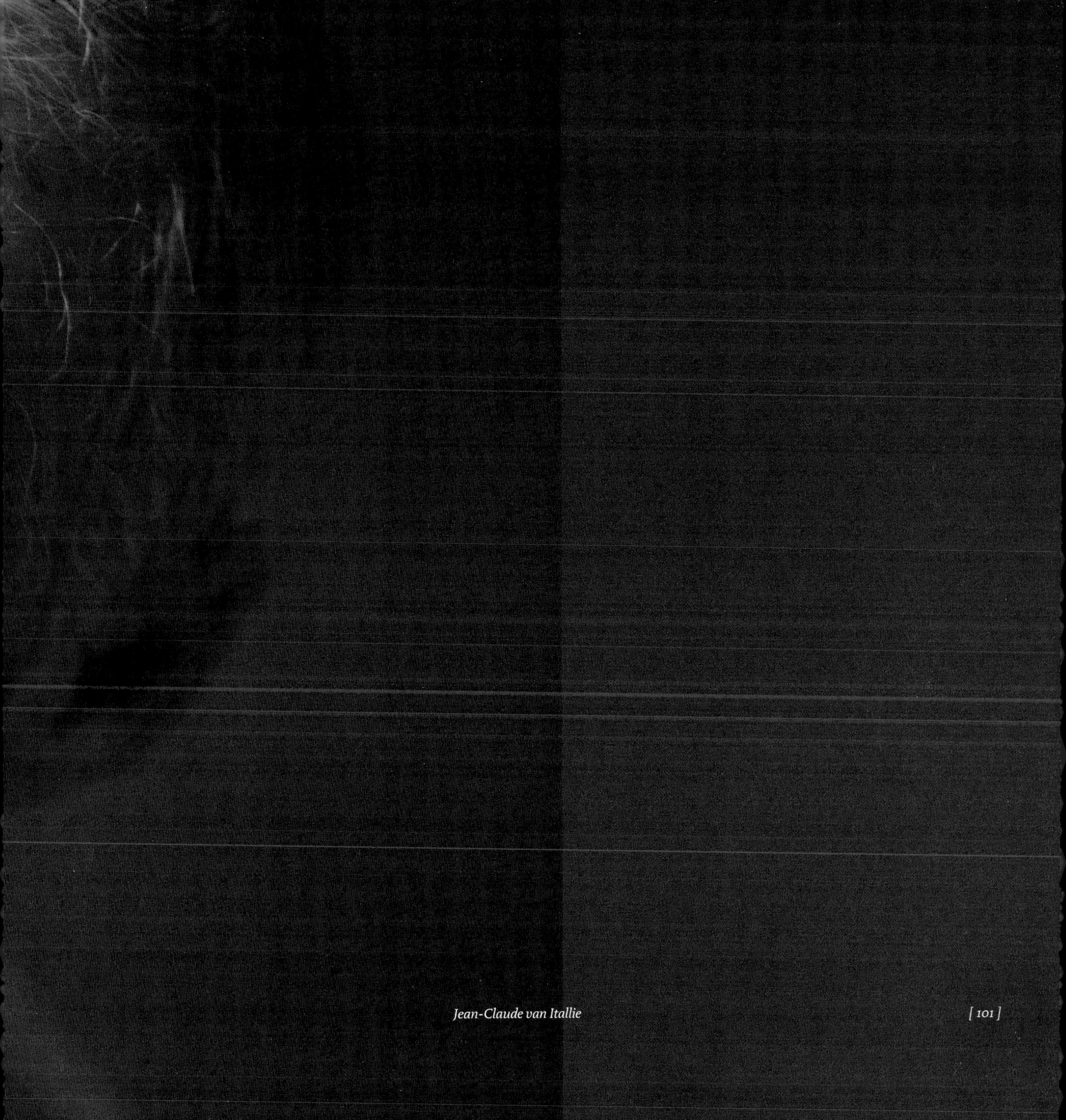

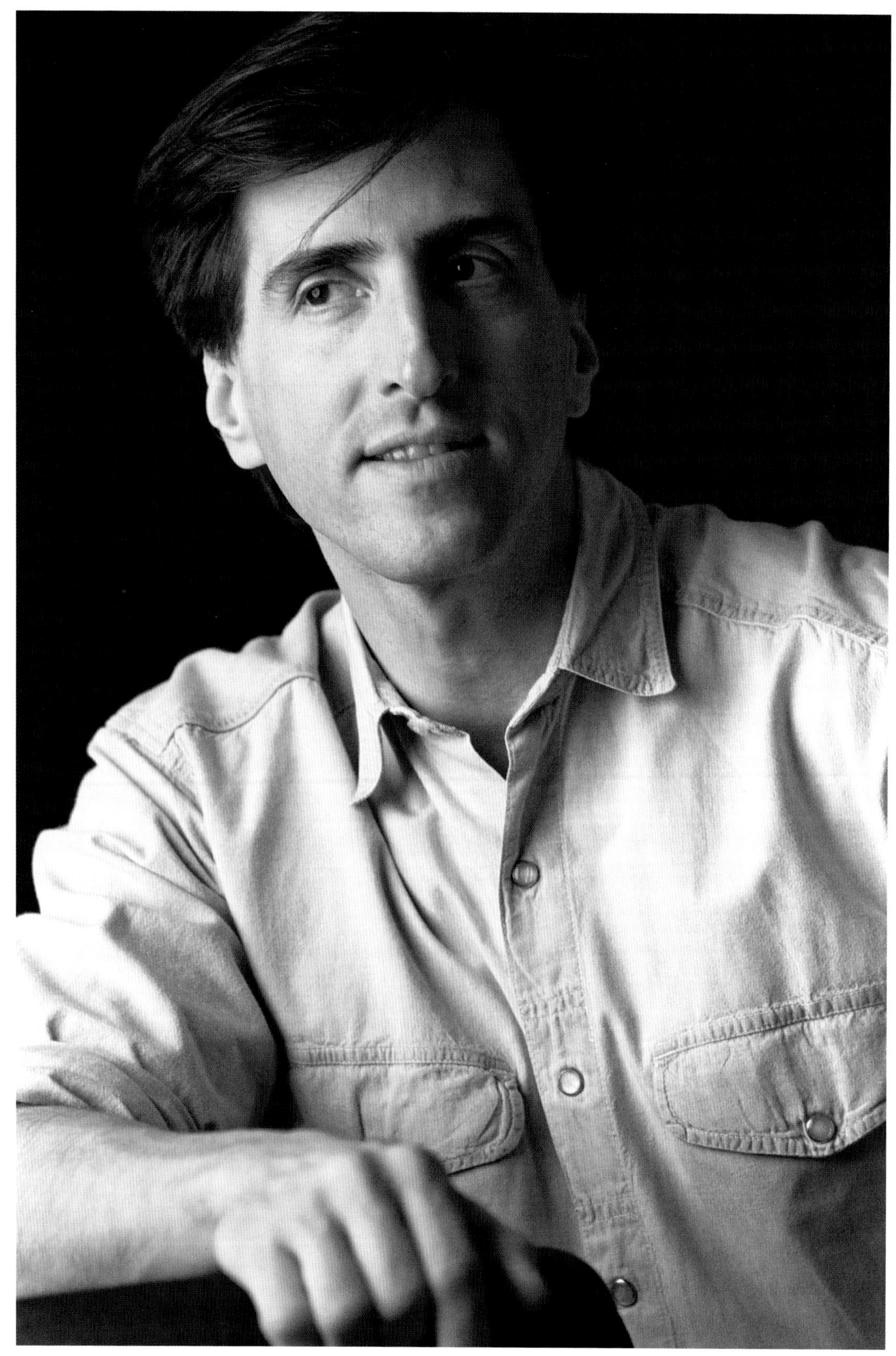

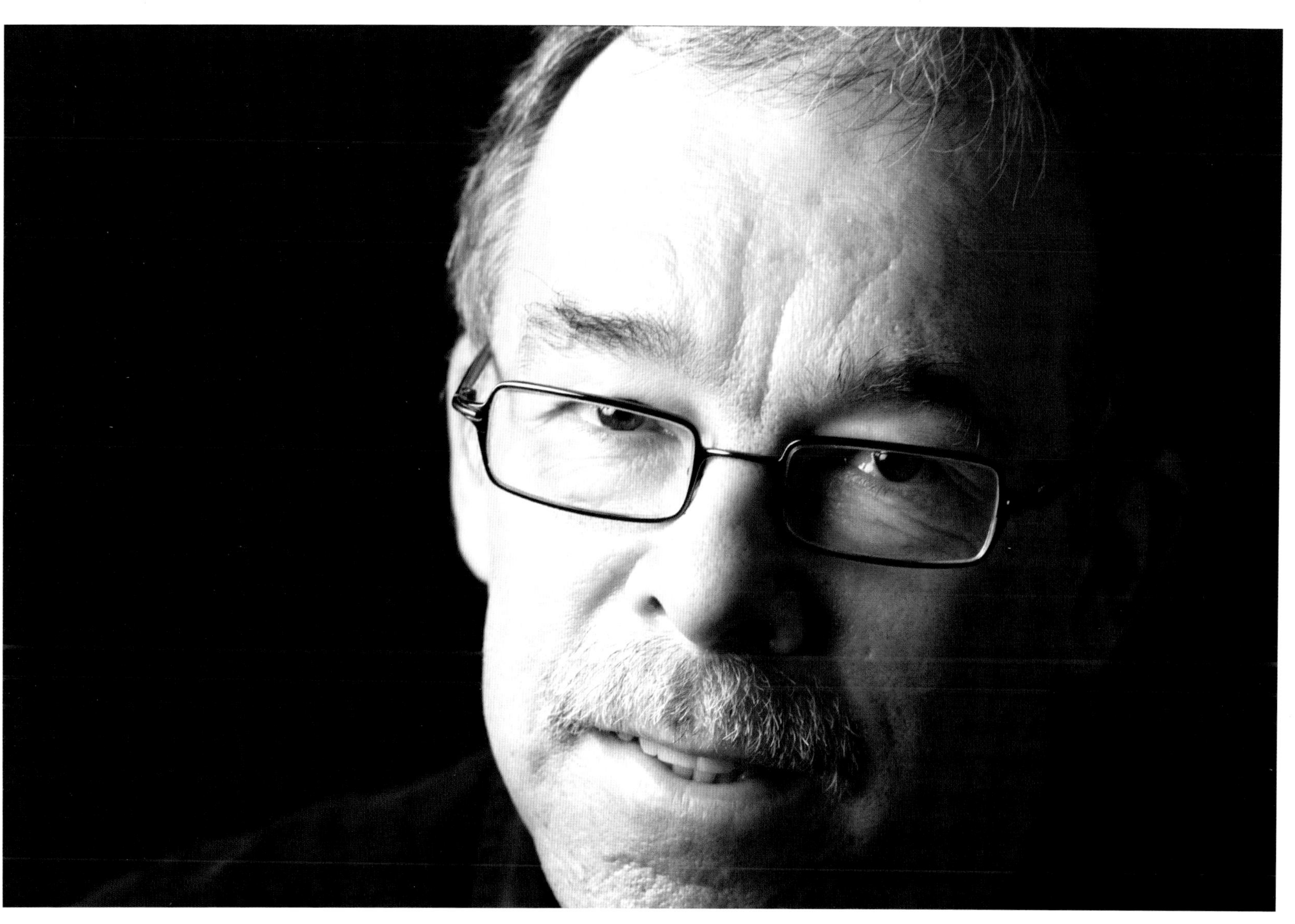

Paul Rudnick (opposite) — Richard Dresser

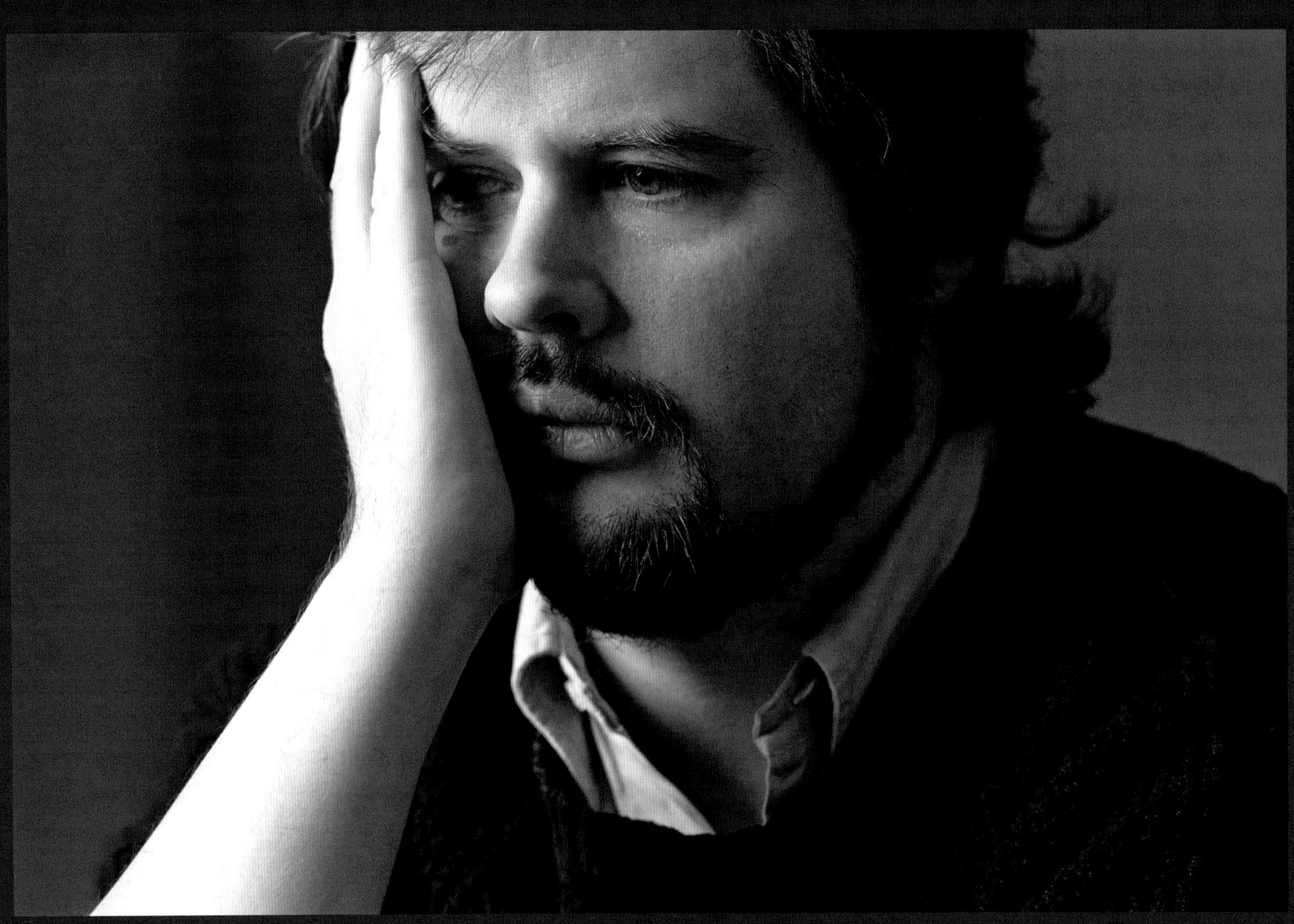

CHRISTOPHER DURANG

(Born 1949—American playwright and co-chair of the playwriting program at Juilliard, awarded first Luminary Award for his work Off-Off Broadway, numerous Obie Awards and the Tony Award for Best Play for Vanya and Sonia and Masha and Spike.*)*

Soft-spoken and not overtly comic, Christopher Durang has been performing since he was a child, when, to his family's surprise, he asked if he could sing at his aunt's piano students' recital. He looks back with wonder that they said yes, but his mother went so far as to buy him a white suit to wear for the occasion. It became an annual event and probably the beginning of his performing career. When asked how playwriting began for him, Chris said, "I wrote plays when I was very little, which was both precocious of me and sort of peculiar as far as the family was concerned. The first one was in second grade, and then I kept writing little ones in school. I wrote one in seventh grade called *Banned in Boston*. The play was extremely innocent. Later, my play, *Sister Mary,* was almost banned in Boston so it was sort of like a foreshadowing." His conversation, like his plays, has a cumulative effect, often with a sedate beginning, wild tangents, and then just the right word, phrase, or gesture to make it land.

There was another play his junior year in high school, and it was through these plays that Chris found his ticket to the Ivy League. His high school guidance counselor suggested the Ivies would be interested because of his abilities as a fledgling playwright. It was at Harvard that Chris, "basically moved away from the conservative ways of thinking of my mother's family, the sort of Catholic conservatives who supported Joe McCarthy. McCarthy was someone who was often referred to by the family as 'someone whom society had wronged.'" Durang's battle on several levels with the Catholic Church dates back to his Harvard days, first with a musical called *The Greatest Musical Ever Sung,* which included such numbers as The Blessed Mother singing, "The Dove That Done Me Wrong" and then with his play, *The Nature and Purpose of the Universe.*

From his first writings, Chris has been exorcising demons of repression and rigidity. "So much of the Catholic Church is Irish and Italian men making up strange stories and passing them down as facts. I was a very believing child so I believed everything I was taught—hook, line, and sinker. The extraordinary thing about getting over this teaching is the shock of having all these facts just fly out the window. Even in high school, though still a believer in much of the Church, I stopped believing in Hell. I just can't believe that at the end of the world, God in all his lovingness doesn't decide to forgive everybody. I don't believe He decides, 'Okay, you got it now—forever and ever and ever—ENDLESS TORTURE!'

"In my freshman year, there was a writing class taught by Bernard Malamud, and I couldn't get into it. In my middle two years, they had a class called English Composition. A lot of my friends who got in didn't intend to be writers. I couldn't get in. I would write a little essay or something, maybe they were darkly humorous. Maybe the person who read them didn't like the humor, or maybe I was going through a period where my writing wasn't that good. I took it that maybe I wasn't going to be a writer."

He thought about film school and even social work, because he had "this other part that was active—a humanitarian bent." His last year at Harvard, Chris got into playwriting again through a class with William Alford, who wrote *Hogan's Goat.*

When Chris was accepted to Yale Drama School for his post-graduate study, he thought, "Well, I'm going to see if I get encouragement here. If I don't, then I'll see what I should do next." At Yale, he got great encouragement from Robert Brustein, Howard Stein, Richard Gilman, and Jules Feiffer. Satirists and others who aim at sacred cows are not always easily accepted. Speaking of his time at Yale, he said, "I'm just so lucky because . . . there was this feeling that fifty percent of the people didn't like my work and fifty percent liked it a lot. And in the fifty percent that liked it were my significant teachers. Jules Feiffer was a writing teacher. Like the actors at Yale, he would give me real feedback. 'In this scene, I don't like this line.' Or, 'I like that line.' I found it helpful to have it that specific."

After Yale, Chris worked another year in New Haven, at the Yale Rep and at other odd jobs, postponing the inevitable idea of heading to New York. "I found it very intimidating. I felt shy. The notion of contacting some stranger and saying, 'Hello, you haven't heard of me. I write such and such and such,' just struck me as so hard. Once I came to New York, I was quite tenacious and really pursued different pathways and got a fair amount of no's. Yale Drama School ended up being extremely lucky for me, because one of the reasons I had confidence to do that was because I had gone to Yale."

The early plays produced in New York were *Titanic, The History of the American Film,* and the very successful *Sister Mary Ignatius Explains It All for You.* Because of the controversy surrounding that play's outspoken satire, Christopher Durang became somewhat notorious. His Catholic family and especially his favorite aunt, Marion, were definitely upset with what they read about the play. Aunt Marion left messages on his answering machine saying, "You have created a sacrilege. If you look up sacrilege in the dictionary, you will see that is what you have done."

"Of course, it was based on what she read *about* the play, although I must admit I knew she would not like it. I would just say to her, 'I am not asking you to agree but you have to realize I am serious, and I come at this sincerely." I think sacrilege is when you believe in something and make fun of it. If you don't believe in it, I don't think sacrilege is possible. I *can* see that you can upset people's sensibilities."

Alcoholism and its attendant monsters are themes Durang explored in *The Marriage of Bette and Boo,* a highly autobiographical play. Chris even acted the leading role in the production at the Public Theater. "My father seemed to be an alcoholic although he never admitted it, and other family and parents of friends were alcoholic, so an awful lot of my childhood revolved around alcoholism. It was after the *Marriage of Bette and Boo* that I attended Adult Children of Alcoholics. As anyone who has read the literature knows, there are family roles children have. I definitely fit the hero role, which is the very responsible child who doesn't cause trouble because there is so much trouble around him. That is one way I became so serious. My childhood lightness ended very early, and part of my adulthood is trying to rekindle part of that. It was really hell around holidays and very unpredictable. What my mother and I would share every so often in the midst of some real upset about my father's drinking—something would seem so bad it would strike us as funny. I think particularly with dysfunctional things, the mood shifts are just startling. That's what makes it both funny and real. As to why something strikes you as funny . . . really kind of a mystery of humor. It is sort of a distancing. Sometimes, and this seems intuitive with me, there's this phrasing or a word—the kind of word that has a ping to it and lets the audience get the same thought or feeling simultaneously. It is sort of mysterious."

One of the influences on his writing was Joe Orton. "My early plays had a quick-paced ferocity that is sort of like his." Fellini movies were also inspirational because, unlike the Hollywood movies, which seemed to Durang 'very non-denominational Protestant,' Fellini mentioned his Catholic background and brought in all these Catholic quirks—like guilt."

When we spoke of the critical reaction to his works *Laughing Wild* and *The Marriage of Bette and Boo,* Christopher said they were "double whammies in terms of the fact I was in them as well. I think the stakes got uncomfortably high for me. And *Bette and Boo* was very personal to boot.

"One doesn't write in order to receive critical acclaim—one has an itch to express something. You do like the praise because it gives you an outward sign you are valued or something has come across. Most of the time, you get mixed reviews. The consensus of the critics is a valuable thing, but what I wish is that the theatre audience would get in the habit of seeking one or two critics they trust and throwing that into the pot and not always trusting the *New York Times*. There is an unfortunate disparity in the power of the *Times*."

On at least one occasion, Christopher Durang, the actor, has stumped Christopher Durang, the playwright, and even sent him back to the typewriter. While in rehearsal for *The Marriage of Bette and Boo*, Chris, playing the central character, Matt, was uncomfortable with one of his speeches. "It's a speech I'm so glad I didn't cut. After the divorce scene, Matt has a monologue, as he does throughout the play, where he tries to write this essay for college. He gets off the point and starts talking about crazy people. When I wrote the scene, I thought it was good, but then at the first reading of the play, something went off, and it didn't feel right. I felt embarrassed by it and went home and rewrote it.

"One of the other actors said, 'Oh, I like your new speech, but, boy! I really loved the first one.' I'm really grateful because nobody had told me it went badly—I just felt it had. Jerry Zaks [the director] thought I should try the first one a bit longer, and it turned out to be just an acting thing. In watching other actors do it, I can see it's hard. In ninety percent of the lines, I have the sense of how they should be said, but that leaves ten percent where I really don't know.

"I've been told repeatedly that I don't look like the person who wrote my plays. People are often surprised I don't look wilder or angry."

Without the religion of his childhood, he found "suffering—mine, others', the concept of—totally paralyzing." He credits the writing of *Nature and Purpose* with bringing him out of his depression during college. "I cackled aloud as I wrote it. Suddenly the extremity of suffering made me giddy, and I found the energy and the distance to relish the awfulness of it all."

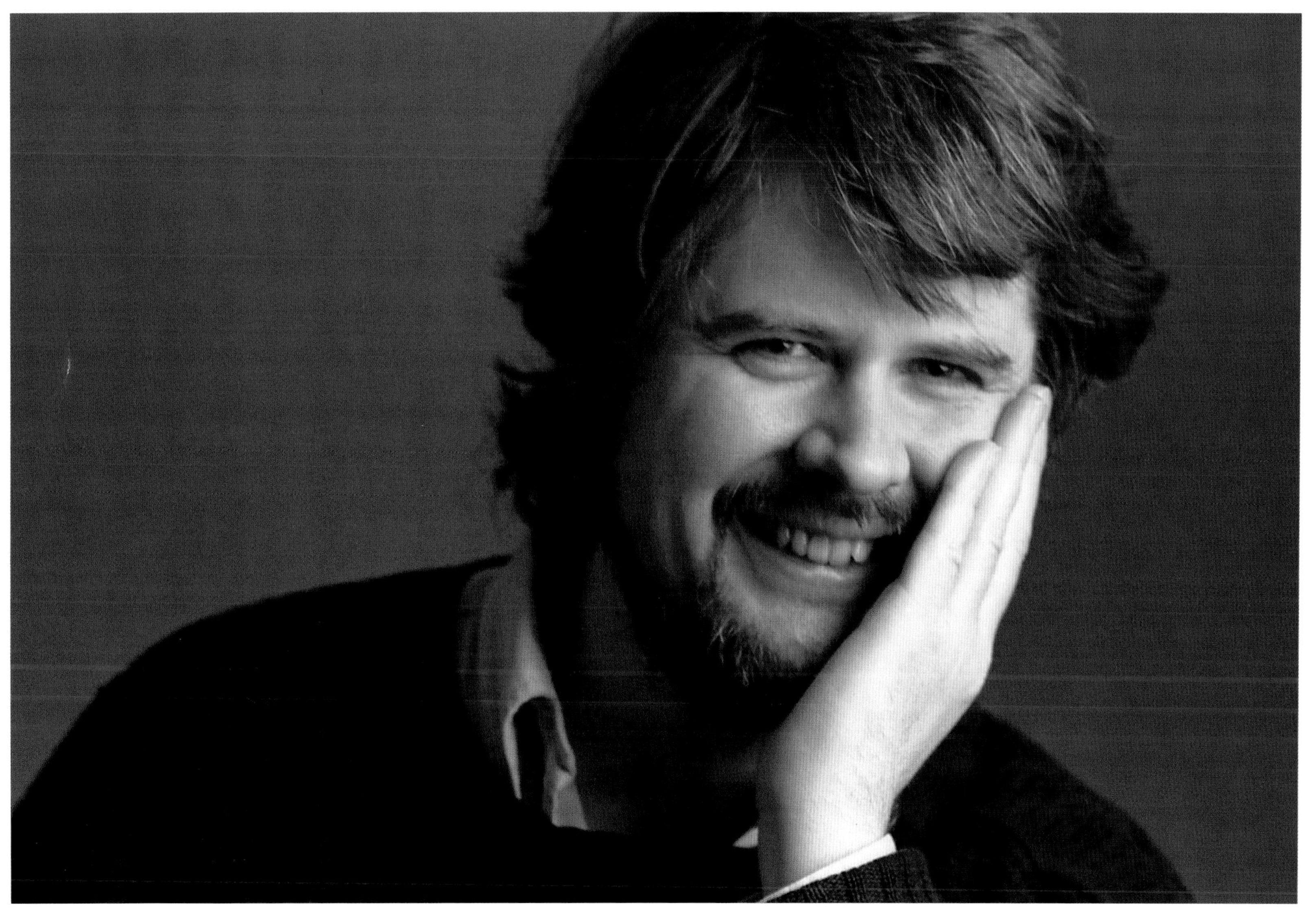

Christopher Durang

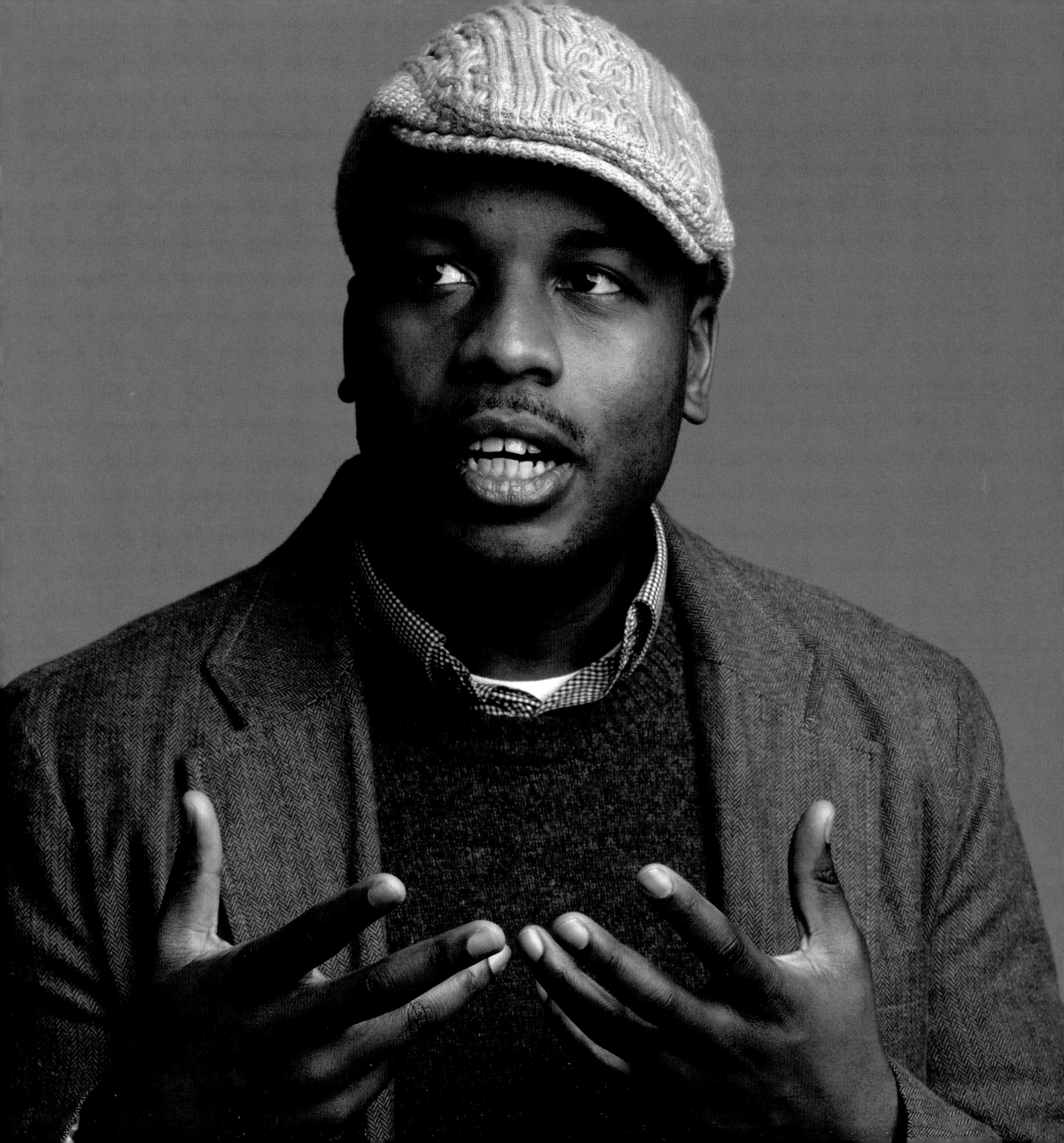

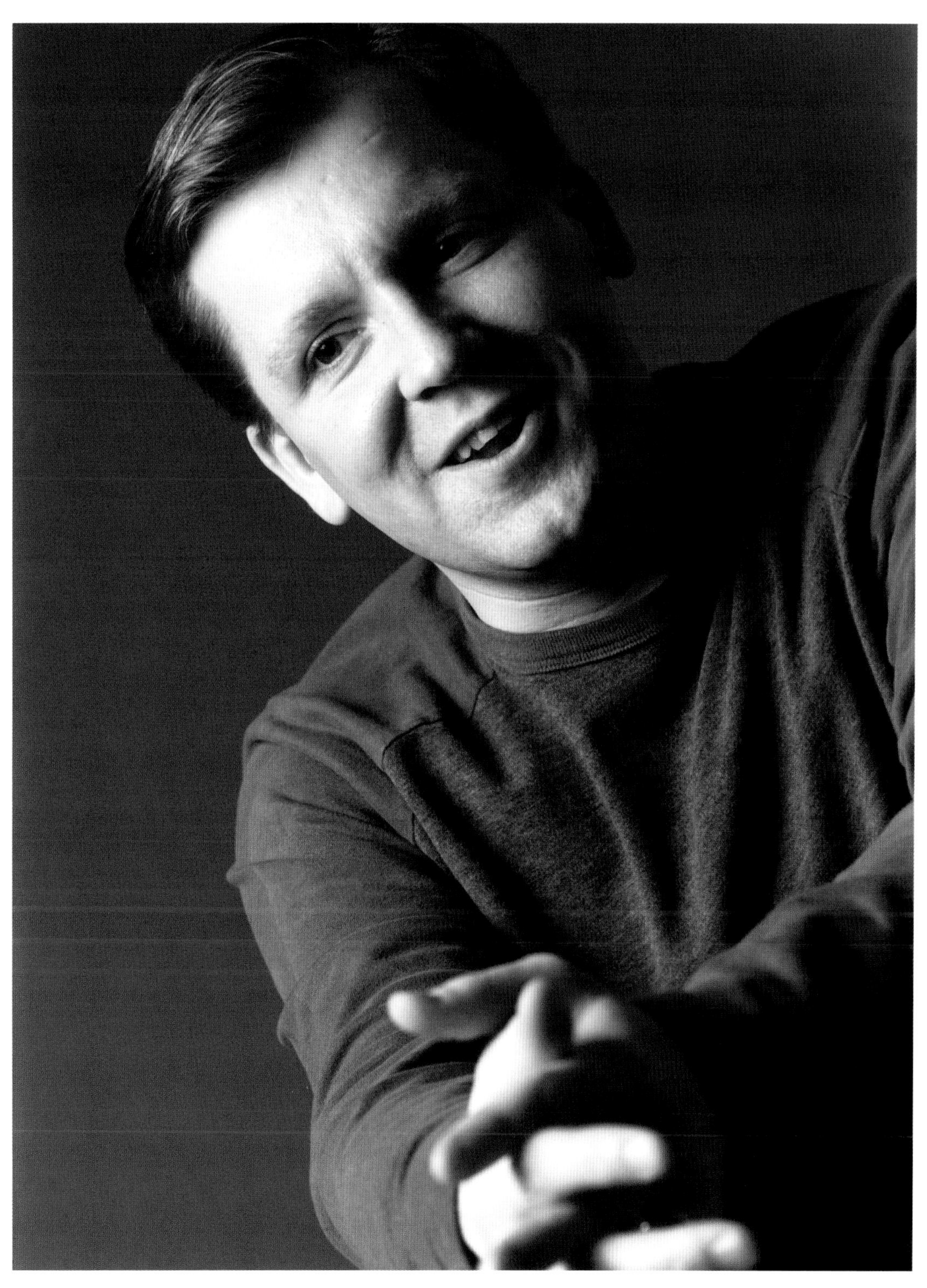

Marcus Gardley (opposite) — David Lindsay-Abaire

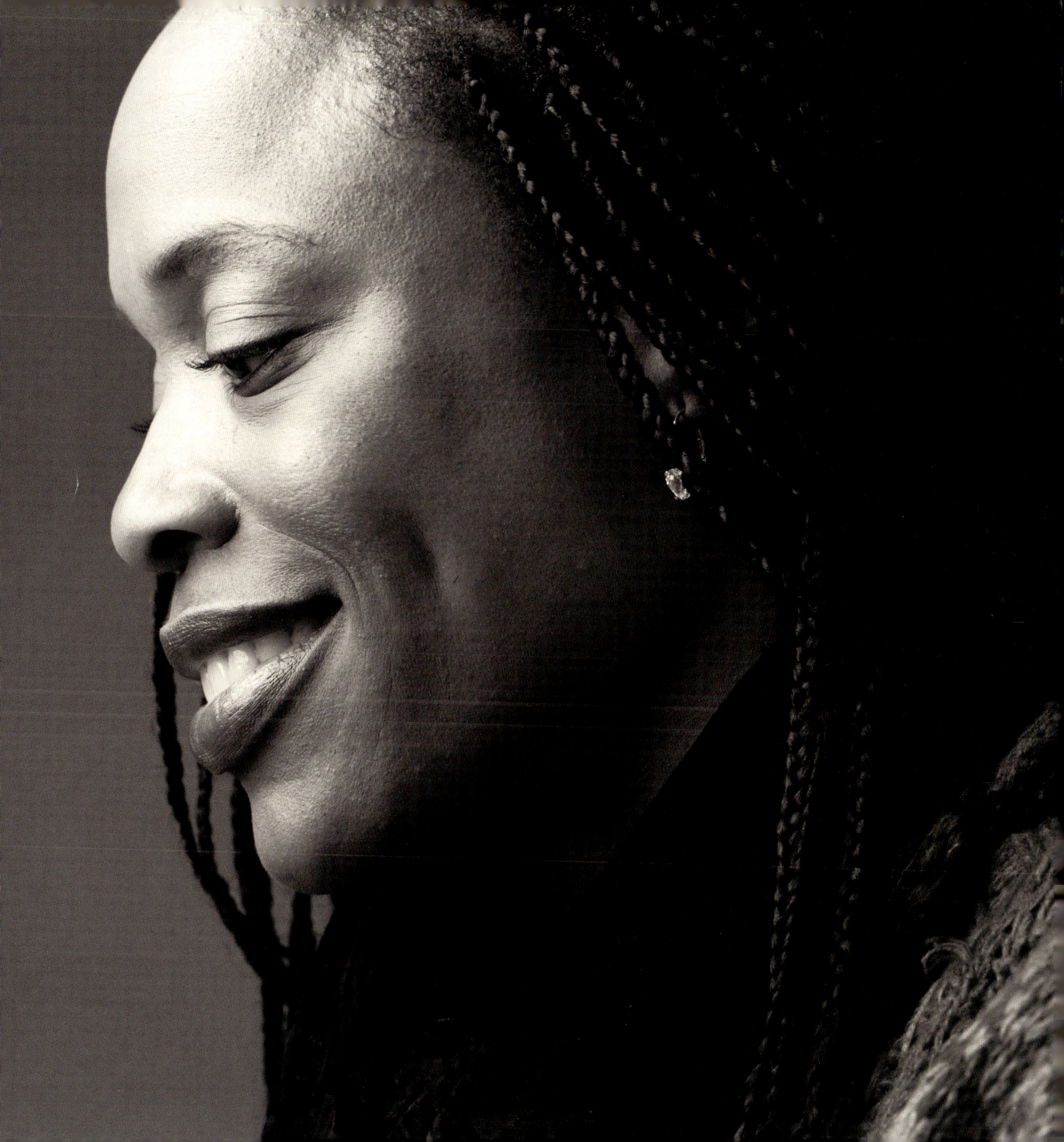

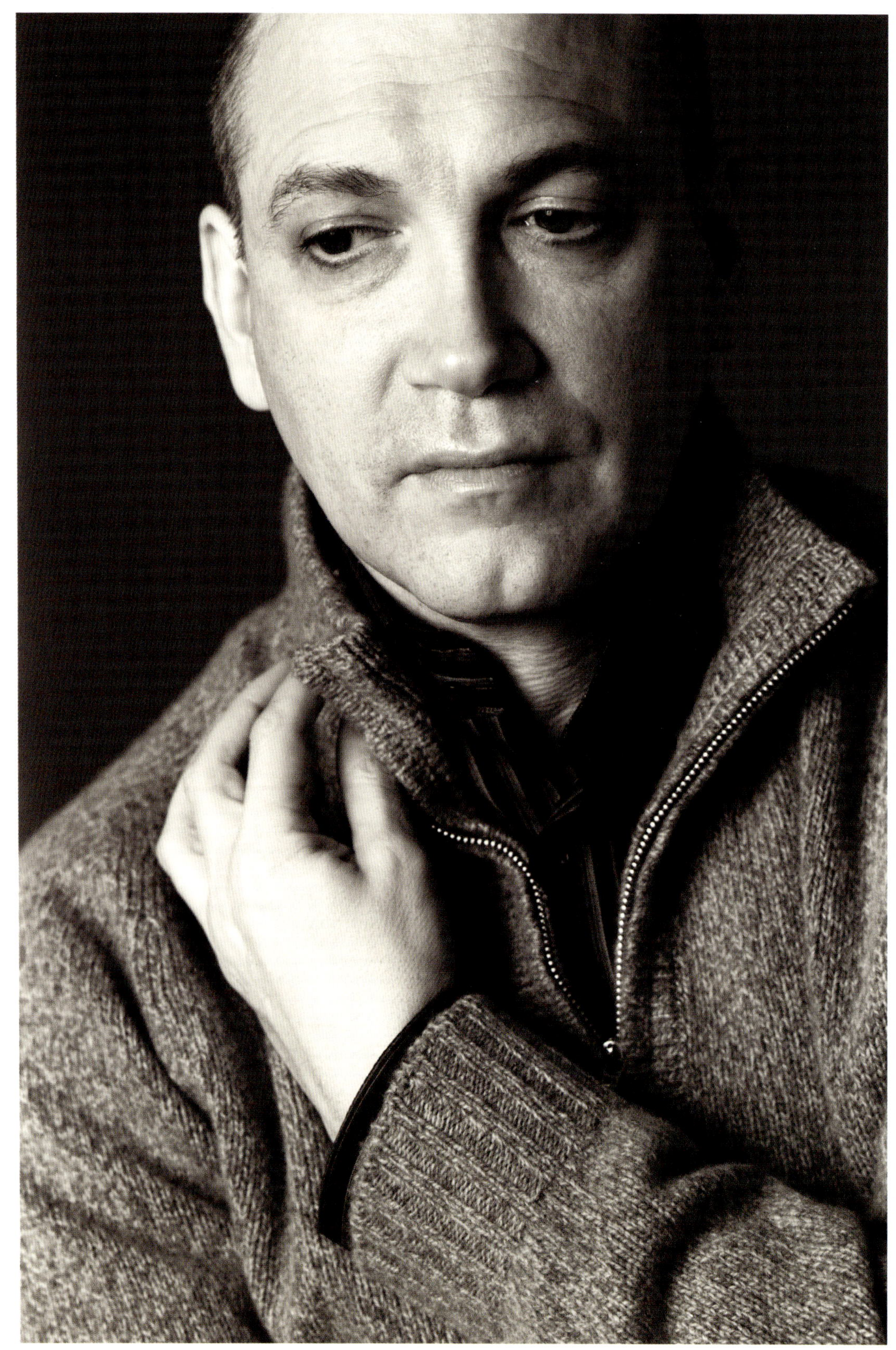

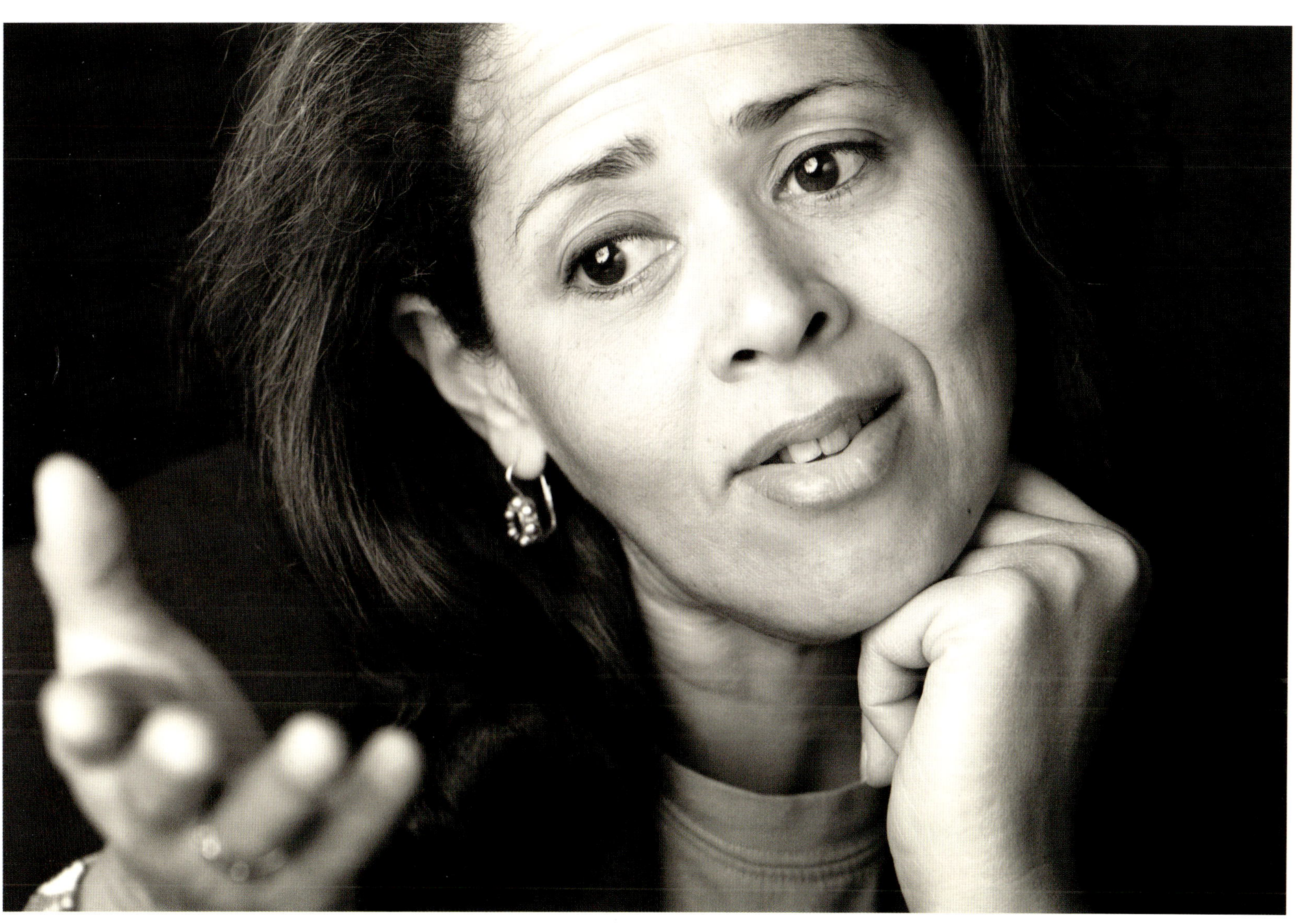

Charles Busch (opposite) — Anna Deavere Smith

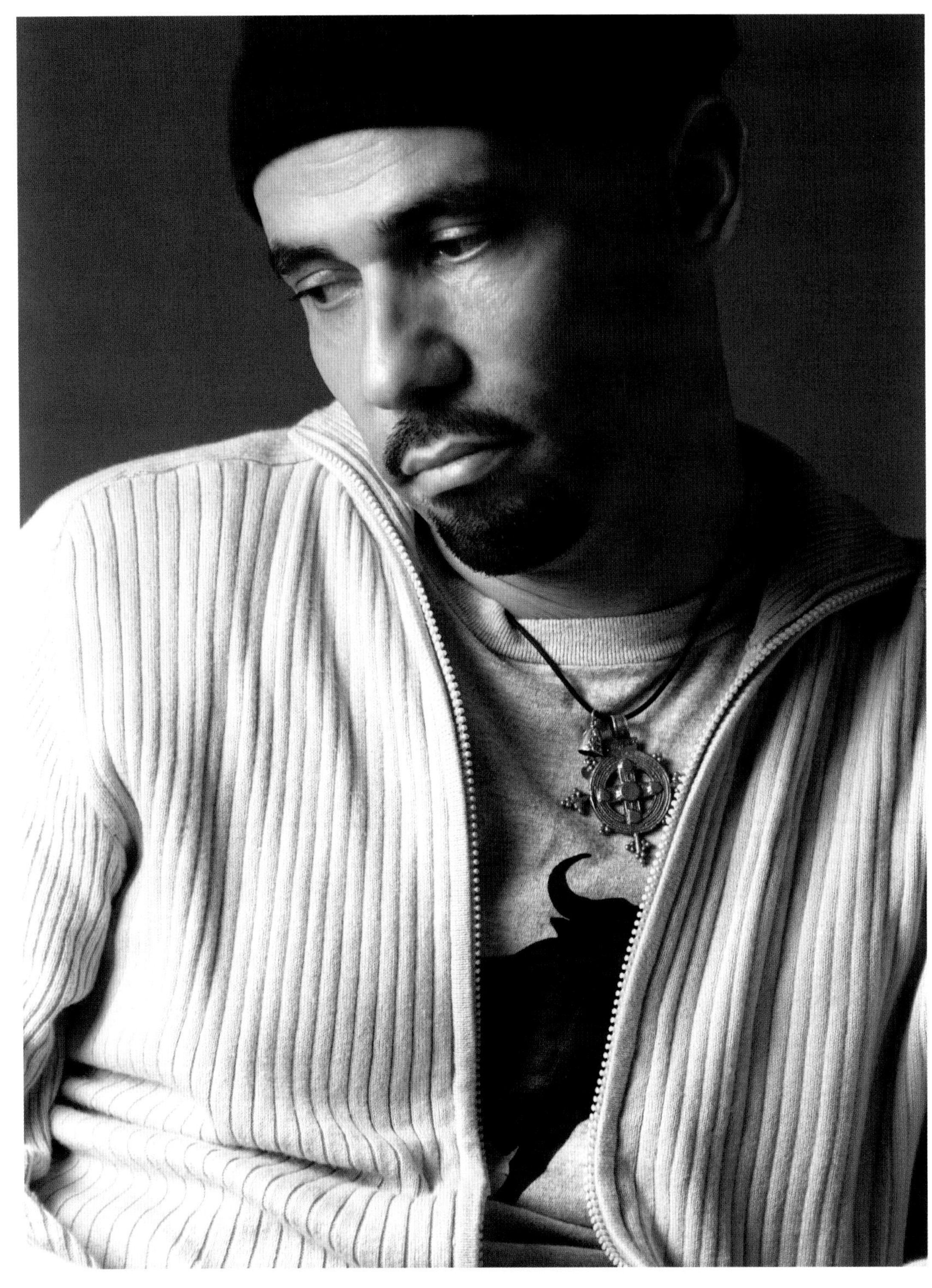

Nilo Cruz — Lanford Wilson (opposite)

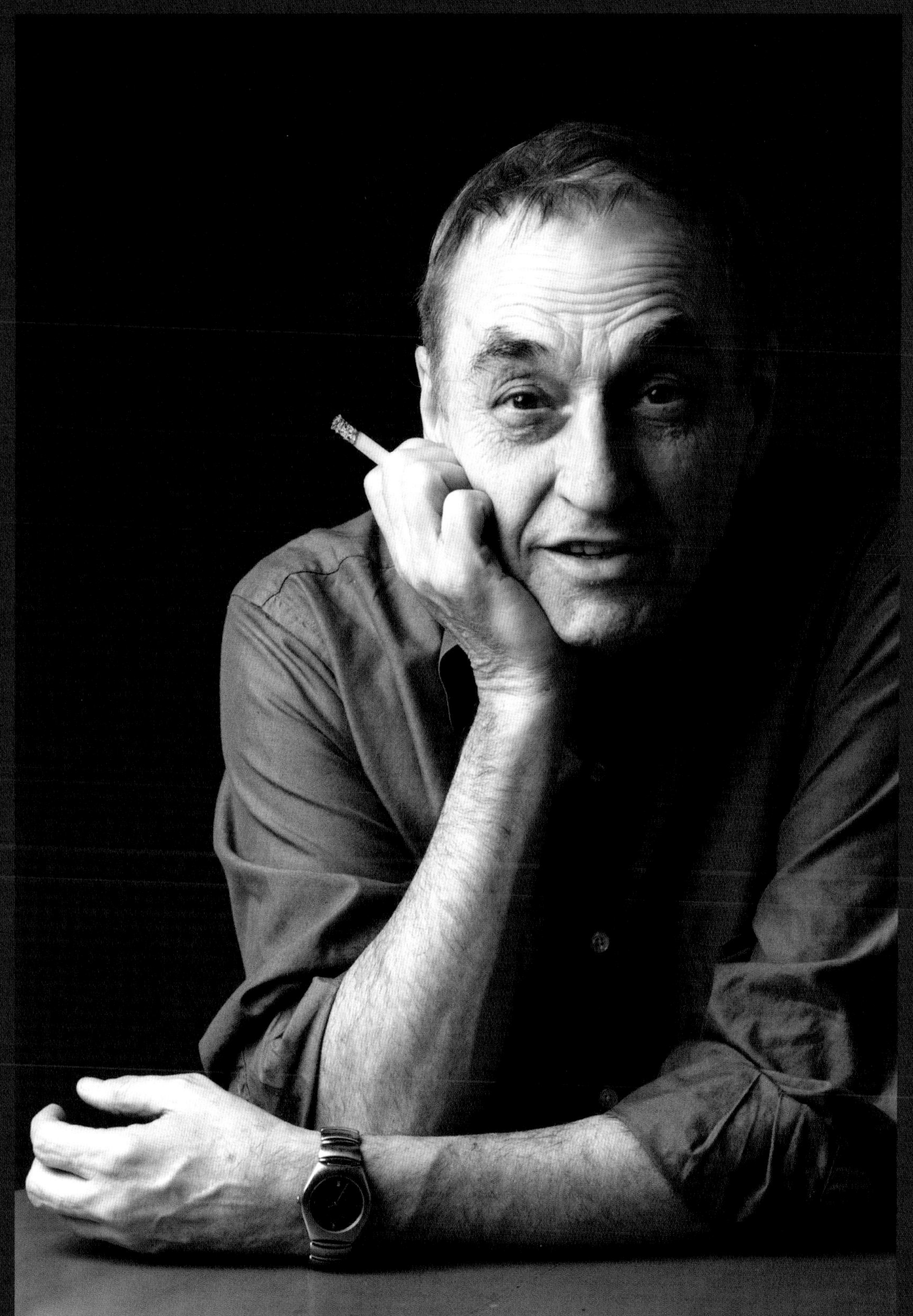

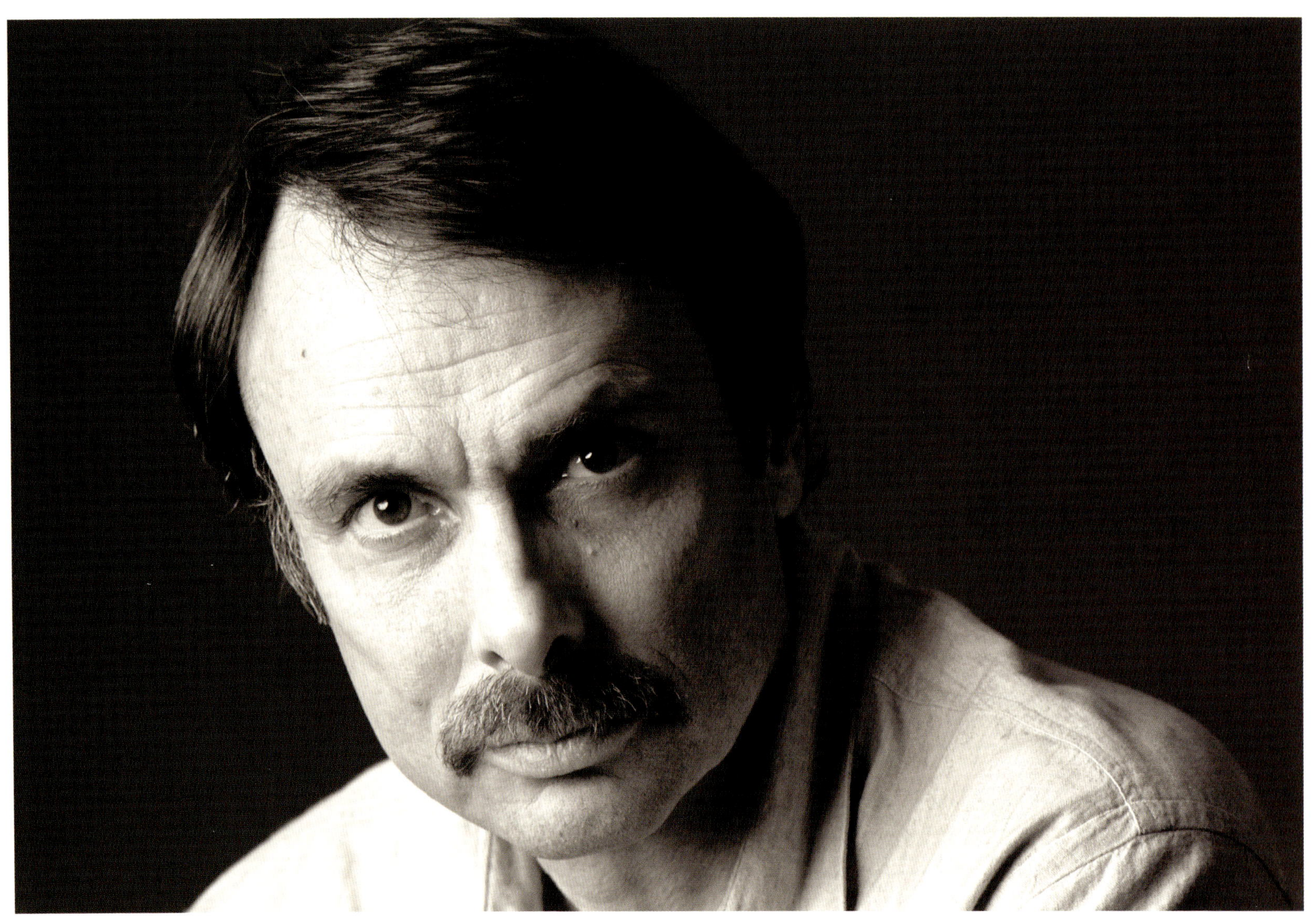

Arthur Kopit — John Pielmeier (opposite)

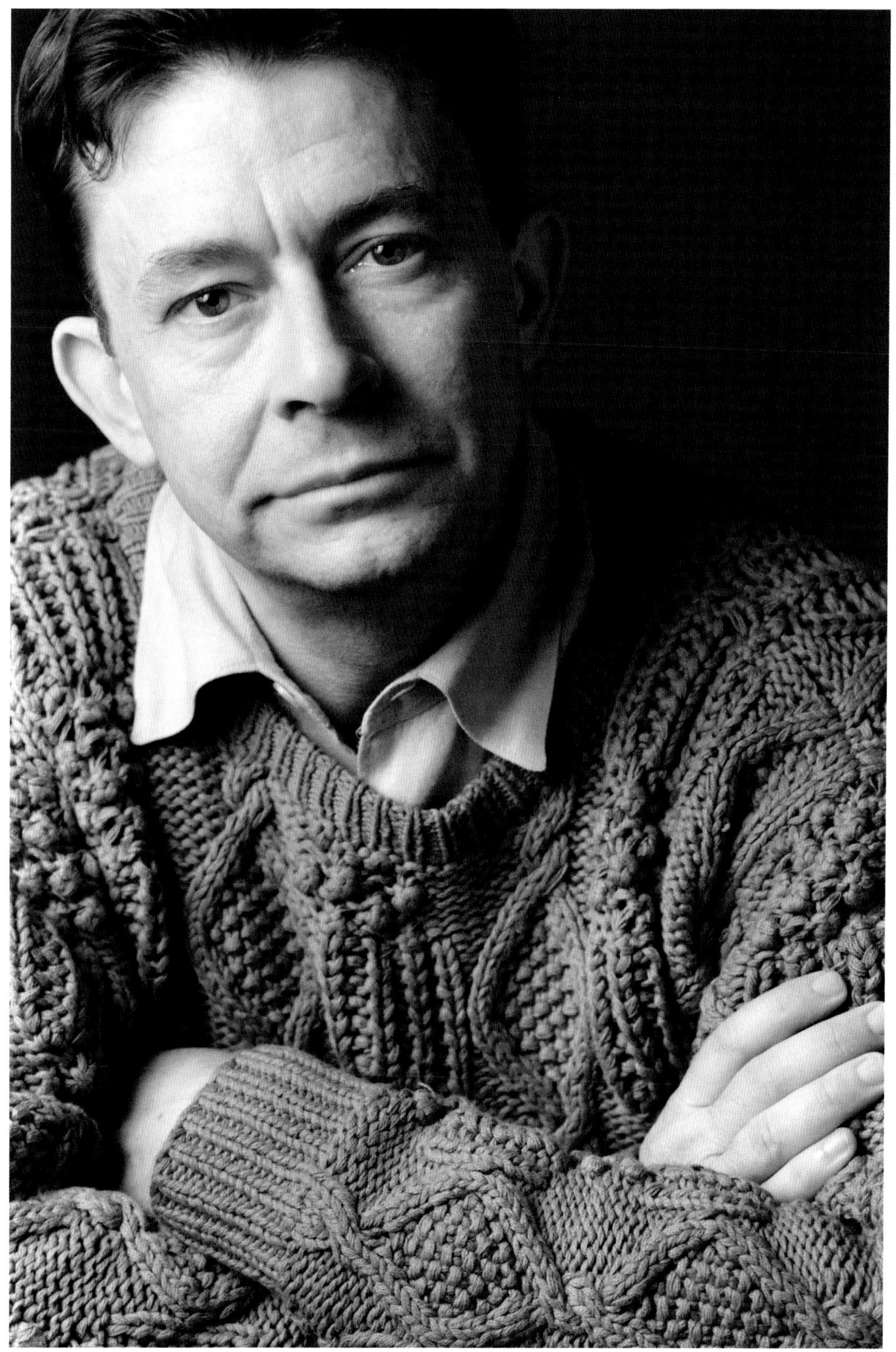

SIDNEY KINGSLEY

(1906–1995—American playwright awarded the Pulitzer Prize for Men in White *in 1934, inducted into the Theatre Hall of Fame in 1983, and awarded the William Inge Award for Lifetime Achievement in the American Theatre in 1988.)*

Edward Albee suggested it would be important to ask the "old-timers" to be part of the portrait series and he mentioned Sidney Kingsley as someone on whose shoulders much of the social justice work in theatre had been built. Kingsley was one of the initial members of The Group Theatre and was blacklisted by the House Un-American Activities Committee. His play, *Dead End*, is said to have influenced national policy on slum housing. Eleanor Roosevelt saw the original production repeatedly and then arranged the first-ever command performance of a play at the White House. Subsequently, President Roosevelt convened a commission that resulted in the Housing Act of 1937. Very few plays can claim such a profound impact on so many lives. Kingsley was eighty-three when I photographed him and six years later he was gone.

Kingsley came to his photo session and interview in December 1989, on his way to dinner at the Algonquin. He had suffered a stroke the year before but was recovered and sharp. The only trace of disability, and nod to infirmity, was the cane he carried.

Sidney Kingsley's Pulitzer Prize–winning play, *Men in White*, was controversial at the time of its first production in 1934 and, since it deals thoughtfully and sensitively with the issue of abortion, it would probably have protestors from the far-right picketing in front of theaters even today.

"I was twenty-six when *Men in White* was produced. One of the indirect rewards of *Men in White* was that it was refused permission to be produced in Nazi Germany."

"Who directed it?"

"Lee Strasberg."

Along with Harold Clurman and Cheryl Crawford, Lee Strasberg was one of the founders of The Group Theatre, characterized in those days by their reputation as "angry young men."

"They were, I wasn't. I was a delighted young man. They were doing my play."

Men in White was the first, big, commercial success for The Group Theatre. In his autobiography, *A Life* (1988), Elia Kazan seemed to feel that The Group Theatre never gave Kingsley his due as playwright. The

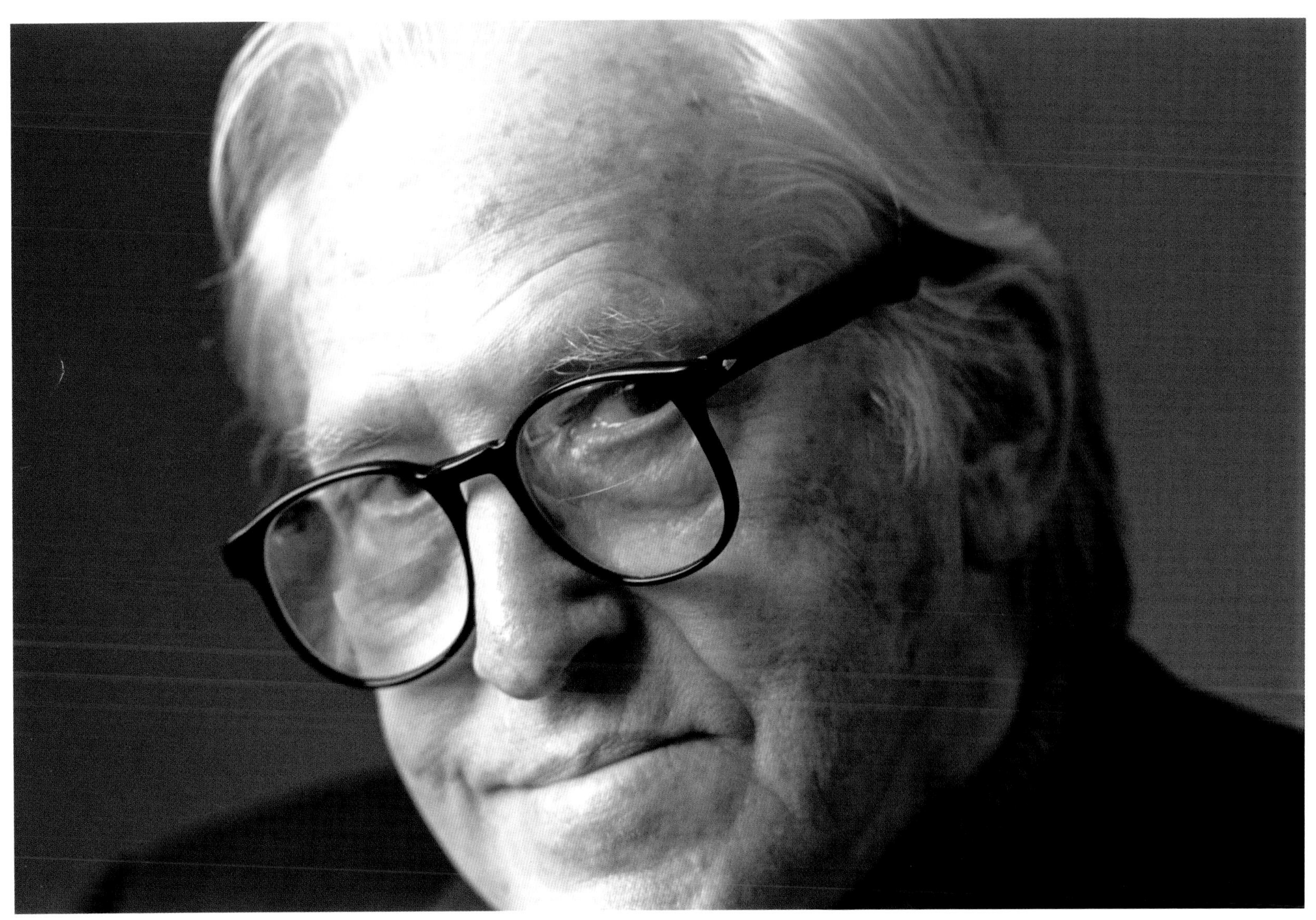

members of the Group attributed its success and the crowds flocking to see the play to their ensemble acting and Strasberg's direction. According to Kazan, Kingsley resented this and directed all his other productions.

"They were really good actors," Kingsley said of Strasberg, Luther Adler, and Sanford Meisner and the rest of the Group. Then he corrected himself. "Sanford wasn't really a good actor. He became a good teacher, they tell me."

The phone rang. It was Mr. Kingsley's secretary confirming his dinner reservations at the Algonquin. He nodded toward the phone, "Since I had a stroke about a year ago, when I come into town I try to do everything. We're going to have dinner and then go the theater. *Orpheus Descending*."

For a moment, I thought when he said "we," he might have been speaking of his wife, Madge Evans, the beautiful Hollywood ingénue he had met and married in 1939. "Do you have children?"

"No, unfortunately my wife and I decided we were too happy together to risk it. We decided not to have children. It was a bad decision. She died a number of years ago and I miss her and I wish I had a child."

"Perhaps your plays are your children, in a way?"

"Oh, yes they are. Very much so. Even as a youngster I knew I wanted to be a playwright. So when I went to Cornell I won a few prizes and decided to be a playwright—kind of a wild decision for a poor young man to make. I was fortunate *Men in White* was my first play."

"Then for it to win a Pulitzer! Did you expect that?"

"Let me tell you a story. At Cornell I studied with Professor Drummond, who was a great theatre man. He taught public speaking as well, and one day he gave us an exercise. He said, 'Improvise a speech which will be your address to your class at the twentieth reunion.' So he had me improvise this speech, and I said, 'We meet again today after twenty years. Twenty years ago, when we last met, we sat on the steps of Goldwyn Smith Hall, sang "Far above Cayuga's Waters" and we went into the world and practiced the arts and disciplines we learned here at Cornell. And I went into the theatre—as I had been working in the theatre at Cornell, as you all know—and I was fortunate enough to have some success and to have won the Pulitzer Prize.' And five years later, I did win the prize. I was in Europe at the time and I asked Professor Drummond to accept the prize for me. No, I didn't expect it, but I had the gall and a lot of audacity, which you need in the theatre."

So only a few years out of Cornell, still in his twenties, he had won the Pulitzer and two years later directed his next play, *Dead End*, which was another hit—this time on Broadway. It dealt with the relationship between slum housing and crime. We spoke of the film that followed and the continuing life of the Dead End Kids in a series of Hollywood films about a group of children growing up on the streets of New York.

He smiled. "My little babies."

I wanted to know about some of the kids in the show who became well known thereafter—like Sidney Lumet who made his Broadway debut at the age of eleven as one of the original Dead End Kids.

"Still my friend. He's a fine director, and he's grown."

"Did you base any of your characters on family or friends?"

"In *Detective Story*, the detective there has an obsession about his father. My father deserted us when my sister and I were children. My mother raised us and made a living as a dressmaker. There is some hint of that in the detective's feelings about his father. And in *Dead End*—I knew that environment personally. I used my childhood there. I grew up. . . . My boyhood was spent in Harlem, 113th Street. That's where I spent most of my boyhood and youth. That was fun—writing *Dead End*—I just drew on what I knew."

In other plays, he had a pattern of spending a few years researching and then writing, including an historical play called *The Patriots*.

"I wrote it in the army, which wasn't easy. The Jefferson Memorial was created around that time. And they asked if we could perform the play in Washington, which we did. I was invited to sit in the President's box at the inauguration of the Jefferson Memorial. It was a lot of fun."

"Ten years ago, there was talk of a play of yours about the art world. Was that ever produced?"

"No, I never produced that. Wrote it and worked on it, then let it go. I was never satisfied with it. I'm working on a couple of new plays now."

"Do you write every day?"

"Well, I work even if it's not writing. I work all the time, basically. Another play that has had a phenomenal life today is *Darkness at Noon*. In the last six months, I've had a dozen offers to buy it for film—from Yugoslavia, from France, from Germany. It's about the Soviet Union. It was based on Arthur Koestler's book and won the Critics Award, but since Gorbachev, it has been sought after all over the world." Kingsley did the stage adaptation of *Darkness at Noon* in 1951 and was pleased to have it suddenly in demand again. "Just a few weeks ago, *Detective Story* was done in Tokyo, and before that, Turkey. And now there is this interest in *Darkness at Noon*. It's fabulous."

But it was hardly his first brush with the film industry. I asked about the film version of *Men in White*.

"Oh, yes. With Clark Gable."

"I would have thought that the prizes and prestige and the film would have guaranteed the play a life in print but found I had to read *Men in White* in manuscript."

He was not surprised. "Five of the prize plays are being published in France. Here, there is a great aversion to publishing plays."

Kingsley plays are characterized by a strong, human story, not just period pieces but plays with a strong sense of social ills. I wanted to know if he had grown up in a political family.

"No, but I was very active in debating both in high school and at Cornell. As such, one became involved in great public issues, so what I learned was to look for the big questions."

They are still big questions. Sidney Kingsley plays are also notable for their touching and passionate love scenes. I was particularly thinking of the scene in *Dead End* where the criminal, played by Bogart in the film, meets his old sweetheart who has become a prostitute.

He nodded, "That was a two-minute scene. That was a wild one. It really worked. Shocking. In the play she died of syphilis. But they changed it in the film to consumption."

"Naturally, the old standby. Were the critics as powerful then as they seem to be now?"

"There were more newspapers. There were eight or ten important critics and today there are one or two. I got a bad review from Brooks Atkinson for *Detective Story*, my biggest hit. It didn't matter because there were eight or nine other good reviews. Also, in those days the gossip columnists were critics. Walter Winchell was a powerful critic. Almost single-handedly, he could make a play. Leonard Lyons, Ed Sullivan, all wrote very vividly of the plays and they were regarded as good critics. The power Walter Winchell had is inconceivable today. He could make. . . . His political power was enormous."

Before Kingsley left for his evening of Tennessee Williams, I asked him, "Many of your plays were turned into films. Did you like Hollywood?"

Given his treatment there in the heyday of McCarthyism, his answer was not surprising. "I loathed it."

Jon Robin Baitz (opposite)

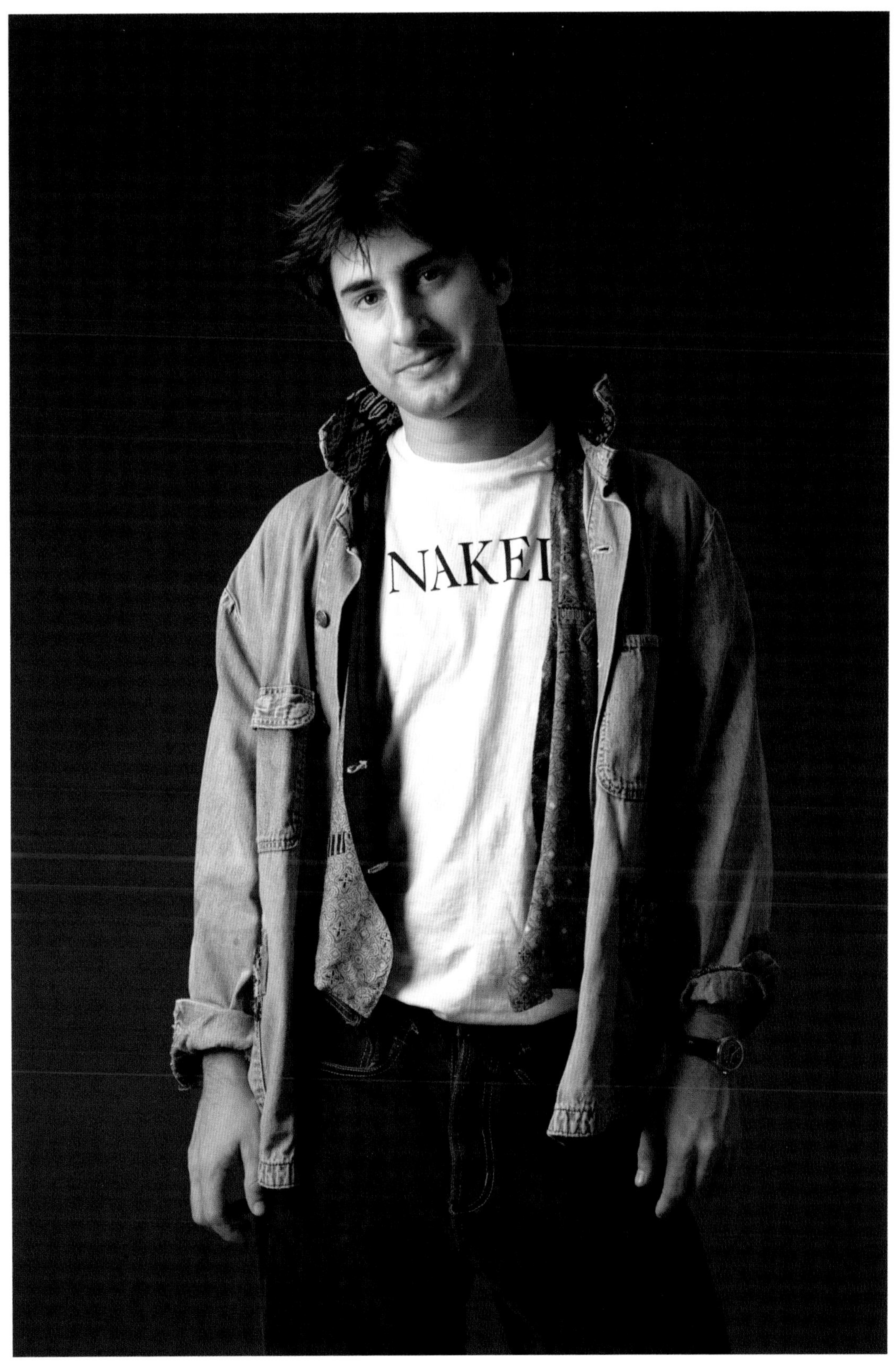
NAKEI

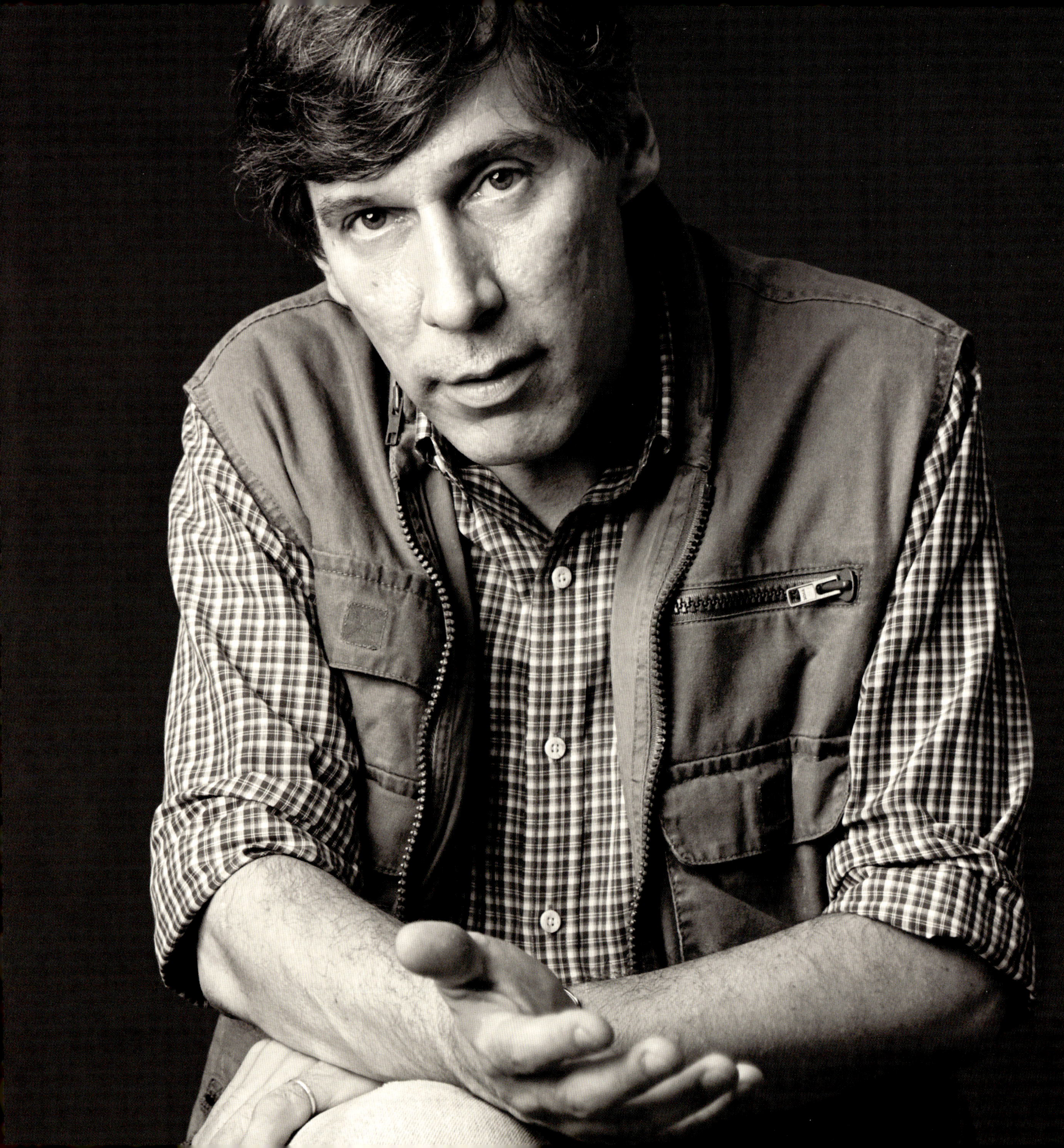

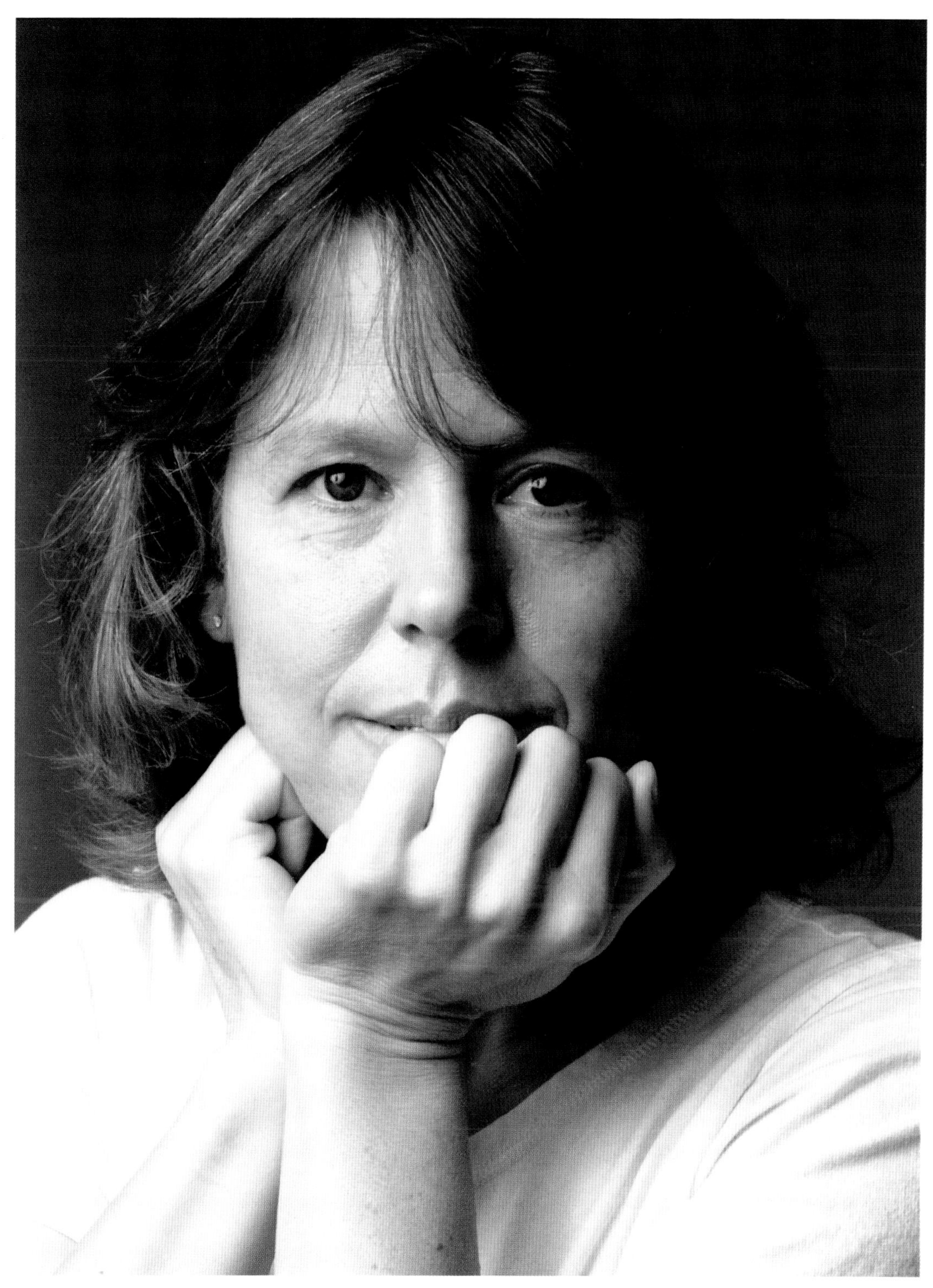

Thomas Babe (opposite) — Joan Ackermann

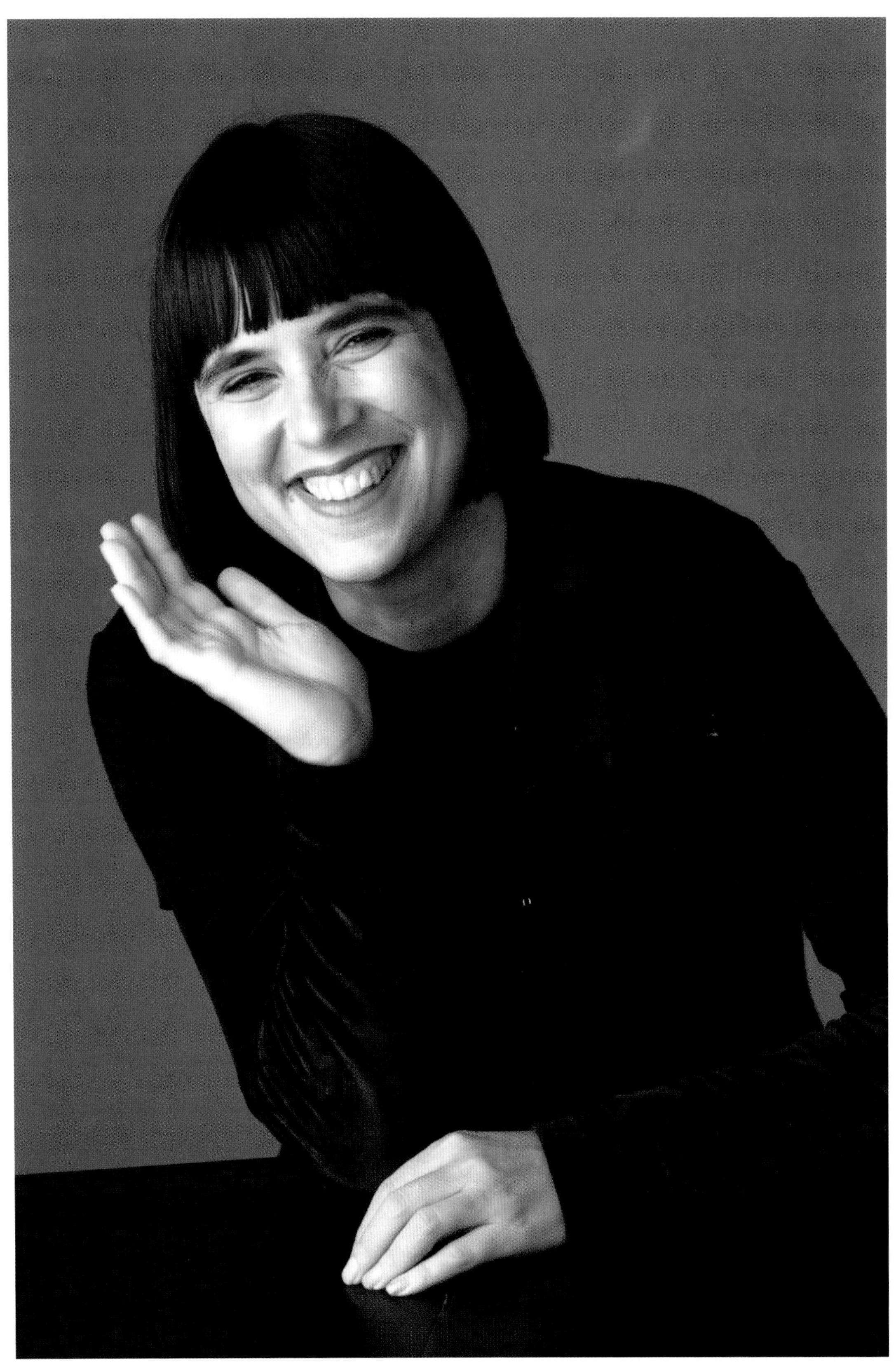

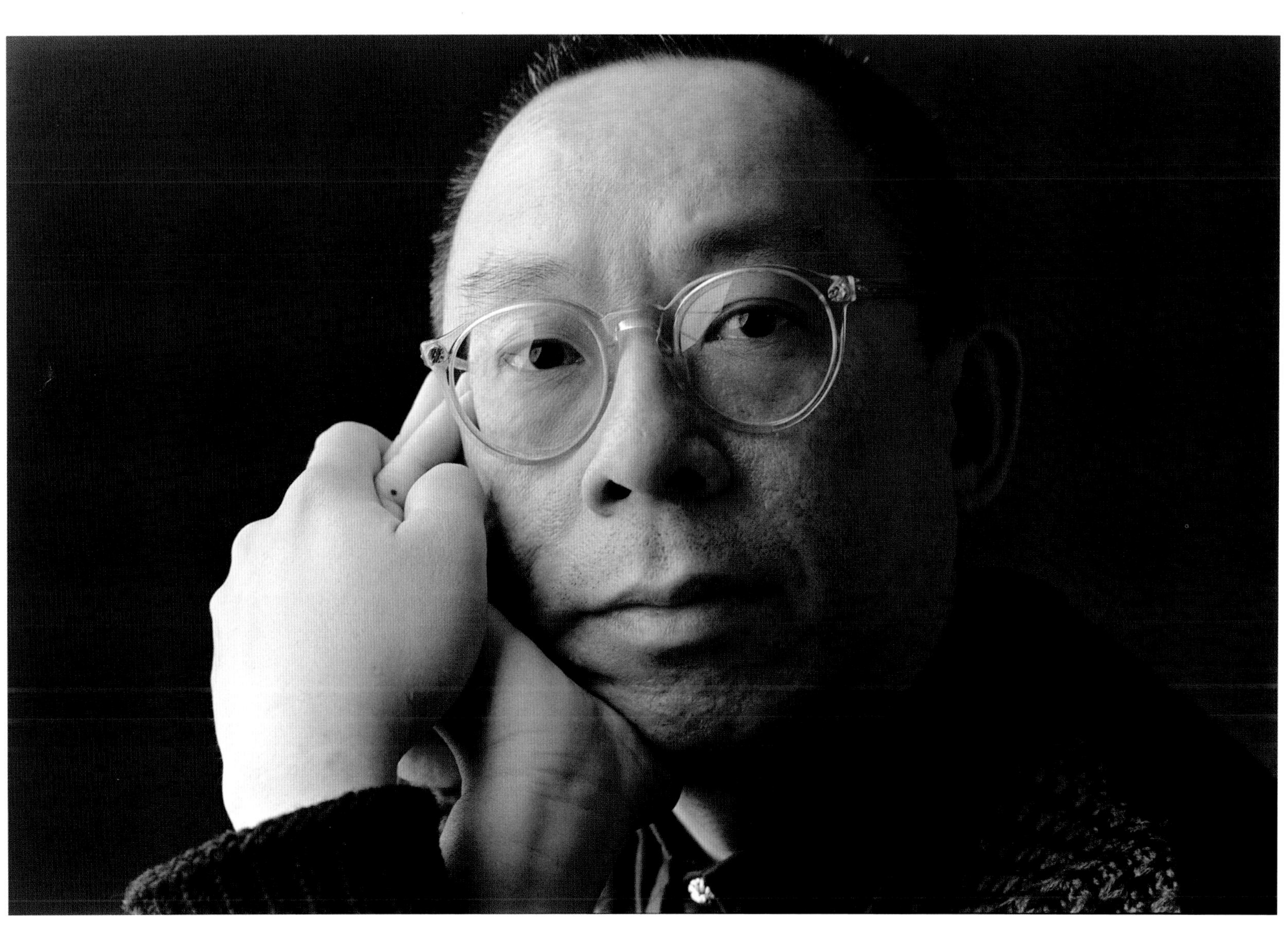

Eve Ensler (opposite) — Ping Chong

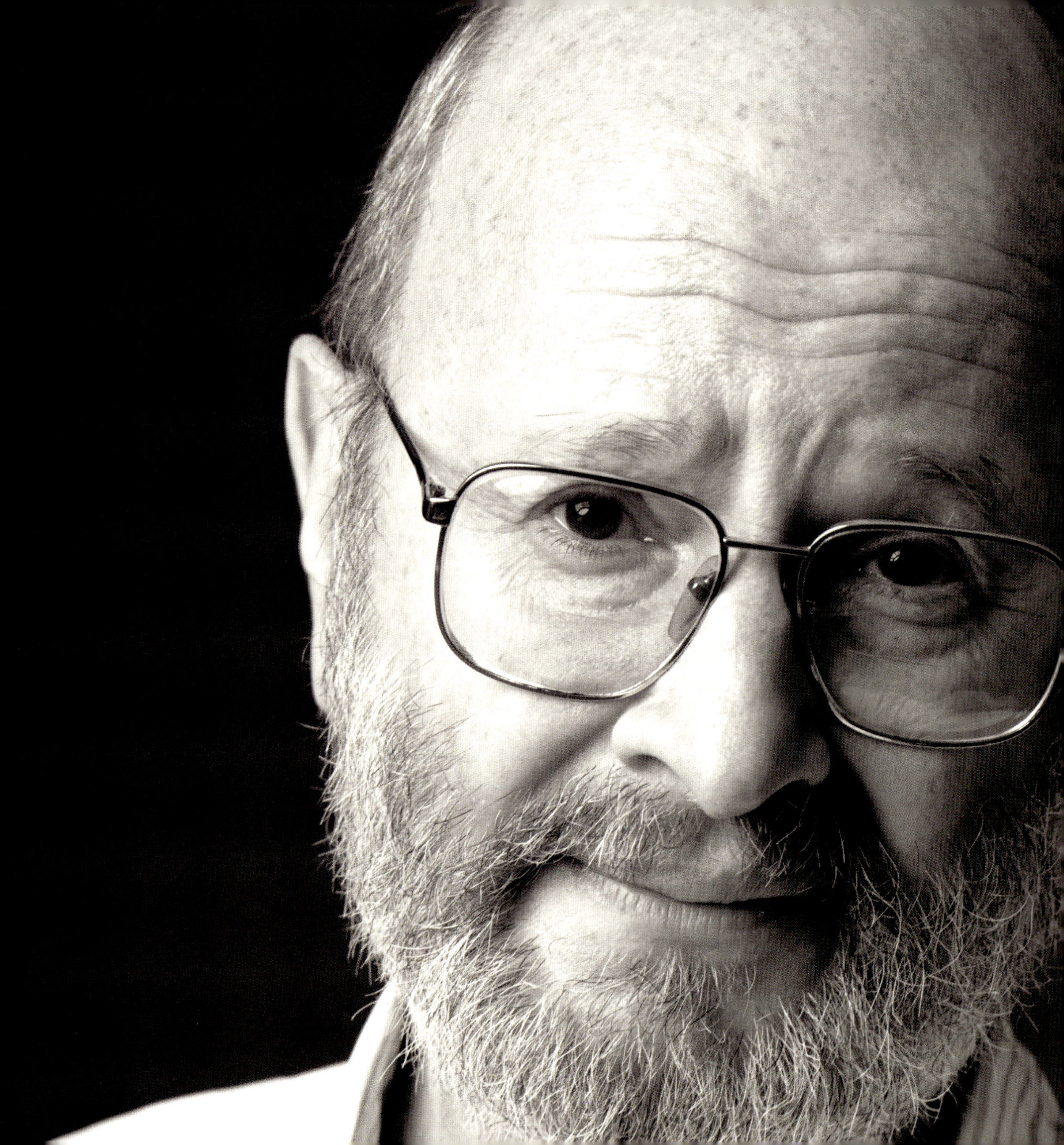

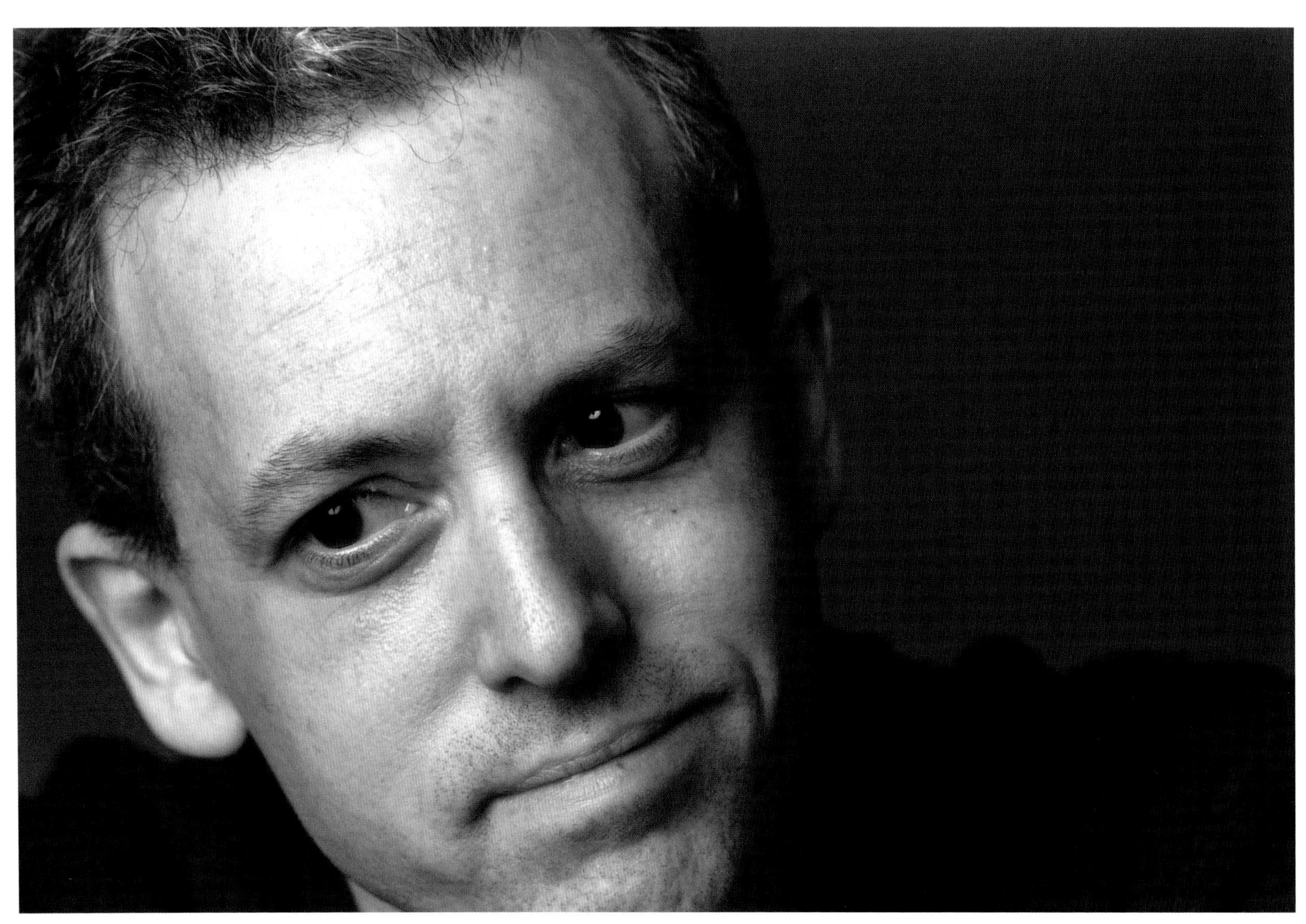

Donald Margulies — Terrence McNally (opposite)

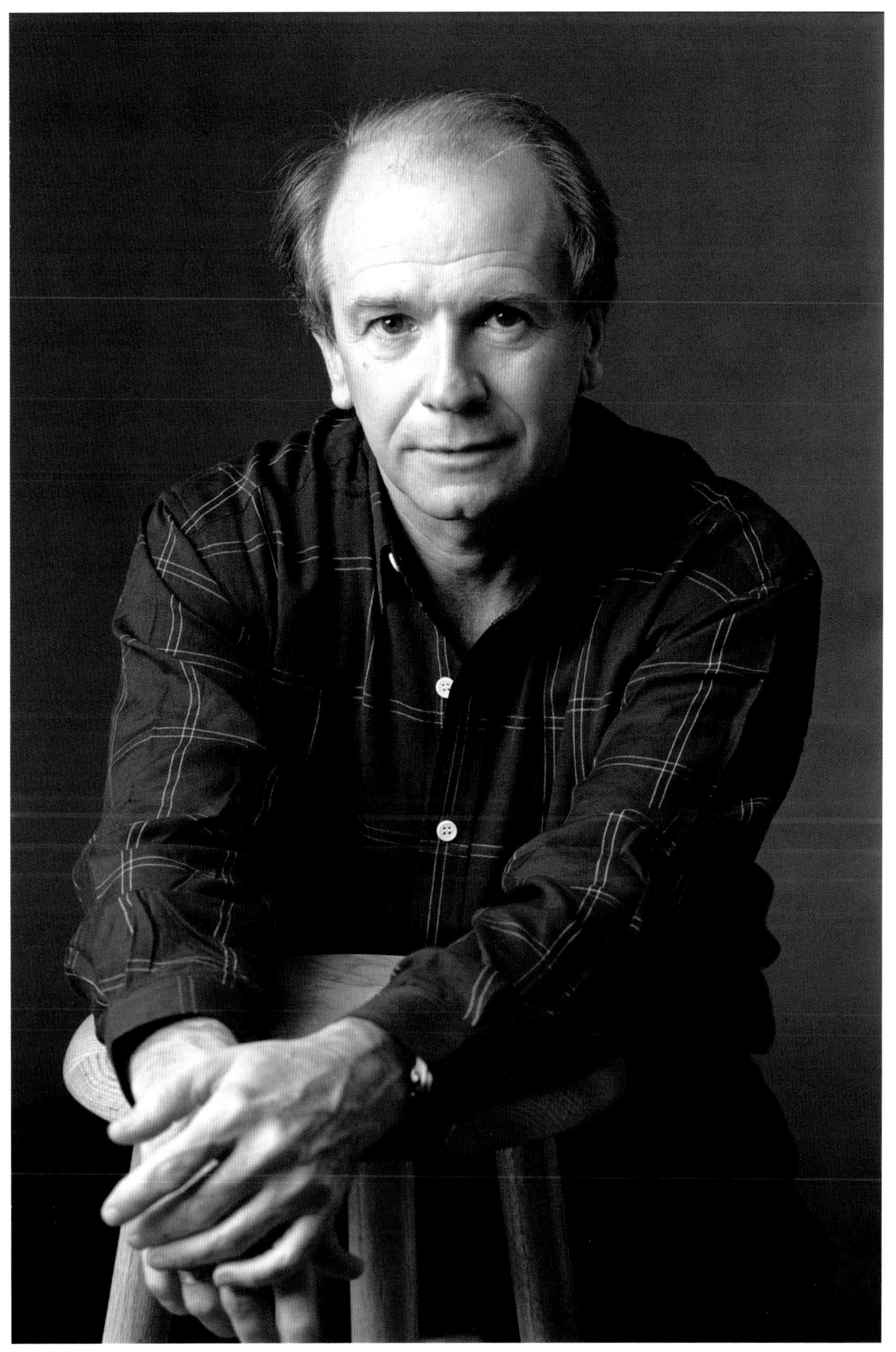

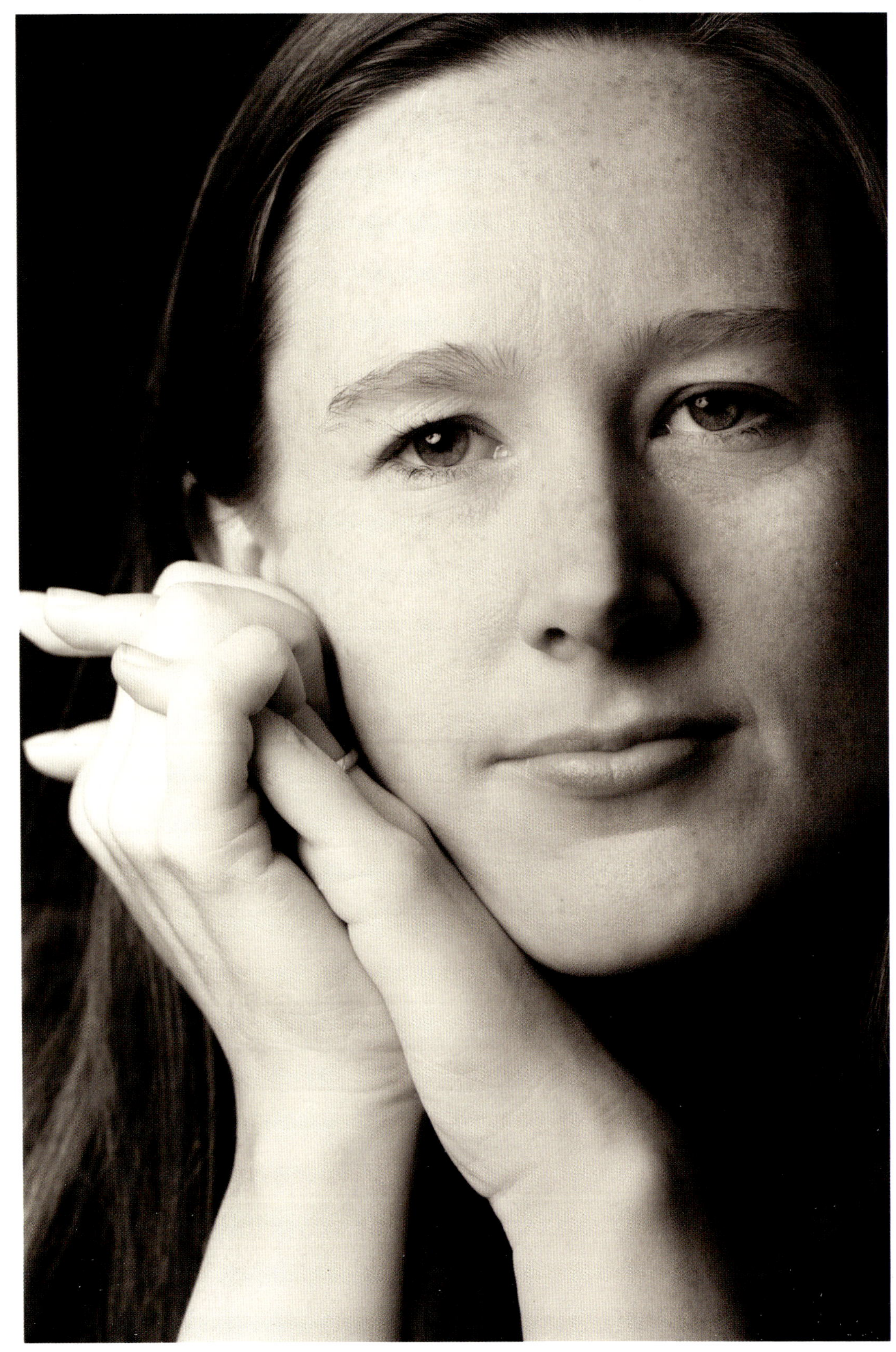

SARAH RUHL

(Born 1974—American playwright awarded a McArthur Fellowship and the PEN/Laura Pels International Foundation for Theater Award for a playwright in mid-career.)

In July 2012, as I was looking back over decades of photographing and interviewing playwrights, I felt the book could not be complete without certain compelling, newer voices, like Sarah Ruhl, whom I had photographed in 2007. When I got in touch about an interview, Sarah was in the middle of rehearsals for a remounting of *Melancholy Play* in New York and suggested we settle for a virtual exchange, via email.

* * *

SJ: A face-to-face or even voice-to-voice interview is so different from the cyber-space interview, which seems more formal, less digressive, and obviously less conversational. For me as interviewer, it means trying to be concise. I am trying to understand playwrights and playwriting. How and why theatre is important still. What led you to playwriting, as opposed to some other writing?

SR: Paula Vogel. It was meeting the right teacher at the right time in my life at Brown University; she convinced me I had the mettle for it. Had I not met Paula, I would have continued to write fiction and poetry.

I was also deeply affected by going to rehearsals from a young age with my mother who is an actress in Chicago.

SJ: Thinking back—are there productions that stand out in your mind? What was it about going to the rehearsals that made you think you wanted to be part of this?

SR: My mother played the nurse in *Romeo and Juliet*. I was terrified by her grief. She also directed productions of *A Midsummer Night's Dream* and *Enter Laughing*. From watching those productions over and over again, I probably developed an attachment to magic and to vaudeville.

SJ: How old were you when you went to Mom's rehearsals?

SR: From the age of five to presently . . .

SJ: You mention her grief as the Nurse in *Romeo and Juliet*? Why does that stand out?

SR: I think it disturbed me to see her lose a daughter figure . . . and to see her grief *in extremis* . . .

SJ: Grief in all its forms seems to be a big topic in all your plays. What or who are the major influences for you—past or present, people or things? Other writers, teachers, family, friends?

SR: Besides Paula and my mom . . . Maria Irene Fornes, Mac Wellman, Nilo Cruz, Caryl Churchill, Virginia Woolf, Katherine Mansfield.

SJ: What is your process like? For example, do you write daily, or sporadically?

SR: I used to write daily before I had children. Now I write whenever I can, whenever someone is not vomiting on me or near my computer.

SJ: Do you think women are more impacted by being mothers and writers than men are by being fathers and writers? Or is there any difference? Have we finally erased these distinctions in 2012?

SR: I think we have come a long way. Still, we are not Scandinavia . . .

SJ: How do you come up with the ideas for your plays? Are they visual first, or an emotion, or a phrase you heard?

SR: Each one is different. *Eurydice* started with an image, as did *Dead Man's Cell Phone. Clean House* started with a phrase. And *Melancholy Play* started with an idea.

SJ: John Lahr has called you a fabulist. How might you describe yourself?

SR: I like that. I like it better than the term "magical realism," which in some ways, I think, is a contradiction in terms.

SJ: Your plays seem to me to be both visionary and fantastical. As though the playwright has a shamanic role of reaching into the void and bringing back visions that explain us to ourselves. Do you see the role of the playwright (yourself in particular) or the purpose of theatre art today in such a way?

SR: I think the playwright, especially now, has this crazy obligation to the live arts now that we live in a digital age. It is a rare honor these days to bring people into a room together, whether they are sleeping or not; at least we are all dreaming together, or breathing together.

SJ: Where do you see yourself in twenty years?

SR: I hope I'm still writing and living in Brooklyn. I think a lot about longevity, about how we develop artistic stamina over time. I hope I'm teaching a little bit. I hope my kids are happy.

Richard Foreman (opposite)

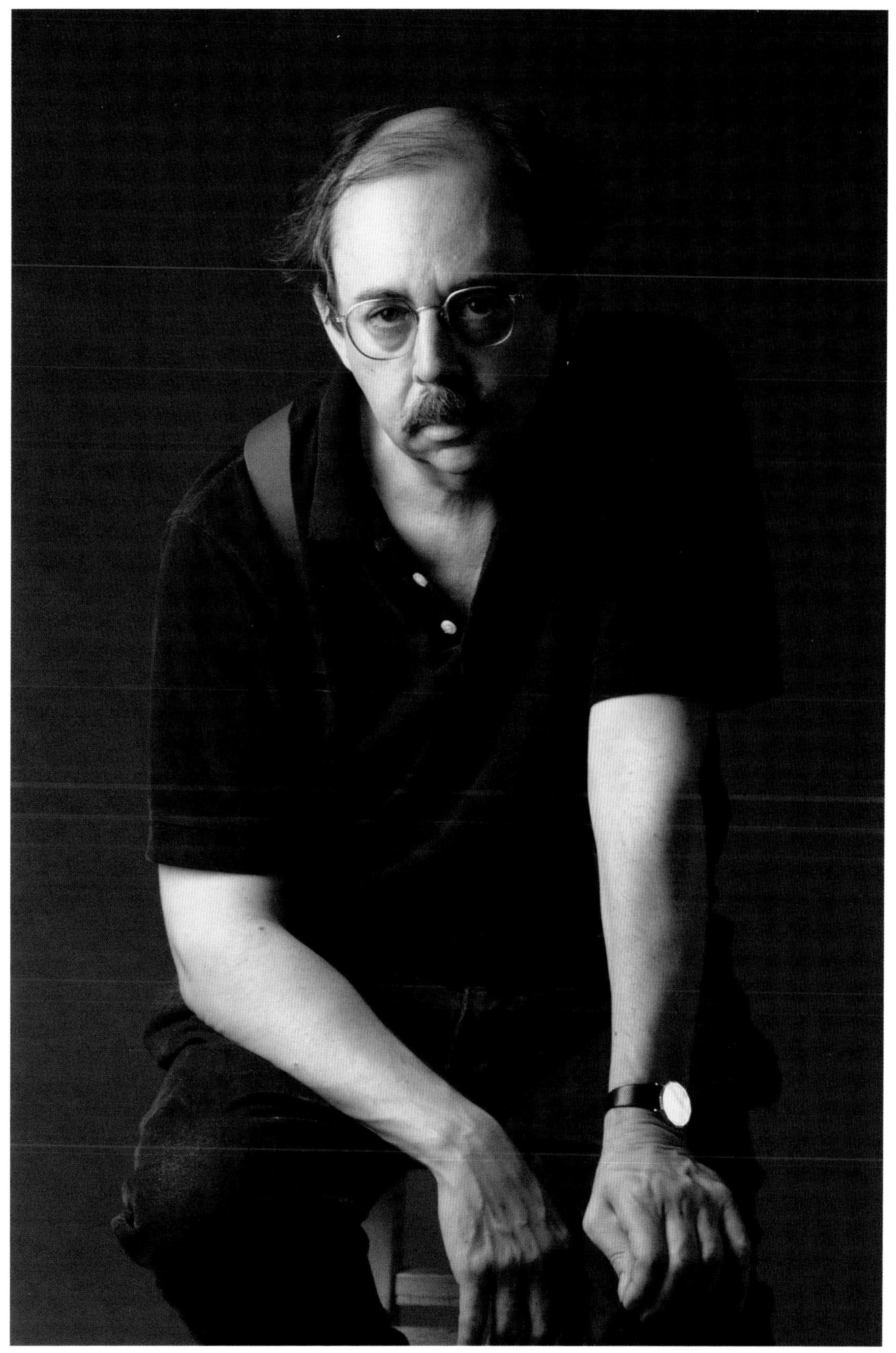

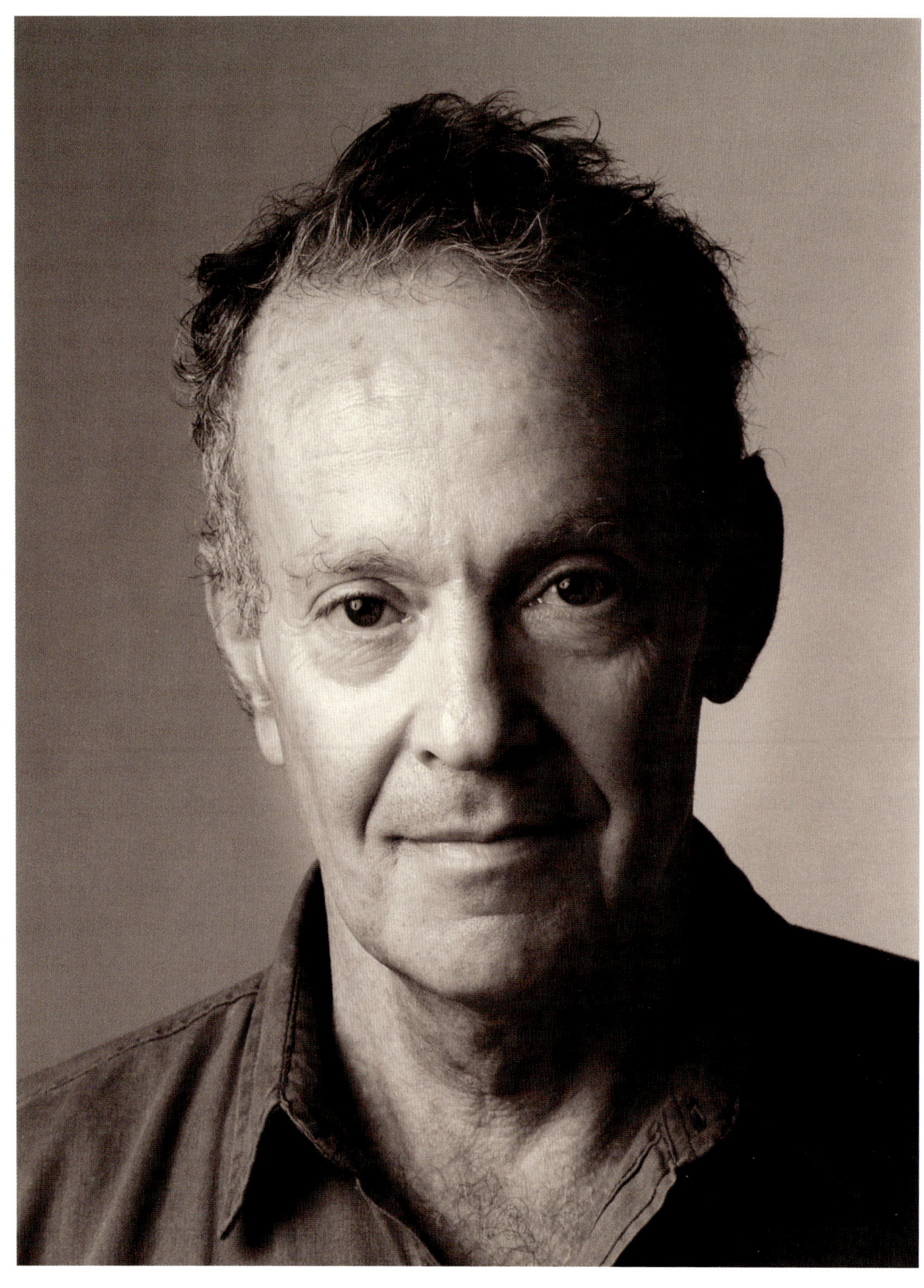

Joe Chaikin — John Guare (opposite)

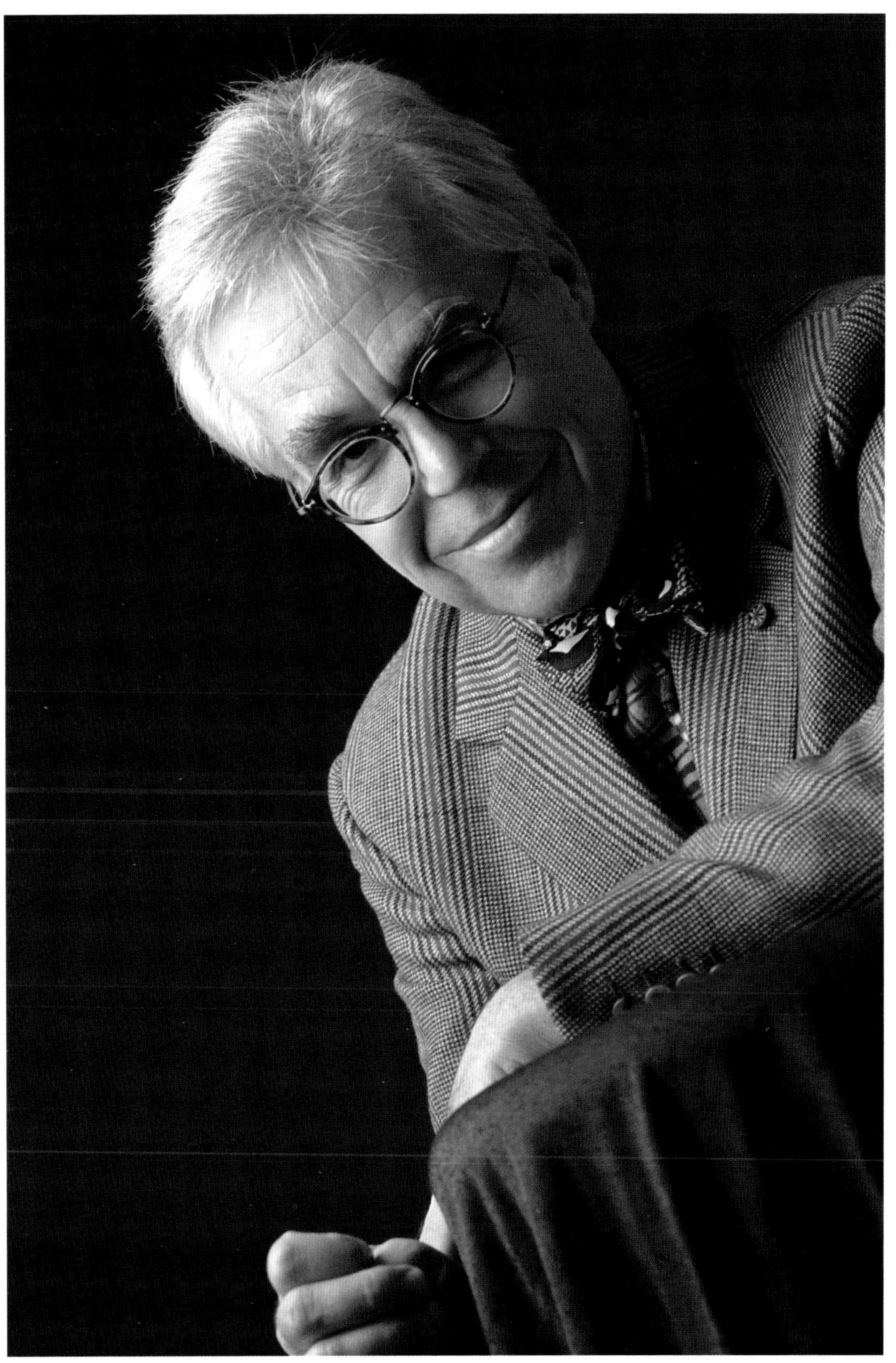

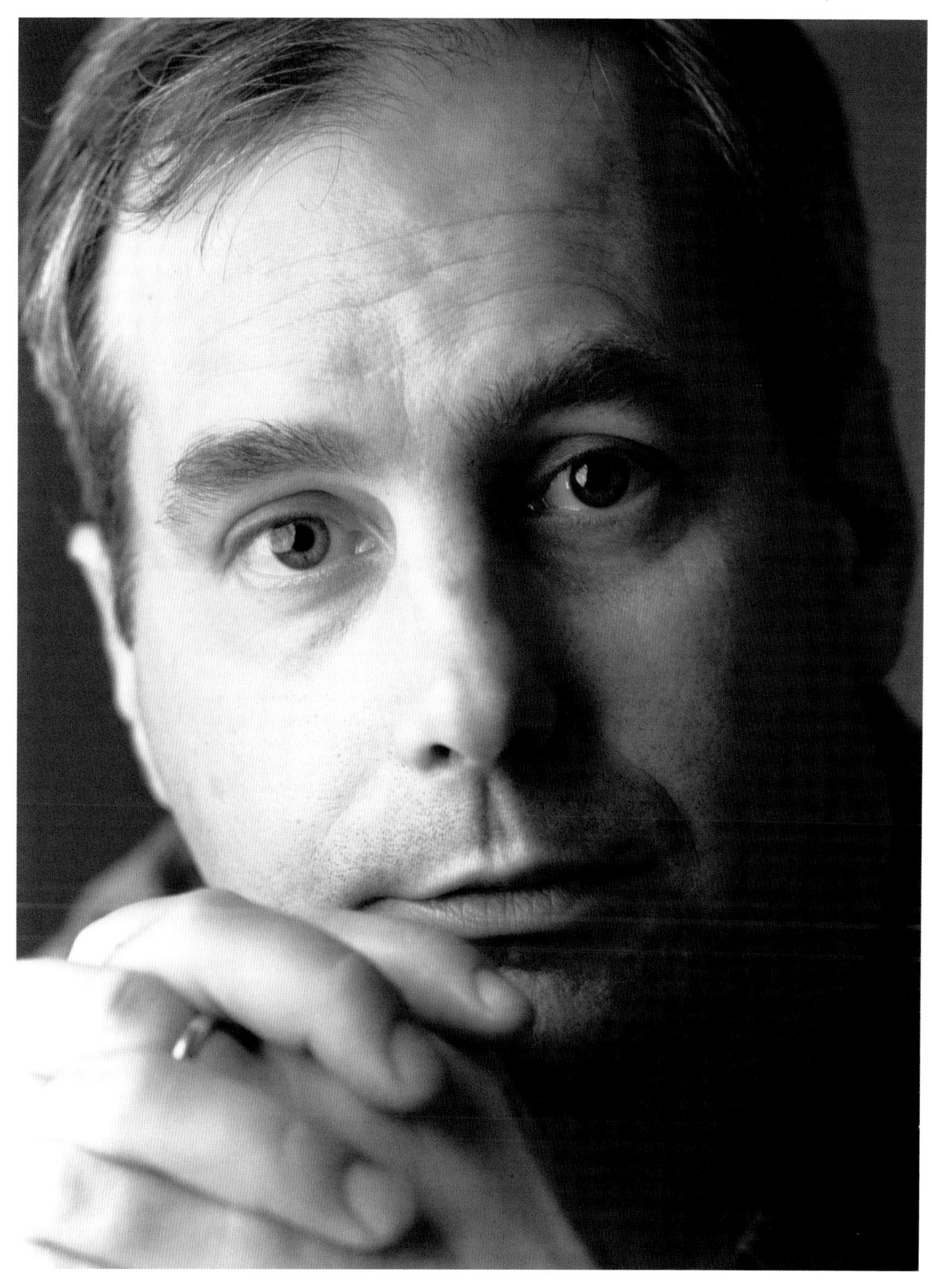

Young Jean Lee (opposite) — Lee Blessing

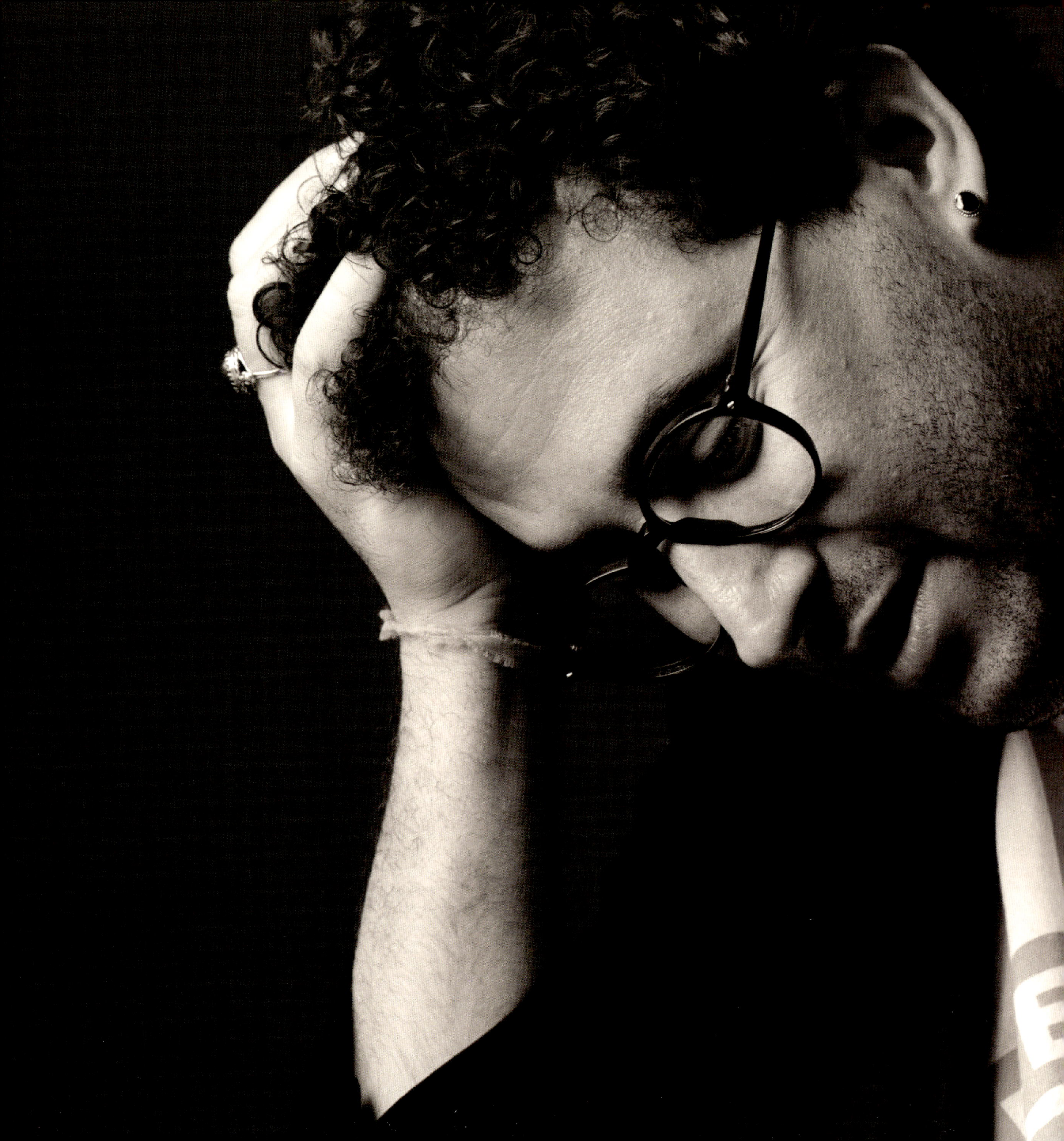

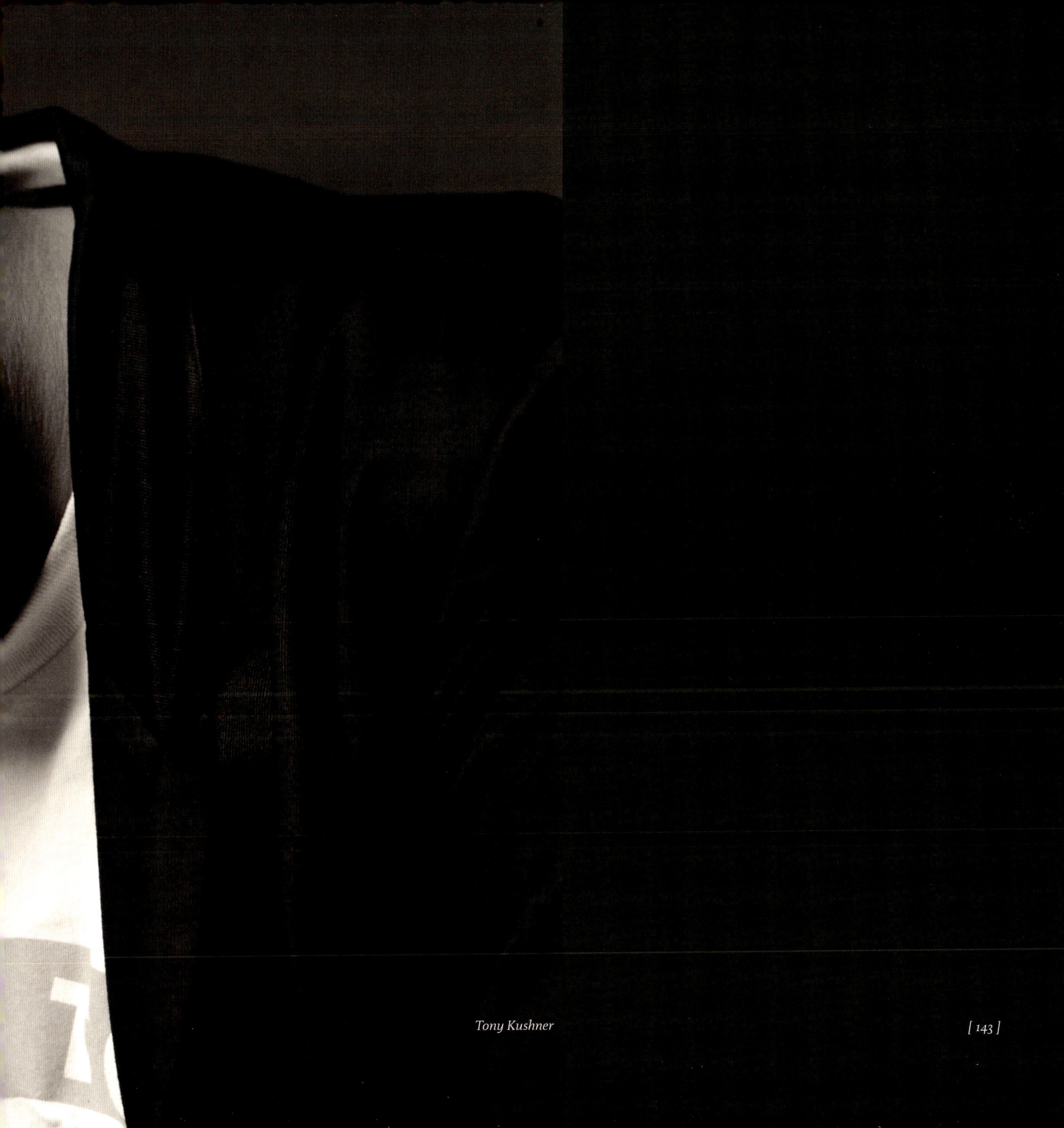

ARTHUR MILLER

(1915–2005—widely considered one of the greatest dramatists of the twentieth century, American playwright and author of All My Sons, The Crucible, *and* Death of a Salesman, *which won the Pulitzer Prize in 1949.)*

I pursued Arthur Miller for years and got polite letters saying, "No, thanks. I have enough pictures of myself." Then in 1996, Arthur Miller accepted the invitation from Signature Theatre to be that year's playwright-in-residence. He had declined an earlier invitation. Having been Signature's photographer since 1991, I thought this would be my chance. The company made an appointment with Mr. Miller for our photo session, but then he cancelled. Later, he sent me a note giving me his phone number in Connecticut, and early one afternoon, I dialed it. A woman with an accent answered.

"May I speak with Arthur Miller, please?"

"Who is calling, please?"

"My name is Susan Johann. I'm the company photographer for Signature Theatre. I am supposed to do a portrait of Mr. Miller. I have done this for all past playwrights-in-residence."

"Oh. He *hates* to have his picture taken. But just a moment, please." I heard her voice again, some distance from the phone. "Ar-*thur*!"

Miller's wife, Inge Morath, was a fine photographer in her own right, and I have always imagined that she said something to encourage him to agree because suddenly Arthur Miller was on the phone. He agreed to a session at his place in New York City, but first asked, "You're not bringing a lot of equipment, are you?"

"No. No. Just me, my cameras, and one light."

We set the time for a week later at noon. Having a fear of being late, I arrived twenty-five minutes early and sat in the park across from Miller's building on one of the warmest February days I can remember in New York. At precisely five minutes before the hour, I dragged my equipment cart to the building and rang the intercom bell. Mr. Miller buzzed me in. Eight years of pursuit, and there I was—on my way.

Miller answered the door. He was tall, reserved, still handsome and strong-looking—a giant of a man. Here was someone who has plumbed the depths, who found and grappled with the big issues, who looked for answers through his work and through a life that informed his work. Here was a man of stature in every way.

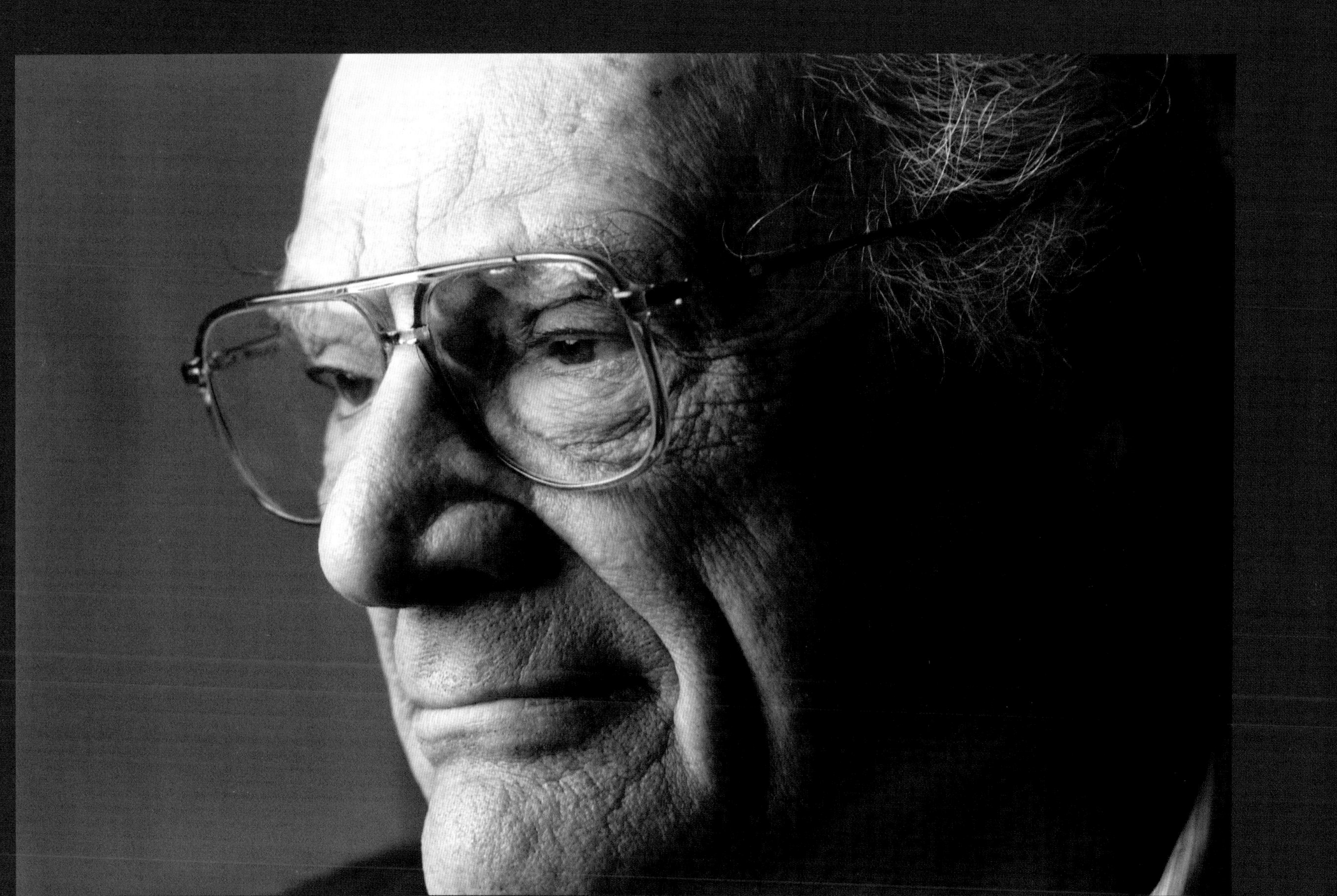

I pulled in my little equipment cart and assessed the situation as I unpacked. It was high noon. The sun was streaming through the window and bouncing off the very large, old table where Mr. Miller was now sitting. It seemed a natural place for him to be.

From this simple apartment in Manhattan, one could conclude Arthur Miller lived like a monk. Most of his time was spent in Roxbury, on the same property where fifty years ago, with his own hands, he built a ten-by-twelve work shack to write in. It was there that *Death of a Salesman* was written. The house and shack sit on three hundred acres with thousands of trees that Miller himself planted.

By contrast, his Manhattan place was Spartan. When I admired the table, he said it was from a sixteenth-century Spanish monastery. There were colorful paintings on the wall, but the rooms were basic, small. The sense was one of utility, with white walls and touches of red and black. This was a place of purposefulness.

Everything was just about ready. I had set up the light and was looking for a three-prong plug outlet. But it was an old building. Miller started to root around in a kitchen drawer for a converter plug. Nothing. I was getting nervous. Then he pulled the couch away from the one wall we hadn't checked, and there it was. We were set.

It was quarter past noon when I took the first picture. I mentioned a friend who had interviewed him at The Chelsea Hotel where Miller had lived in the sixties. We spoke of a play at BAM, one I had seen the night before and he had seen in London. He thought the actor was wonderful, the play a bit too long.

When I had taken forty frames, he said, "I think you must have enough. I had surgery last month, and I should have my feet up."

Oh, dear—guilt warring with fear of missing what I came for. I quickly pulled the light to the left.

Mr. Miller volunteered that the surgery was for his spine and that he had been discharged on the fourth of December. He was growing impatient. He said, "Well, you must have enough now."

I asked him to look to the right. Three more clicks, and that was it.

In forty-three frames, I finally had pictures of Arthur Miller. It was all over. In the next ten minutes, I packed up and was gone, hoping the picture I had pursued for eight years was in the camera. This was before digital, of course. At the time, other than a Polaroid, there was no way to know what was in the camera until the roll of film was developed. A portrait of Arthur Miller would be the capstone to my ongoing photographic documentation of contemporary American playwrights.

Before leaving, I asked Mr. Miller if I could interview him.

"No. I've given that up."

"May I quote you?"

"Yes. Perhaps it will discourage others from asking."

With fifty years of interviews and his own very astute essays on theatre, with an autobiography, and the best of his plays, Arthur Miller's work speaks for him.

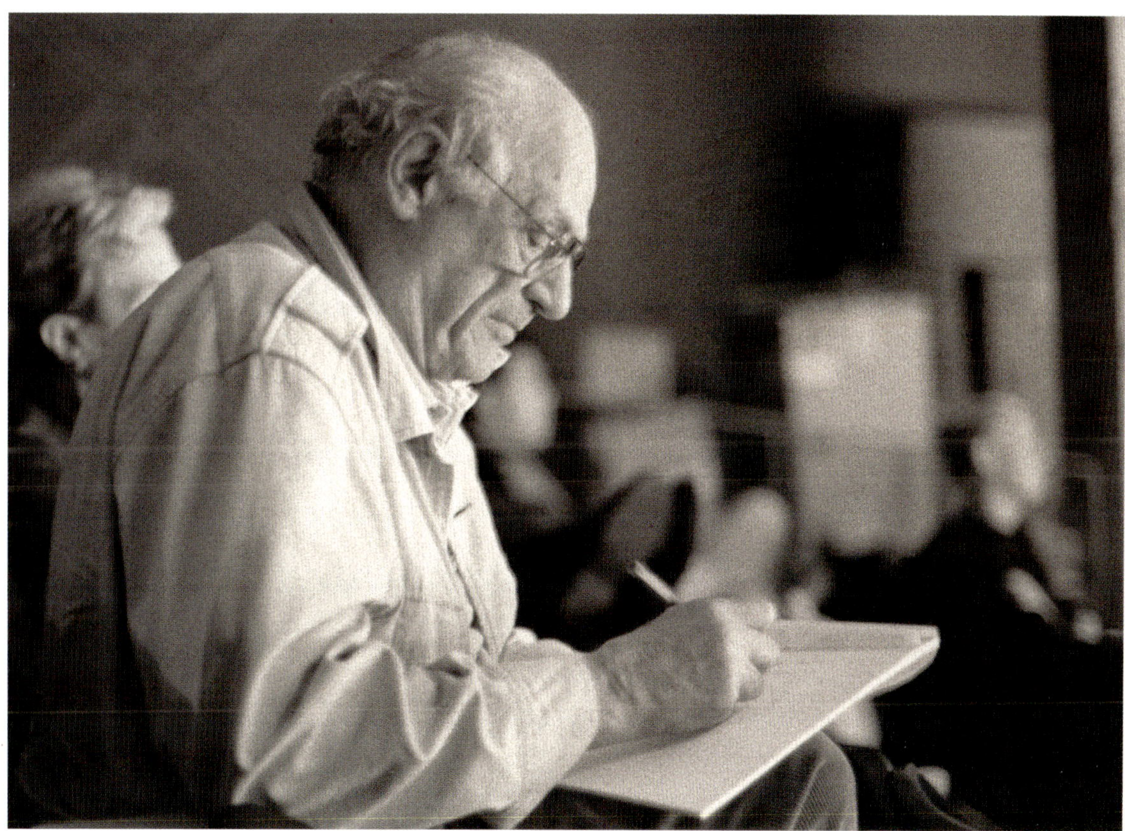

Arthur Miller in rehearsal at Signature Theatre, 1997

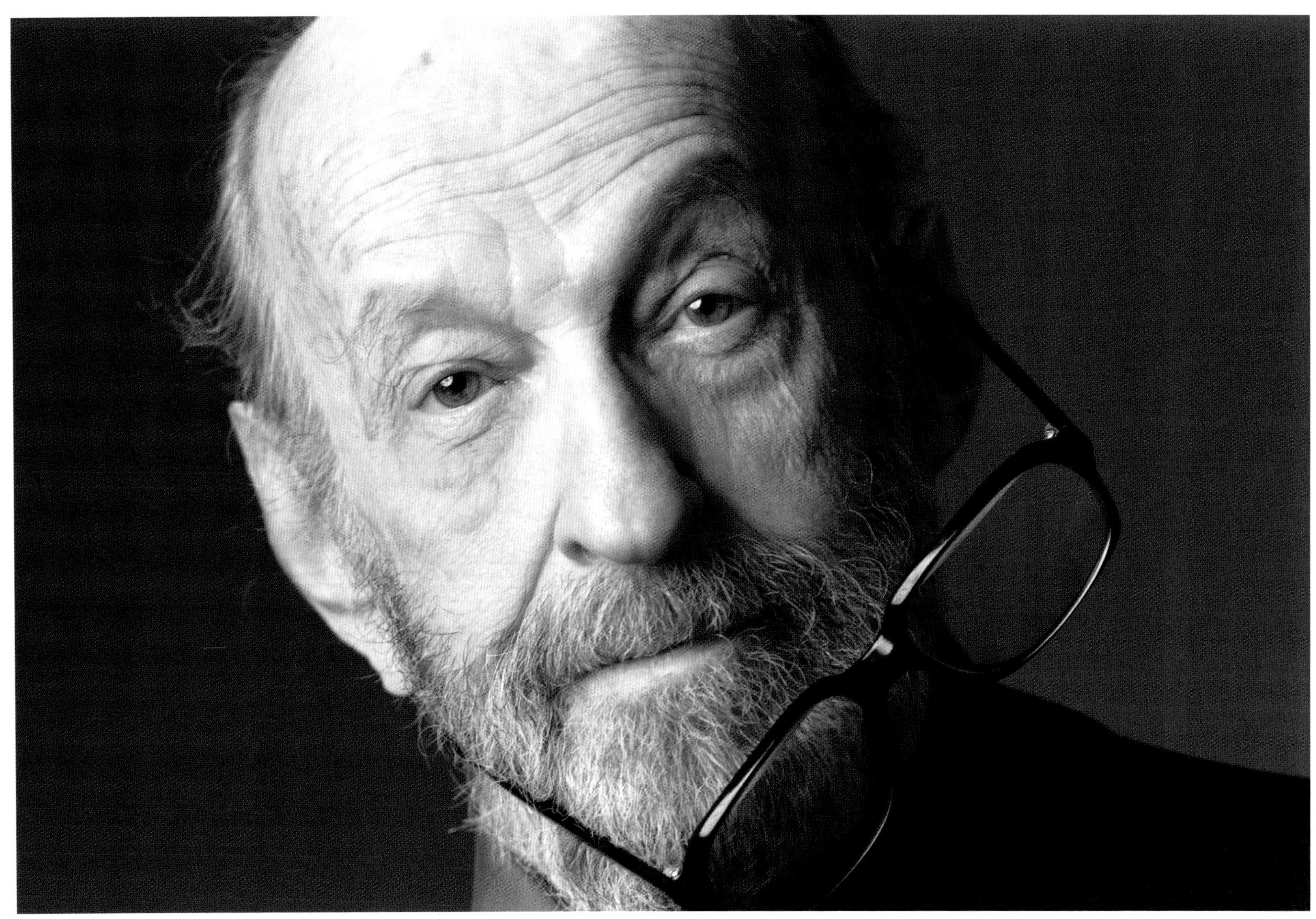

GARSON KANIN

(1912–1999—A prolific American writer and director of plays and films, including his 1946 play, Born Yesterday, *he was nominated for three Oscars and won three Tonys.)*

On a balmy June afternoon several years ago, I had lunch at the New York Athletic Club with Garson Kanin and his wife, Marion Seldes. We talked about theatre, ate oysters, and ended the day with a song. Along the way, I tried to get Garson to talk about himself and his work. It wasn't easy.

This beloved writer began his life in theatre as a scrappy young man who never graduated from high school and always felt the lack. For the rest of his days, he attacked learning with the fever of the autodidact. Garson was the author of *Born Yesterday* and, with his first wife, Ruth Gordon, co-wrote the films *Adam's Rib* and *Pat and Mike,* as vehicles for Katherine Hepburn and Spencer Tracy.

I asked Garson how he became a playwright.

"No idea. I have no idea. But I do know that when I decided to write plays, I made it my business to learn something about the art, its structure, and how other playwrights were doing it."

Garson recalled his teenage years and the weekly walks when the family would have trouble deciding which of twenty plays to see at one of the many Yiddish theaters lining Second Avenue. Enchanted by the theatre, they did not always have ticket money for the whole family, so sometimes just the brothers would attend the performance then hurry home to re-enact the whole evening for their parents.

Garson's tuition at the American Academy of Dramatic Arts was funded by Mike, his older brother. Garson was hired as an actor by George Abbott and then continued to work for him for five years as a stage manager, as an unofficial casting director—getting the best young actors from his group of friends—and as a script reader and assistant.

"There is a bit of luck in all success. You see, I was born in Rochester, New York, and that's where Abbott comes from. When he learned that. . . . Well. At first, when I started at the Abbott office, I would go to the pile of scripts, pick up a couple, and read one. Then I'd write a report or synopsis and leave it on Mr. Abbott's desk." Abbott noted how good the reports were and gave Garson a raise.

Thornton Wilder became a mentor and told him which writers to read. "I never went to high school. I went to the University of Thornton Wilder."

One senses the fearlessness of Garson Kanin, very evident in his books on Hollywood, where he describes meetings with Sam Goldwyn and Louis B. Mayer. Garson was a twenty-four-year-old, holding his own.

"Early on, I learned not to be afraid of anything." Three of the screenplays written with Ruth Gordon for the Tracy and Hepburn team were nominated for Oscars. In the "long stretches of excruciating boredom," he started writing the comedy that became *Born Yesterday*.

With his own Broadway plays, Garson had a little rule. He made sure someone would make a Broadway debut even if it were only in a small role.

When asked if he considered himself a playwright, a screenwriter, a novelist, or simply a writer, Garson said, "I consider myself a dope."

"Why?"

"Because I hardly know anything."

Garson was often asked by interviewers about the basis of Billie Dawn, his most famous character in *Born Yesterday*. He finally said, "I'm Billie Dawn."

"Did you see yourself in all the parts you wrote?"

"In every part, male or female."

"So. How do you write? Do you sit down with a blank page?"

"Not for long! First, there has to be the 'big spill,' without thinking twice, without rewriting, without changing. Just keep going, keep going, keep going. Then, when it has a beginning, a middle, and an end—and only then, go back, begin to edit, consider, and revise. Cut. Mostly cut."

"Then the rewriting goes on?"

"Forever. Forever."

"So how do the characters come to you?"

"From God."

Inspiration comes at any moment, and he wrote the last act of *Happy Ending* in the tiny airport in Martha's Vineyard, with borrowed pen and paper.

Being with Garson Kanin was a humbling experience, not because he was overbearing, not because he had done so many significant things, and not because he has worked with so many significant people in the American performing community, but because he was so humble himself. No airs—just a real straight-ahead guy.

I asked if, like many playwrights, he had some enormous need to explain. "Nope," he said, shaking his head.

"To entertain, to divert, to amuse," said Marian.

"Like Noel Coward?" I asked.

"I wish," said Garson.

Marian and I began to sing Coward's own favorite song from *Bittersweet*—"I believe, that since my life began, the most I've had is just . . . a talent to amuse."

Garson joined us in singing, "Heigh, ho! If love were all."

"So love is all?" I asked. "Then you've been lucky."

Marian smiled. "He's extremely lovable."

Garson looked down. "Aw, shut up."

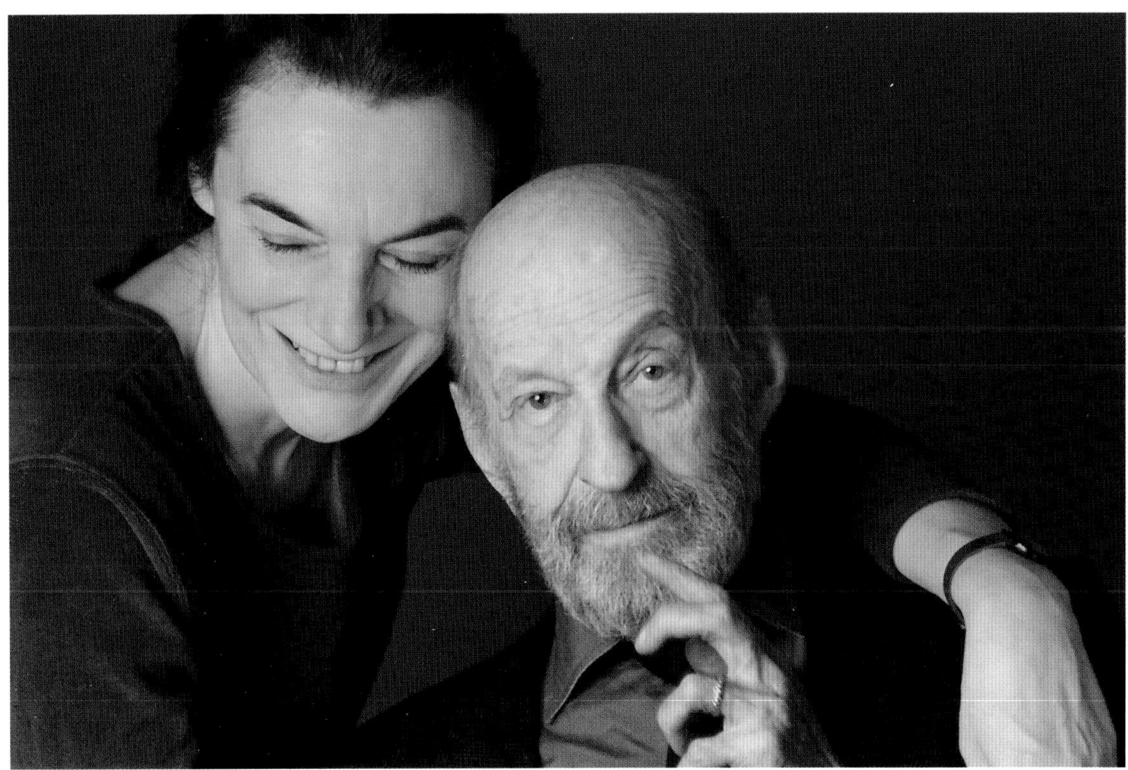

Marian Seldes and Garson Kanin

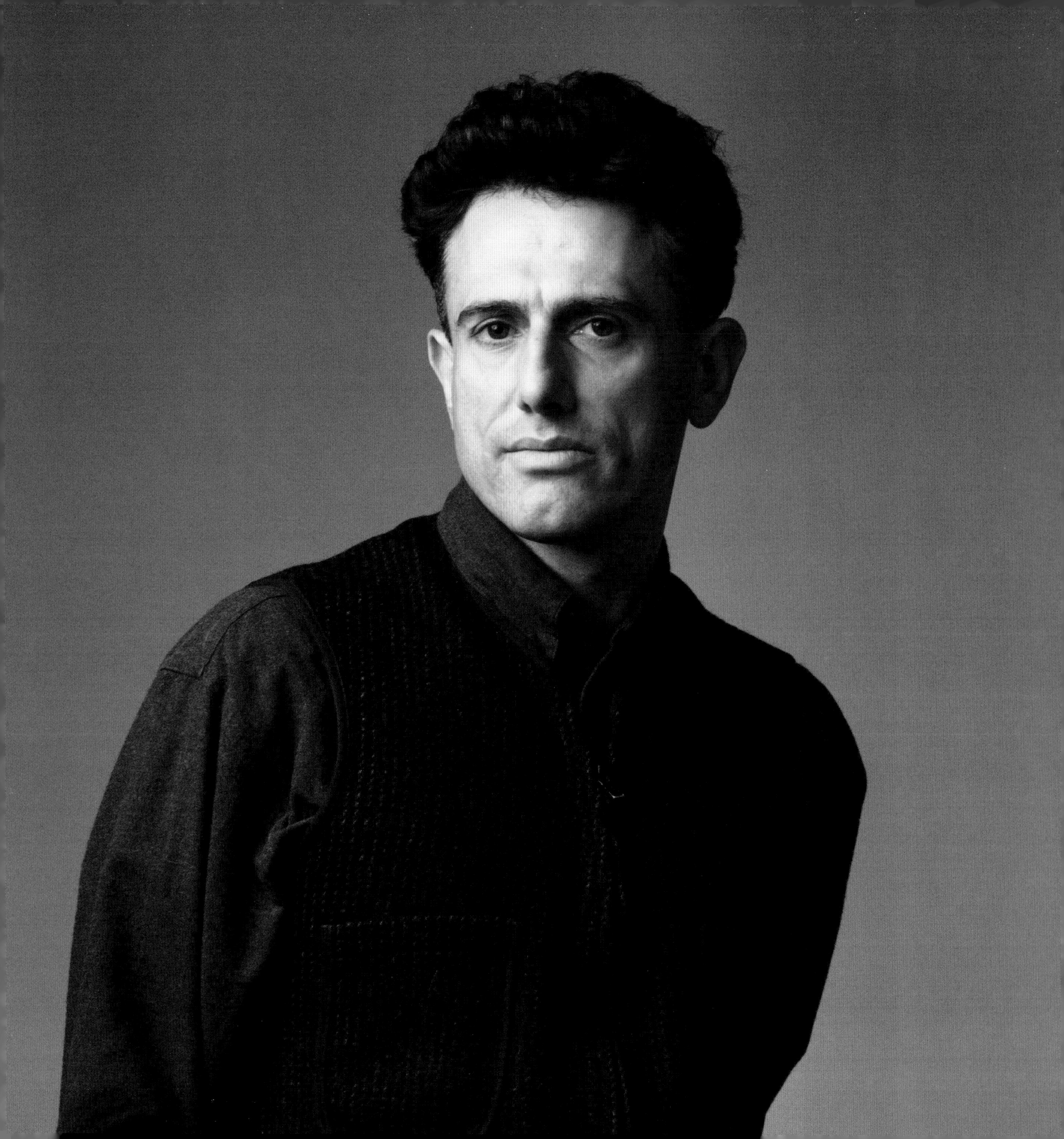

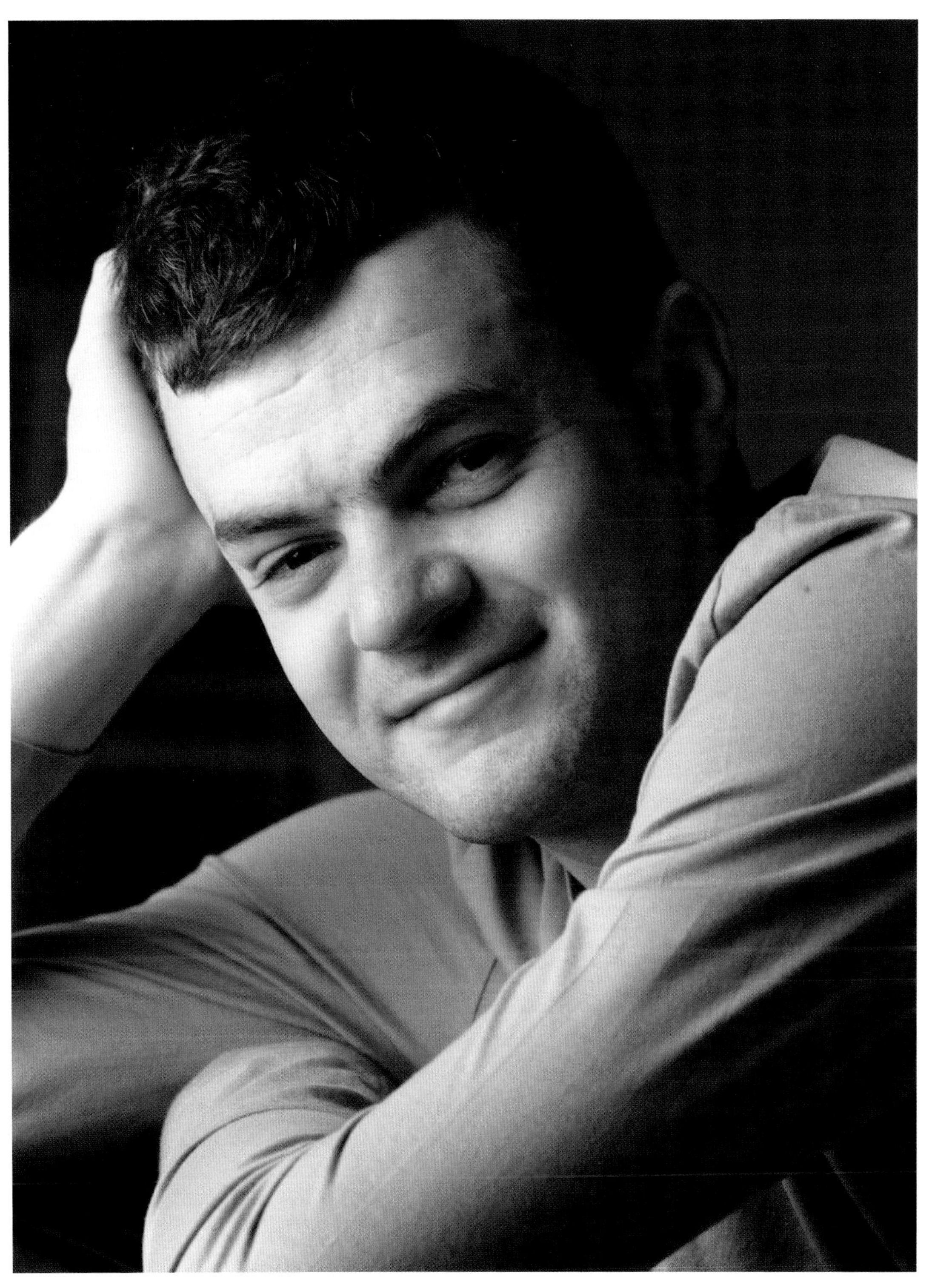

David Greenspan (opposite) — Jonathan Harvey

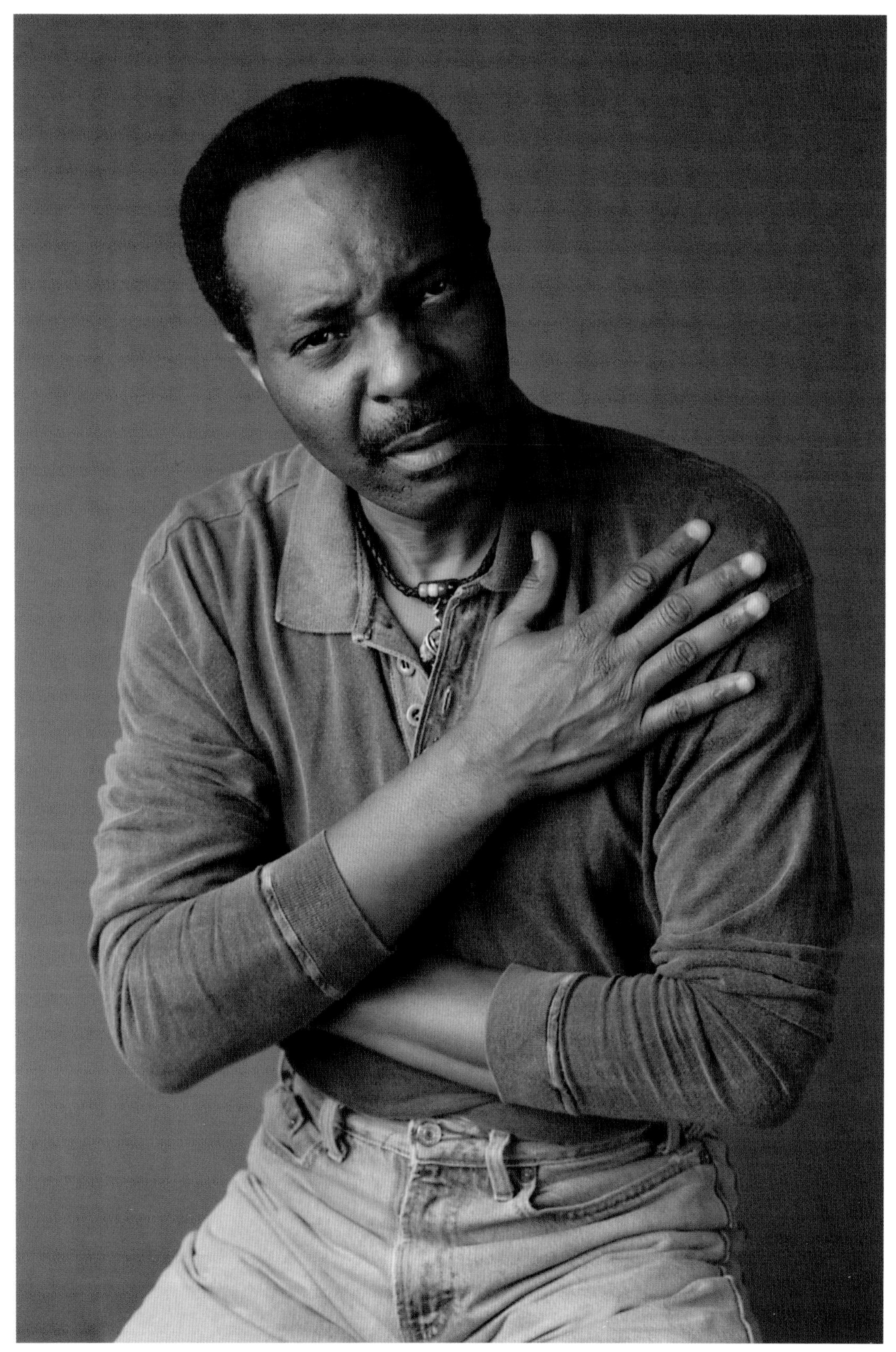

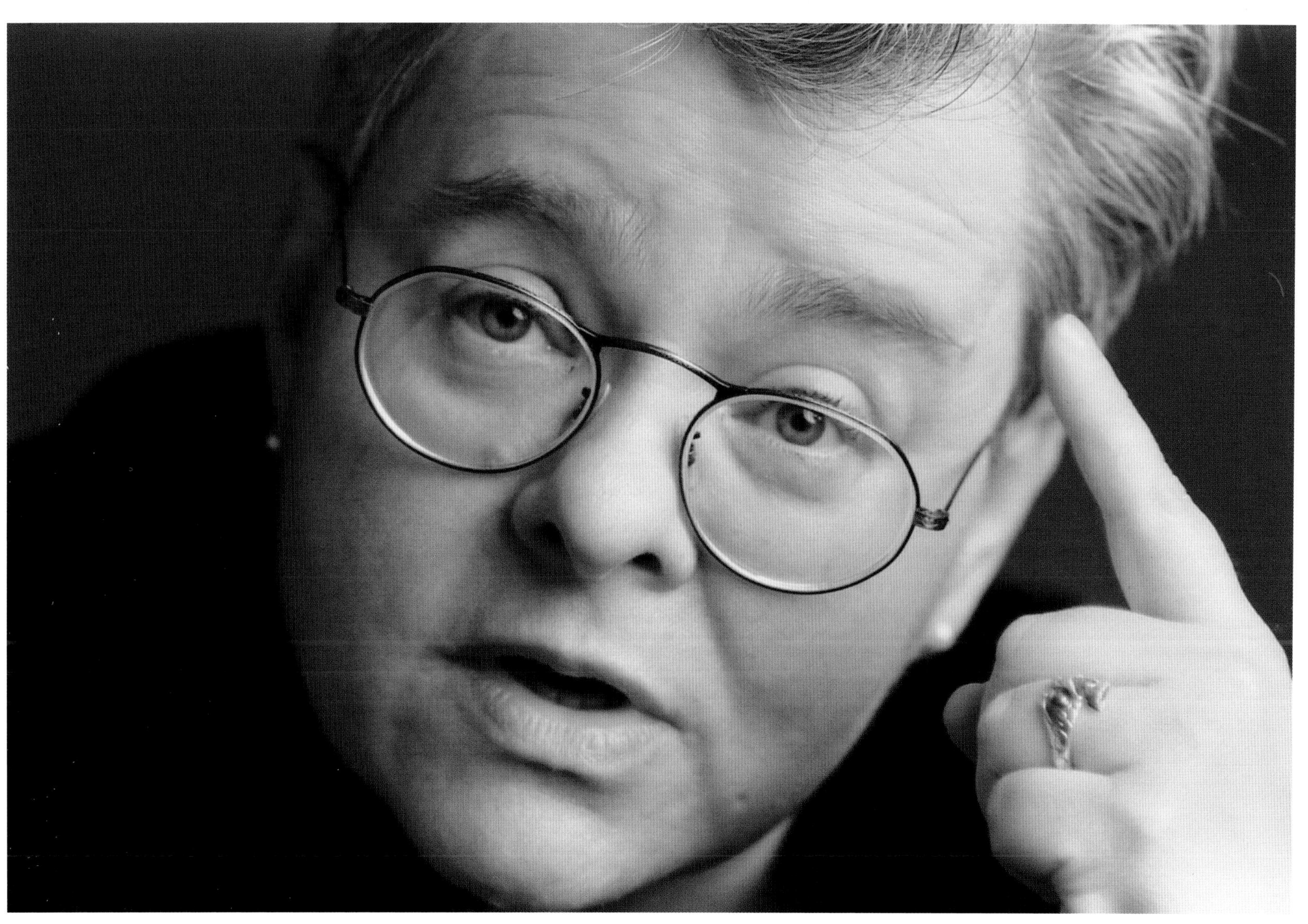

OyamO (opposite) — Paula Vogel

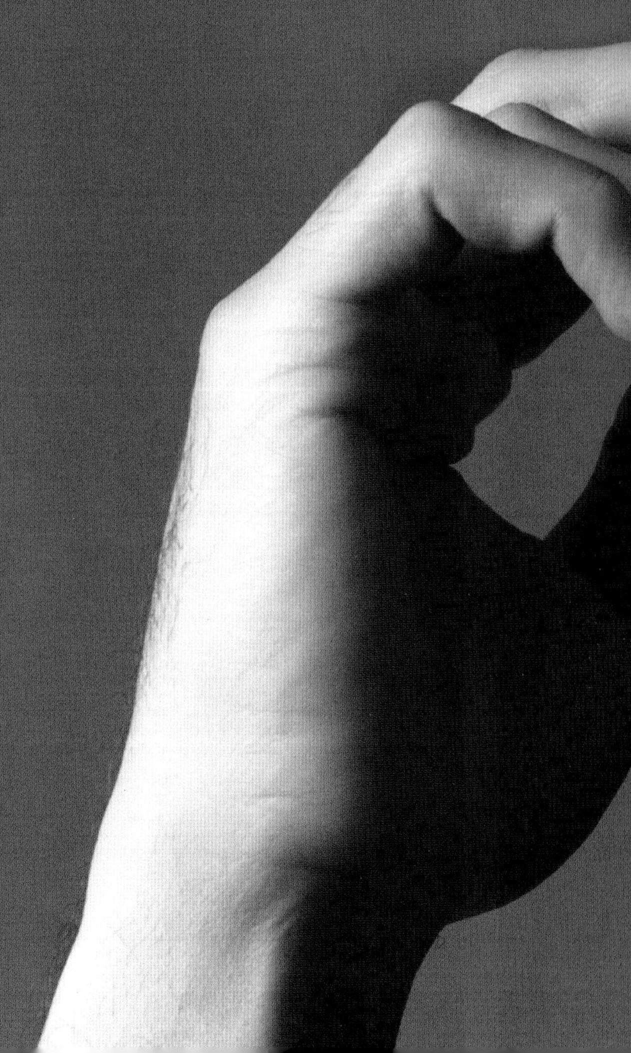

Eric Bogosian

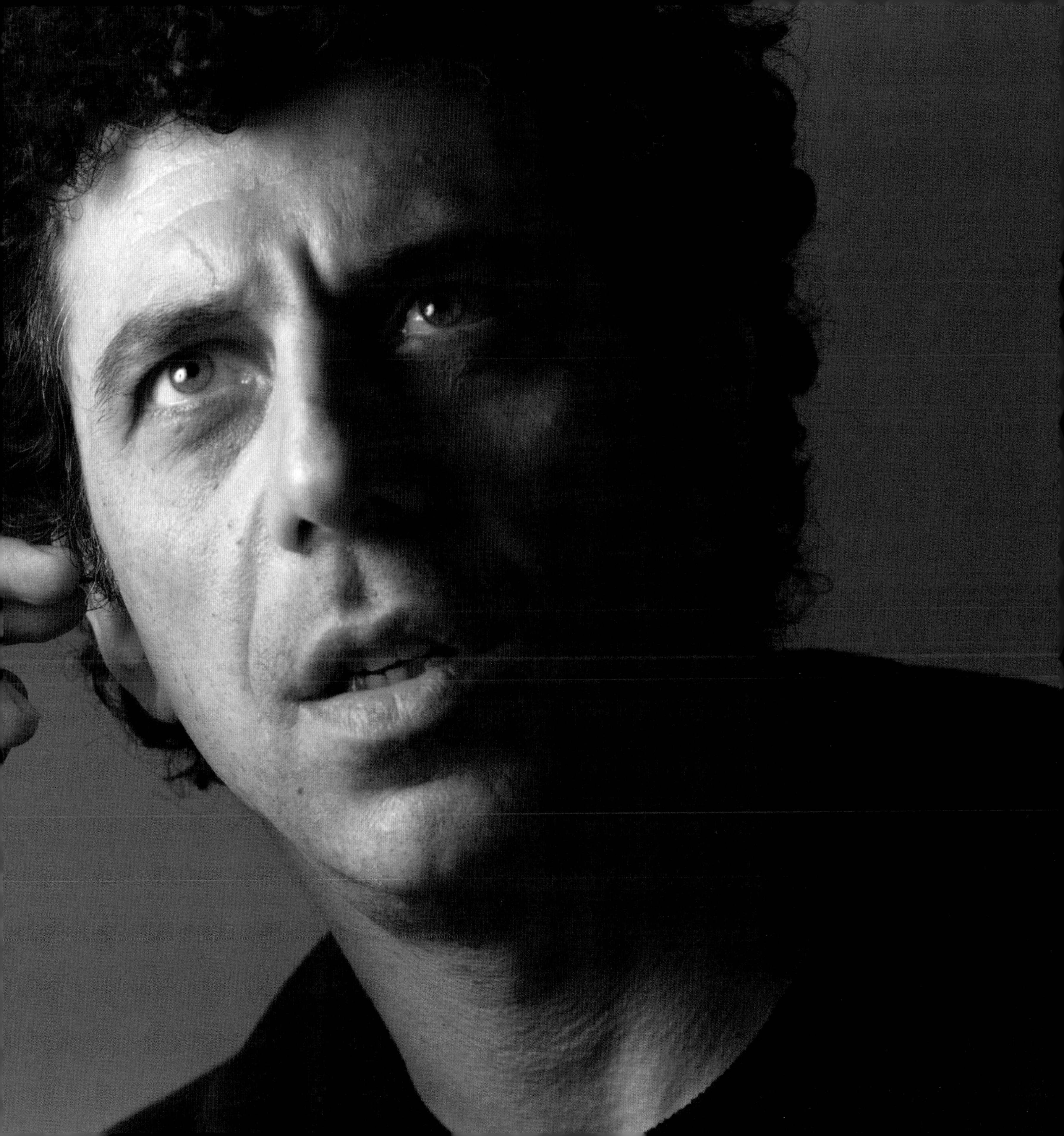

CHRISTOPHER SHINN

(Born 1975—American playwright known for Dying City*, awarded Obie and Guggenheim Fellowship in 2005.)*

On a very warm Saturday in May of 2012, I met Christopher Shinn on the Lower East Side of Manhattan to talk about playwriting. We were to go to a favorite hangout of his, but it had flooded the night before so we walked a few more blocks to a chic, sophisticated Mexican restaurant, Empellôn Cocina, and had brunch. The setting is a cool, modern interior, aqua and white with Latin-leaning jazz.

* * *

SJ: When did you decide to be a playwright?

CS: I think at eighteen when I decided to go to NYU. I applied to Boston University for political science. I applied to Emerson for fiction writing. I thought I might want to be a novelist or might want to work in politics. I had been inspired by Bill Clinton, but I had started writing plays at fifteen and really liked it. So when I was accepted to NYU, I said, "All right. I'm going to be a playwright."

I had also grown up at Hartford Stage and saw great plays from a very young age. That was very influential. I saw *Desire Under the Elms* at Hartford when I was ten. A serious work for such an impressionable age.

SJ: You worked with some very accomplished teachers, Tony Kushner and David Greenspan. What do you think you learned from them?

CS: I think I learned how hard they worked and how deeply they thought. I think that was more important than what they taught me. I saw very clearly that if you wanted to be a great artist, it was not something you could magically do.

SJ: I recently re-read your play, *Dying City*, and when I was out in the city, all the talk I was hearing began to sound like your dialogue.

CS: I have a very bad visual memory. If I closed my eyes and you asked me to describe the restaurant, I'd have a very hard time. But I have an amazing memory for what people have said. So if you told me to go write down our entire conversation up to this point, I would probably be able to do it with almost perfect accuracy. It's always been just a skill I have. I have always been able to remember what people said. That's why my dialogue has that quality. I can literally hear it. It's not only that I hear people say those things, but I internalize how people speak.

SJ: Where do you write?

CS: I write in my apartment.

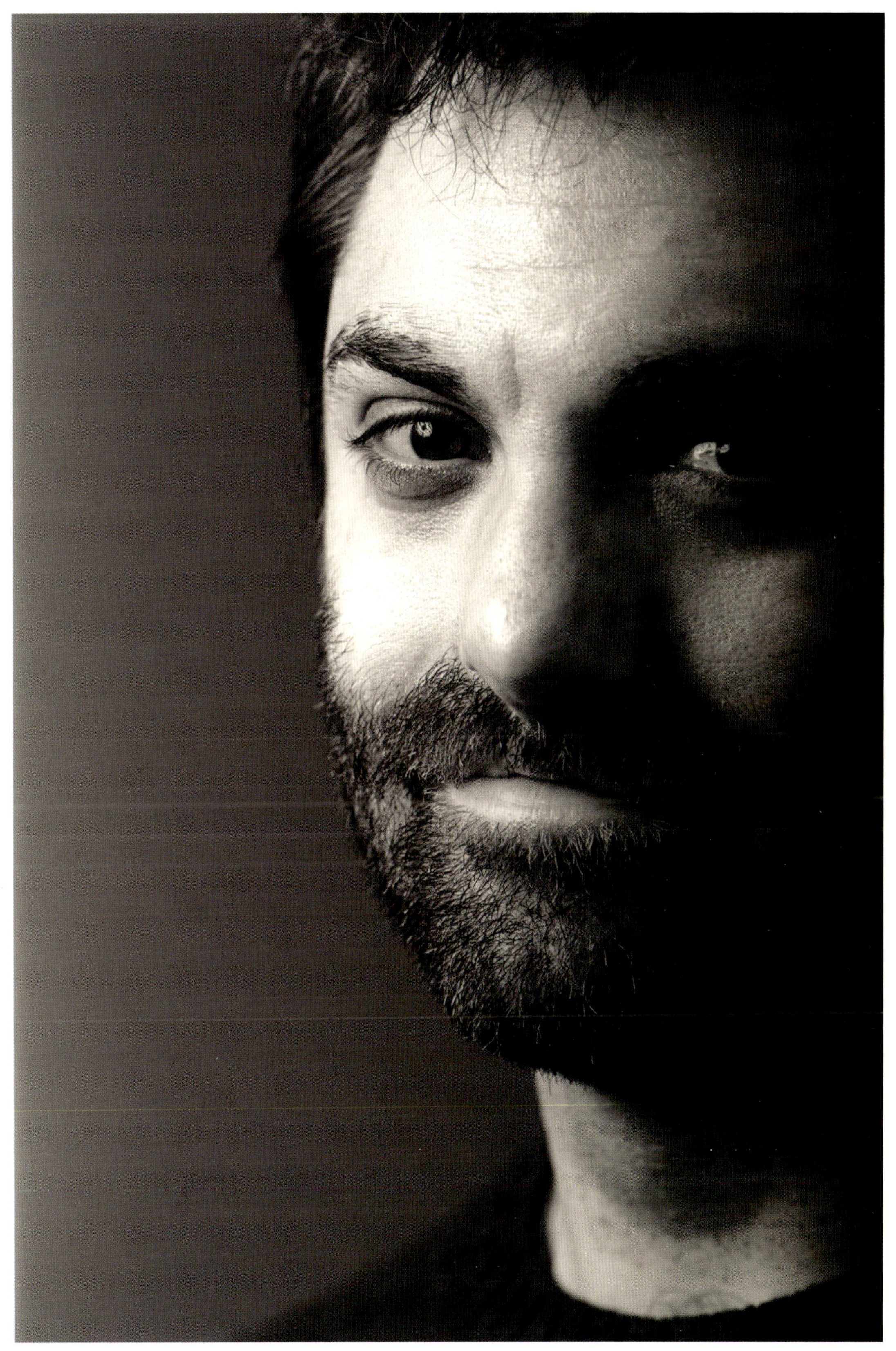

SJ: Other than your teachers, are there other influences?

CS: Shakespeare, Chekov, and Ibsen. Of the Greeks, I'd say Aeschylus would be the one I'd pick.

SJ: And our modern contemporary writers?

CS: Caryl Churchill. I think she was the best, still is, of the twentieth century, second half. I just think she has done things no one else has ever done. And her innovations never feel inaccessible, so clearly communicative. Huge impact. She'd be the one.

Also David Mamet. Whatever you think of his politics, he did change something about dialogue and in a really extraordinary way.

SJ: I could see that. When you did the translation of the Ibsen, *Hedda Gabler,* what did you do differently?

CS: I felt like my job was to be as faithful as possible to the play while making sure contemporary audiences would hear it in a way that sounded new. It sounded new to his audiences when he wrote it, so I thought it was important.

By going back to the original translations, then to two additional new translators, I saw so many things that had become cliché that weren't actually in Ibsen's initial play. What happened is that people had worked from the early Edwardian translations that were so intellectual. They retained a sort of British feel rather than a more direct translation into a more American idiom.

When I went back to the original translations, I found Ibsen was much more contemporary than I expected. One example is the scene at the end of Act Two between Hedda and Lovborg. It's much more frank and sexual and passionate in the Ibsen than in the English versions I read. In Ibsen's version, pretty much you don't even have to read between the lines; it's almost in the language. She basically accuses him of having raped her.

SJ: In the collection of your five plays, there are two plays with twins. What's with the twins?

CS: We live in an age where we value science so much. We're told constantly that human nature can be explained by genetics or by evolution; that certain disciplines can explain why we behave the way we do. That has never seemed true to me, and I think twins are a great way of showing that even when you're the same genetic material, you end up being very, very different. It is proof that it's not all in our genes or even in the way we're raised. Individual people have individual psyches.

The play, *Dying City,* is being revived at Signature Theatre [Arlington, Virginia] this year. The director is gay and his identical twin brother is straight. He read it and is excited to see a story that reflected his own—one twin who was straight, the other gay. It isn't all in your genes. Life is more complicated. I don't know if I'll ever do it again, but it showed up in two plays because it fascinates me how individual people are.

SJ: Your whole twin thing with the doubling of actors—would it make a big difference if the twin brothers were played by two different actors instead of one actor playing the two characters?

CS: I want people to think why they are the way they are and not think anything is what it seems.

SJ: Philosophically, how are you affected by the media? How are your characters affected? In *Dying City,* she seems to be using television to self-medicate.

CS: Very much so. When people say the best art is on TV, I don't deny there is good writing, but to put forward the point of view that the best writing or most extraordinary writing is on TV, I think, is not true. I think the commercial pressures are very much in evidence. I think we have idealized TV. It's very hard. People are busy. It's undeniable that it's easier to watch a TV show. As opposed to a novel, which can sit on a shelf and then find its audience, theatre has to find somebody to put on the play at the time. I wish we had an easier way of popularizing them.

I was just talking to Michael Wilson, the director. He was speaking about a reading he was putting together of a Horton Foote play, as though it had never been produced. And I said, "Has it been produced?" He said, "There was a period when nobody was doing Horton's plays." There was a period when he was working out of HB Studios and this piece got about a two-week run. I got seized by terror, and I thought "Could that happen to me?" Horton was an amazing writer, and there was a period of disfavor when no one was doing his plays, or doing little Off-Off Broadway two-week runs. So you do rely on others to say yes.

SJ: Have you had a problem with the amount of sexuality in your plays? Getting the plays produced?

CS: I think it has hurt a little bit here—the audiences in New York are a little bit older—but all the plays that have been done in London have been done here. It hasn't prevented production, though it has in regional theaters. It's not just the sexuality but also the language.

SJ: When you sit in a theater watching a play of yours, how do you feel?

CS: I love it.

SJ: So where do you see yourself in ten years?

CS: That's a good question. I started young. My career started when I was twenty-three, when I was at the Royal Court. Now I'm thirty-seven. I remember the day the phone call came; I was really walking on air. I'm thirty-seven now, so I'm still young, and I could see six or seven more plays. At about the seven-year mark, I wonder how long I will want to do a play every fifteen months; probably not for the next thirty years.

SJ: What's your beginning process? Do you come up with a concept first? Do you sit down with a piece of paper?

CS: I just open a space internally. It's like meditating, but in a very relaxed way, almost like sleeping. I begin to have images and the images get more and more detailed over time.

SJ: A bit ago you said you were not visually oriented, so are these images . . . relationships? Or are they dialogue?

CS: They're dialogue. They're a glimpse of a face. They're not a picture and a stage; they're more like a dream. Yeah, dreams are visual but have a feeling, a story. It's that element of a dream—the feeling you have when you tell the dream to somebody. If you tell the dream, "I was here and this was happening." It's more like that, and slowly over time, it builds and builds and gets more texture, and when it's very detailed, I start to write it. It always feels like somebody else wrote it. Like when you have your dream, you didn't create your dream.

SJ: How long is the process?

CS: From the beginning to when I send the play to my agent—about twelve to eighteen months. I can dream it for nine to twelve months. Write it in three months. But that twelve months? A lot of work. Sometimes people think I'm just walking around, but I'm still working. Once I have it there, the writing can go quite fast.

SJ: I see you are part of the American Psychoanalytic Society.

CS: Yes. I had a fellowship with the American Psychoanalytic Society for a year. I have been in psychoanalysis for eight years.

SJ: Is that because you wanted to tune into the Zeitgeist? Or how was it helpful to you?

CS: Psychoanalysts are talking about the deepest part of the psyche. Whether one agrees or not with what they say, it was very exciting for me to find another community outside the arts, where people were doing that. I learned a lot.

SJ: Are young people, and people your age, going to the theatre?

CS: I don't know how many. I teach at the New School for Drama. We get dozens and dozens and dozens of submissions of people writing plays in their early to mid-twenties who want to write plays for a living and classes of writers in their mid-twenties who are writing amazing plays. I get fan letters from sixteen- and seventeen-year-olds. I got a fan letter from a fifteen-year-old. I have a friend who works in a youth library in Evanston, Illinois, who says kids check out my plays all the time. It's amazing.

There is something about the theatre that can't die. It doesn't appear to cross that line into real death, however marginal it may be. And I don't think it ever will. How popular it can remain or become, I don't know.

SJ: With the young, there are people who have never been to a theater to see a play. What's different about going to a play from going to a film?

CS: I think because there are real people on a stage. There is something about it. It just is different. I was in a youth theatre that toured schools in Connecticut. When we would perform, the response was extraordinary, mostly from kids who never had seen a play. To see somebody do something for real has an impact. It just does, and I think that will never go away.

There's a fear that people are so involved with technology and images they are going to lose touch with reality. I think it is the opposite. Even as much as we love the virtual world, there will be a hunger for the real world.

SJ: We now have a culture that it seems addicted to fun. Nothing deep in it.

CS: That's why I like tragedy as a form and why I wish we had theaters doing great productions of Shakespeare's late tragedies. I feel that apocalyptic energy where there is such corruption, such destruction and deceit. That is the kind of stuff we need to be thinking about, and often those themes don't get touched. Lots to write about now. That's why it's very exciting to be alive right now, however hard it is.

SJ: It must be interesting to go back and forth to England to the Royal Court. How did that happen?

CS: I just sent them my work and they discovered me. That was the beginning.

SJ: I spoke to Robert Patrick who had a big success on Broadway and then went to England and had success in the West End. He was gone two years, came back and couldn't get produced.

CS: That's why you have to keep writing—because they forget about you. You have to keep doing it no matter what. If you don't have the strength to keep going, or you get discouraged. . . . You stop because it's heartbreaking. It really is. You think, "I made it. They're going to do my work. They really like my work." And then they forget about you. "Whump. I'm just a kind of cog in a machine." It's dehumanizing. You see how they objectify you. You've got to have a lot of fight in you.

SJ: What gave you the idea to write your dialogue using parentheses and slashes to denote the feelings or the rhythm. For me, it was wonderful and made it much easier to hear in my mind.

CS: I hate when writers direct the actor how to say the line within the parentheses, but I also understand the writer wanting to convey the feeling. That was my way of conveying the feeling without saying what it is. It still gives them room. I'm always looking for ways—an abstract way. But it gives them a sense of the rhythm of the feeling.

SJ: And the slash?

CS: You know who invented that? Caryl Churchill.

SJ: We've all gotten used to that in film, people talking over the ends of lines. But the denotations in the script, the slashes and parentheses, make it clear where you want that to start.

CS: It's very important where that moment is. You are telling the actor where the thought comes for them to respond and where you want them to stop listening to the person. Which is fascinating, too.

SJ: I could really hear them.

CS: The parenthesis is mine.

SJ: Well, this has been great.

CS: Thank you for breakfast and for the conversation.

SJ: Thank you. This is why I do this. I love the conversations.

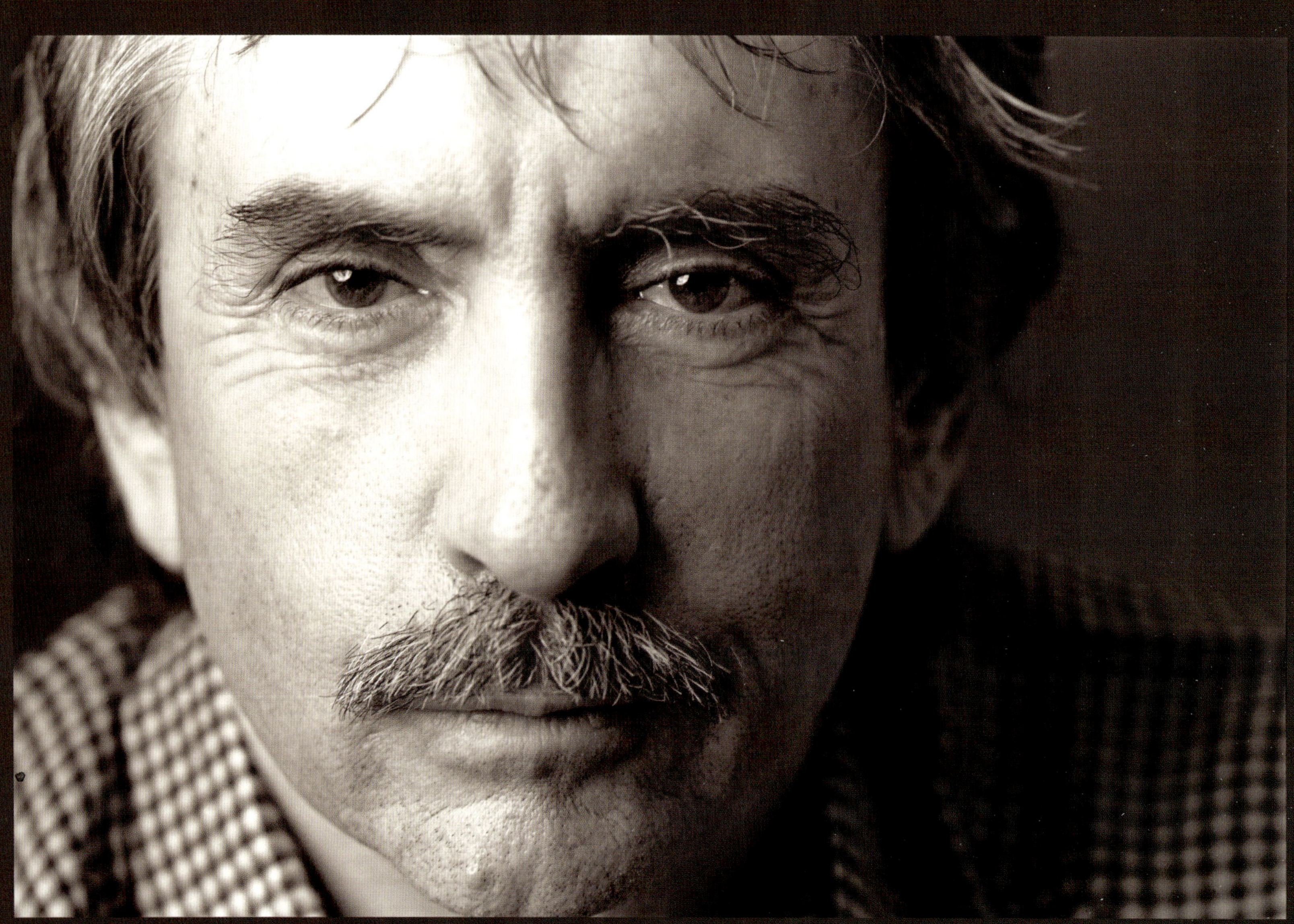

EDWARD ALBEE

(Born 1928—American playwright, awarded three Pulitzer Prizes, the PEN/Laura Pels International Foundation for Theater Award as a Master American Dramatist, a special Tony Award for Lifetime Achievement, a Gold Medal in Drama from the American Academy of Arts and Letters, Kennedy Center Honors and the National Medal of Arts, among many other honors.)

I met Edward Albee at his loft in Tribeca. From outside, his building looks like a warehouse. Inside is a double-height loft, all art with large paintings, sculpture—surprising pieces and those one recognizes—and lots of space. At once simple and grand. We walk down the street to a Japanese restaurant where Albee orders something with spider in the name. "It isn't really spider," he says. It wouldn't have surprised me if it were.

* * *

SJ: I just saw *Thirty-Two Short Films about Glenn Gould.* As a child you were interested in being a composer. It struck me that if you had been shut off in Vancouver with a mother like Glenn Gould's who played the piano, you . . .

EA: . . . would have ended up being a composer. Well, I am in a way. I hear the music that I write. A lot of the phrases in my plays, though nobody would notice it unless they knew it, scan poetically and then come to very specific musical halts. I write that very, very, very precisely.

SJ: As a child, were you somebody who was exposed to a lot of music, painting, sculpture?

EA: You know, the family had a bunch of paintings around. And books. My nanny interested me in classical music when I was this big *[indicates a height of about three feet]*. She'd lay me down and make me listen to the Metropolitan Opera broadcast and concert broadcasts. I started drawing about the same time. I was five or six.

SJ: Were you someone who was read a lot of stories?

EA: Oh, I read a great deal. Classics. And still do. I read all the time—fiction, nonfiction, scientific stuff, history. Everything.

SJ: As a child you found your way to the Turgenev in the family library?

EA: Yes, I liked him a lot.

SJ: Was there a big library in the house?

EA: There were a lot of books, leather-bound books.

SJ: Who read them besides you?

EA: Nobody. Just me.

SJ: Your audience has now gotten a lot about the mother from *Three Tall Women* but the father . . .

EA: Invisible. He was absent even when he was around. He just wanted to be left alone, just alone.

SJ: There are always animals mentioned in your plays. Were there always animals in your life?

EA: Always. I loved them.

SJ: And you liked being out in the country.

EA: Well, Larchmont was suburbs, basically. Not country, but suburbs. I went horseback riding when I was a kid. I was fairly protected. I think they were afraid I was going to get kidnapped because the Lindbergh kid was kidnapped about four miles from where I was growing up and they scared me about that.

SJ: They scared you?

EA: They put the fear in me.

SJ: Did you rebel?

EA: Quite!

SJ: Quite?

EA: Getting thrown out of schools, things like that.

SJ: Did you tell them off, your parents?

EA: Oh, no, no, no. I was much too shy.

SJ: So you were doing . . .

EA: Quiet stuff.

SJ: How did you manage to get thrown out of school?

EA: Wouldn't go to the classes I didn't want to. That simple. They don't like that.

SJ: I've been thinking about some of your plays that seem not to have been properly appreciated, like *The Man Who Had Three Arms*, which was all about a media circus. And here we are now in the middle of such a time of media hype in the United States, about O.J. Simpson, Michael Jackson, scandals.

EA: Vicarious sensationalism. People like it because that is what they are exposed to. I don't notice that, say, a poet, Brodsky, for example, has been made a media star. If they did then people would be reading poetry. It is part of my theory that there is really nothing wrong with American theatre audiences, that if Broadway were filled with great plays for ten years, and only great plays, that would become the taste of Broadway audiences. They'd laugh at these idiotic musicals that are up right now. They wouldn't want to see them. So the public taste is constantly being limited and diminished.

SJ: If we put on *The Man Who Had Three Arms* today, it would have a different resonance because we are now experiencing the things you seem to have seen coming.

EA: I'm always suspicious of plays that come along at the right time. Because they probably should have been written five years earlier.

SJ: The way in which *Three Tall Women* happens with the three women or three parts of the woman speaking to herself—

EA: She's not speaking to herself. They're there. It's the argument I've been having with my British director. It's not in her mind at all. They are there. It's not in the mind of the woman in bed. They are there. They're real.

SJ: On a spiritual plane, on another plane than her plane?

EA: They're there. I mean—having to insist that they are there only because it's in the mind of a woman who has had a stroke!

SJ: Oh! You mean from the existential point. . . . They are there, just as the Edward who wrote *The Zoo Story* at twenty-nine and the Edward who wrote *All Over* are all there as part of Edward. So what would Edward who just wrote *Three Tall Women* and received another Pulitzer Prize say to Edward who's twenty-eight and hasn't written *The Zoo Story*?

EA: Well. "You're going to write this play. And you'll be able to quit Western Union. And you will discover who you are, that you're a playwright, you'll figure that out. That's who you are."

SJ: And what is the twenty-eight-year-old going to say?

EA: "Really? I'm going to do that? What's it going to be about?" "You'll find out. When you're ready, you'll write it."

SJ: Do you think the twenty-eight-year-old would have believed it?

EA: The twenty-eight-year-old always had an expectation of being a good writer. It never surprised him that he wrote *The Zoo Story,* and when it was successful it didn't surprise him.

SJ: Did it surprise him the things that happened to him after *The Zoo Story*?

EA: No. These things happen. He learned very quickly that sometimes things are well received. Sometimes they aren't. Never anticipate anything good because disappointment lies that way. Always expect the worst that can possibly happen, but be pleased when the good comes. But never be grateful. You're pleased you work with good actors, good directors, and have a few intelligent critics around. One's pleased by all that, but one isn't grateful for those things. If you're any good, it's what you deserve. It sounds terrible but it's true.

SJ: You have used the phrase "honorable goal" with regard to playwriting.

EA: Everyone should use that phrase more often. Or think about it a good deal more.

SJ: And the honorable goal of playwriting is . . .

EA: . . . to communicate, to change people's minds, make people think more clearly and deeply about things. Change the world.

SJ: You know some people are really frightened of you?

EA: Why?

SJ: They think anybody who can write such an argument as we got—early on, full blast—between Martha and George, must be able to put us away.

EA: Oh, I'm a nice person . . .

SJ: Oh, I know.

EA: . . . until crossed.

SJ: What I wonder is, are you as good at argument as your characters are?

EA: I'm quieter. I can be a little unpleasant if people are behaving badly. Sure. But it's cold.

SJ: Not hot like Martha.

EA: Cold. More like George I think. The image I like is the image of a man who is in a sword duel with somebody. And there they are. Then *[a sound like "ssshhhwick"]*. Like that. And he didn't know his neck had been severed until he turned his head. Such a clean and swift and subtle gesture. Then he turns, and his head falls off.

SJ: Edward in argument. I'll try not to get into an argument with you. Do you like going to the theatre?

EA: When it's any good. Infrequently.

SJ: When is it good?

EA: If you're lucky, one in every fifty times. When it really changes your life. It really matters.

SJ: What about walking into a theater to go to work?

EA: Oh, I enjoy that. It's where I work. It's where my job is, so I go to it. If you're a playwright, it's interesting to translate your work from the page to the stage. That's interesting. In fact, that's always very interesting.

SJ: Do you have favorite plays of your own?

EA: No.

SJ: Do you like them all equally?

EA: I don't think about them very much.

SJ: A number of people have said you were an anti-intellectual. Do you think you are an anti-intellectual?

EA: Of course not. That's preposterous. Whoever said that?

SJ: I'll get the name so you can write a letter.

EA: If they can read.

SJ: Is it a struggle for you, writing?

EA: I enjoy it greatly.

SJ: If you could sit down with a couple of people who are maybe not around any more, to find out some more about them—

EA: Well, I would like to have spent some time with Jesus. He was a very interesting revolutionary.

SJ: What about Buddha?

EA: I think he would have bored me. I probably would have bored him.

SJ: At heart you are a revolutionary?

EA: I guess. Yes. When I spoke about Jesus, I wasn't talking about wise men and kings but the revolutionary figure. That interests me a lot. Since there is so little known about what Jesus actually said and so much apocrypha and all the rest. Being with the guy, finding what he was really like, how tough a revolutionary he was, I would have found that very interesting.

SJ: What would you talk about?

EA: I'd probably ask a lot of questions about what he was really after. "Stop talking in parables. Talk to me straight." I don't think he did talk in parables. I think that was the people who wrote about him a hundred years later talking about him.

SJ: But people think you're talking in parables.

EA: I'm not. Everything I write is naturalistic.

SJ: On what level and for whom?

EA: Well, there is metaphor in everything. I can't be held accountable.

SJ: Do you have twenty-two more plays that you want to write?

EA: I have two more in my head right now. One of them I'll write this fall and winter, I hope, because we're going to be doing it in April down in New Orleans. I have no idea where this play came from, where these people came from, but there they are in my head. Got to write 'em down. They're sort of where they're yapping at each other and yammering away and I've got to put it down before I lose it all.

SJ: Do you see most of your work in a smaller space now?

EA: No. Three years ago, I wrote a play about Garcia-Lorca with thirty-six characters.

SJ: I don't know this play.

EA: Where would anybody do it except at a university?

SJ: The university is a very vital place for the theatre. Why is it that the young people leave and then—

EA: They run into the real world. You don't have to pay student actors. They don't have to pay thirty-six actors and the sets are built for free. For that production to run, it would cost so much money you'd have to make a damn musical out of it. No. I think it will be done when it's done in national theaters around the world.

SJ: *Three Tall Women* seems well-suited to the Promenade Theatre but it might well be suited to one of the smaller Broadway theaters.

EA: Oh, sure it would be. But nobody wanted it. After it got all the good reviews, nobody wanted to put it on Broadway. Broadway theater managements didn't want it. So we said, "Let's put it at the Promenade." And it's selling out all the time, doing great.

SJ: I don't know what I should ask you that hasn't been asked.

EA: Everybody's asked me everything.

SJ: What struck me in reading past interviews is how consistent you have been from the beginning. The essential Edward Albee hasn't changed much from 1962.

EA: I'm amazed by that sometimes when I look at the stuff I've answered way back. I don't know whether that means a rigid mind that doesn't reconsider anything or—that I was right the first time.

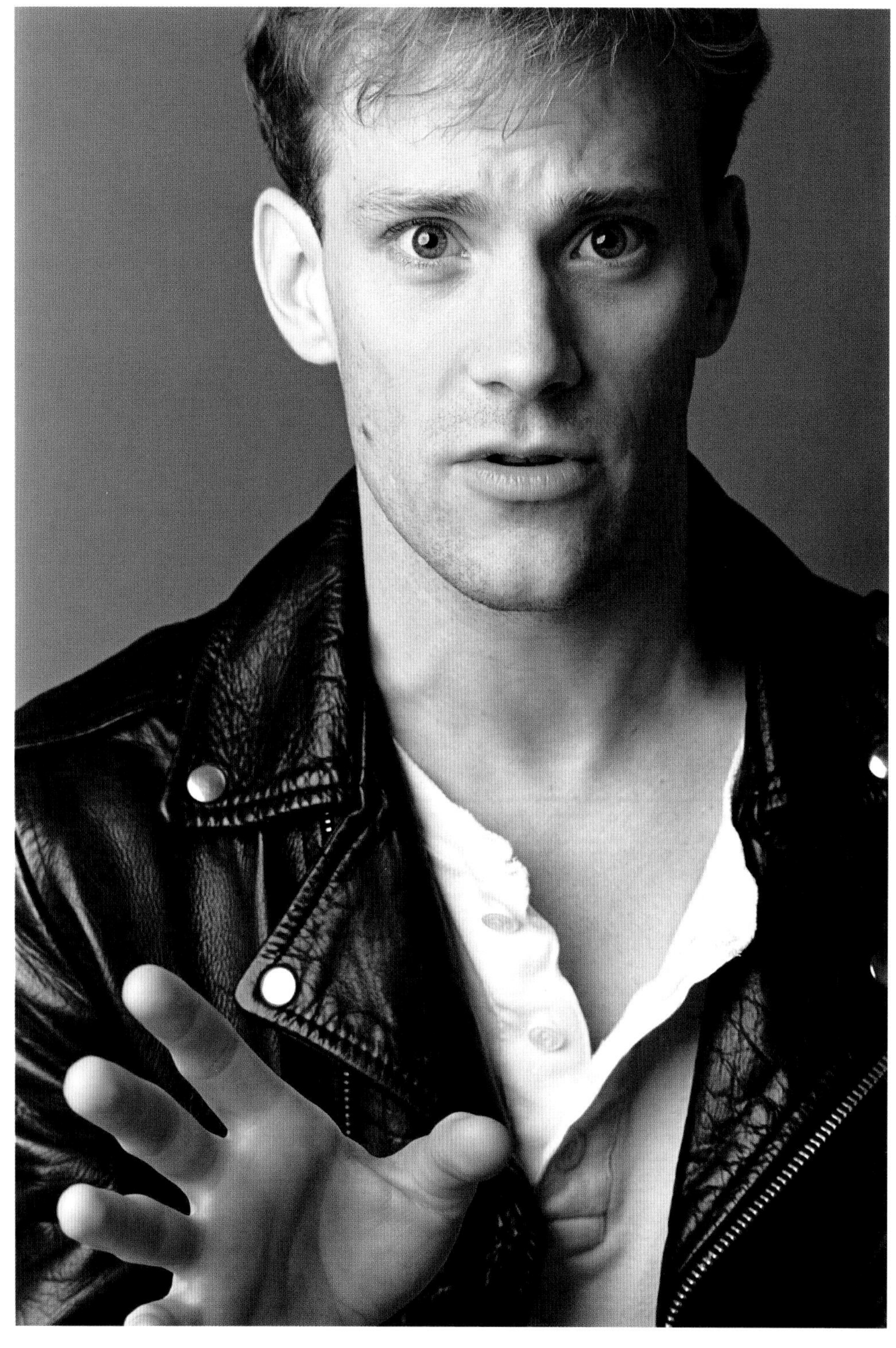

David Drake — Kim Merrill (opposite)

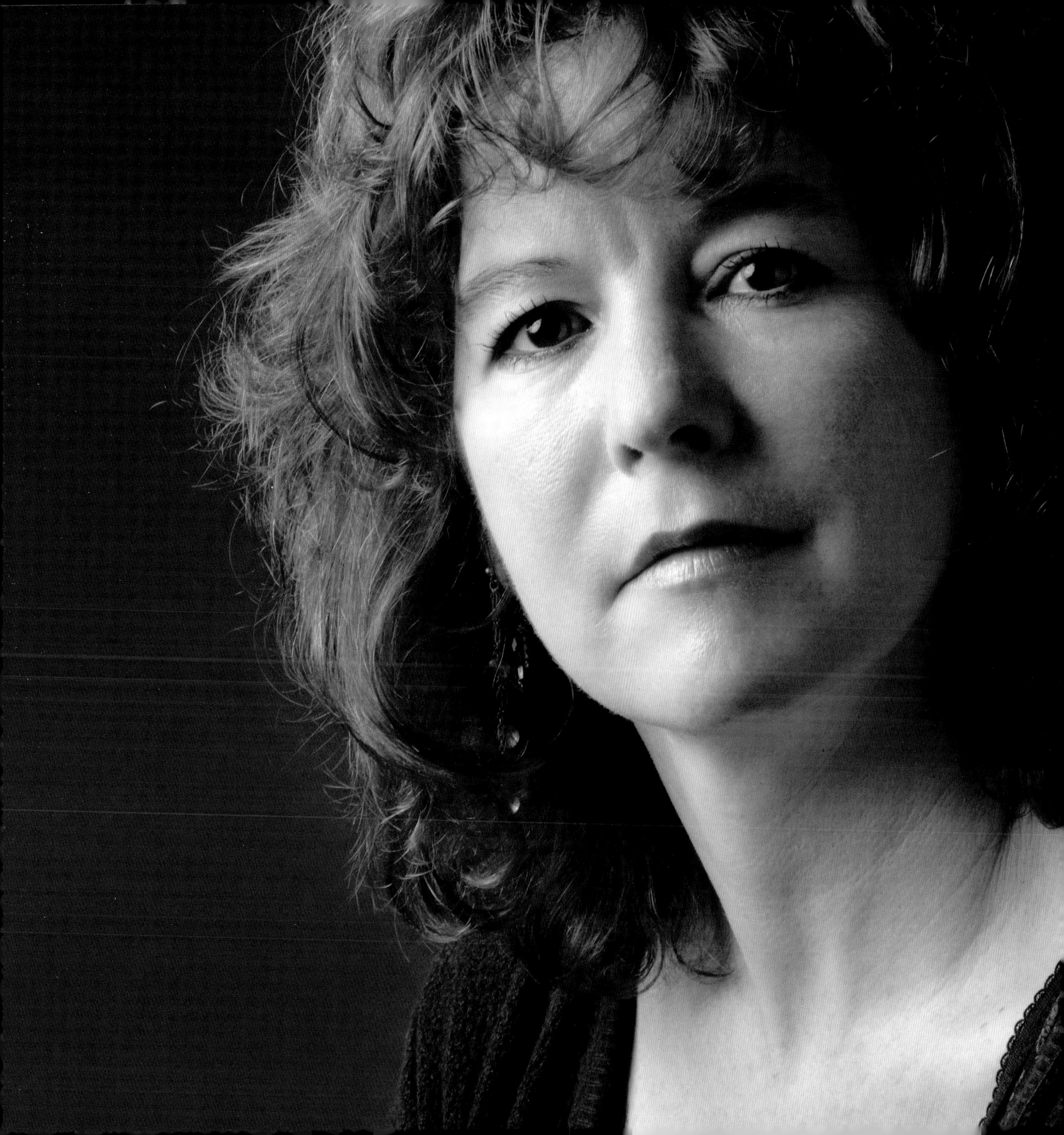

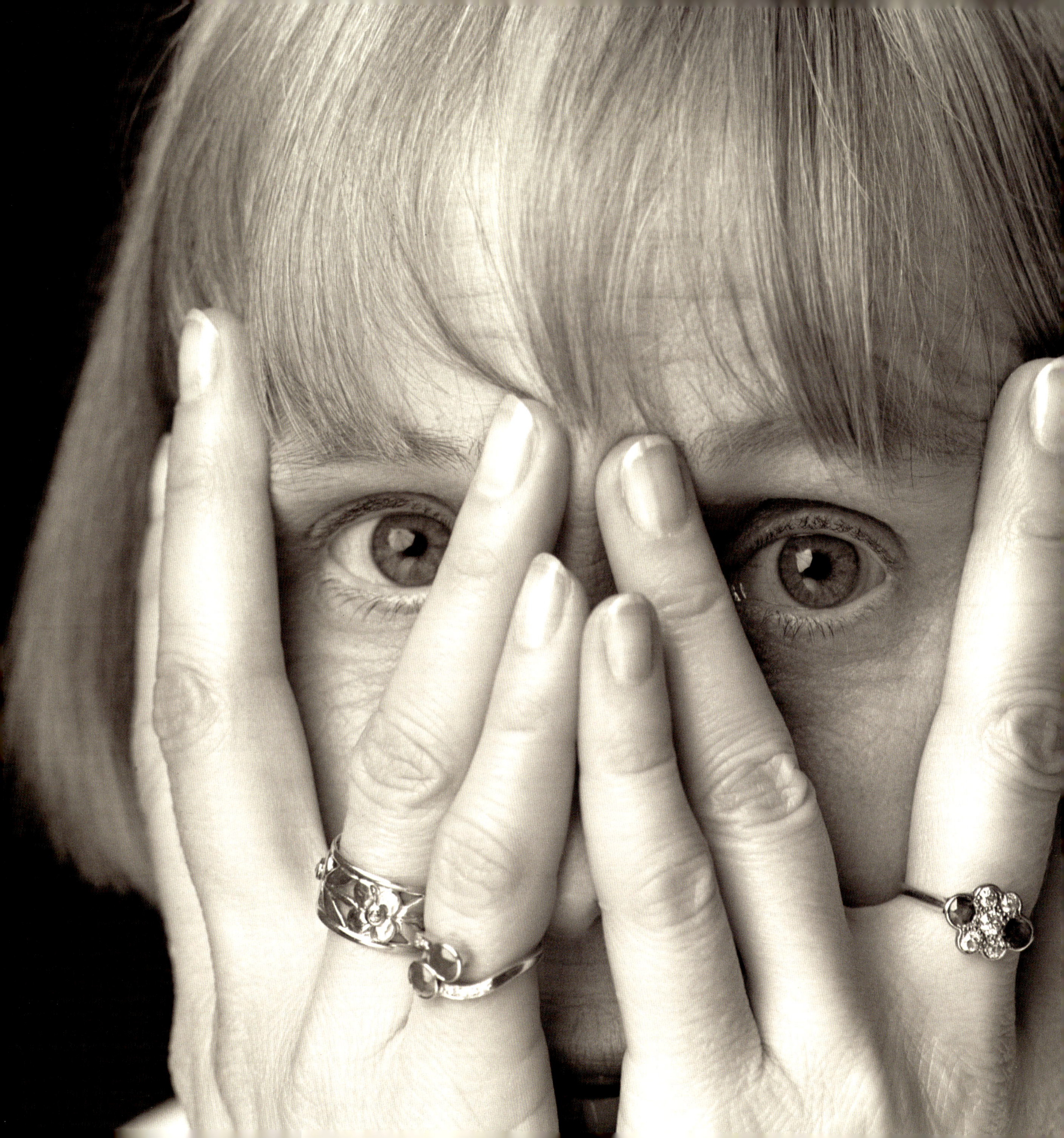

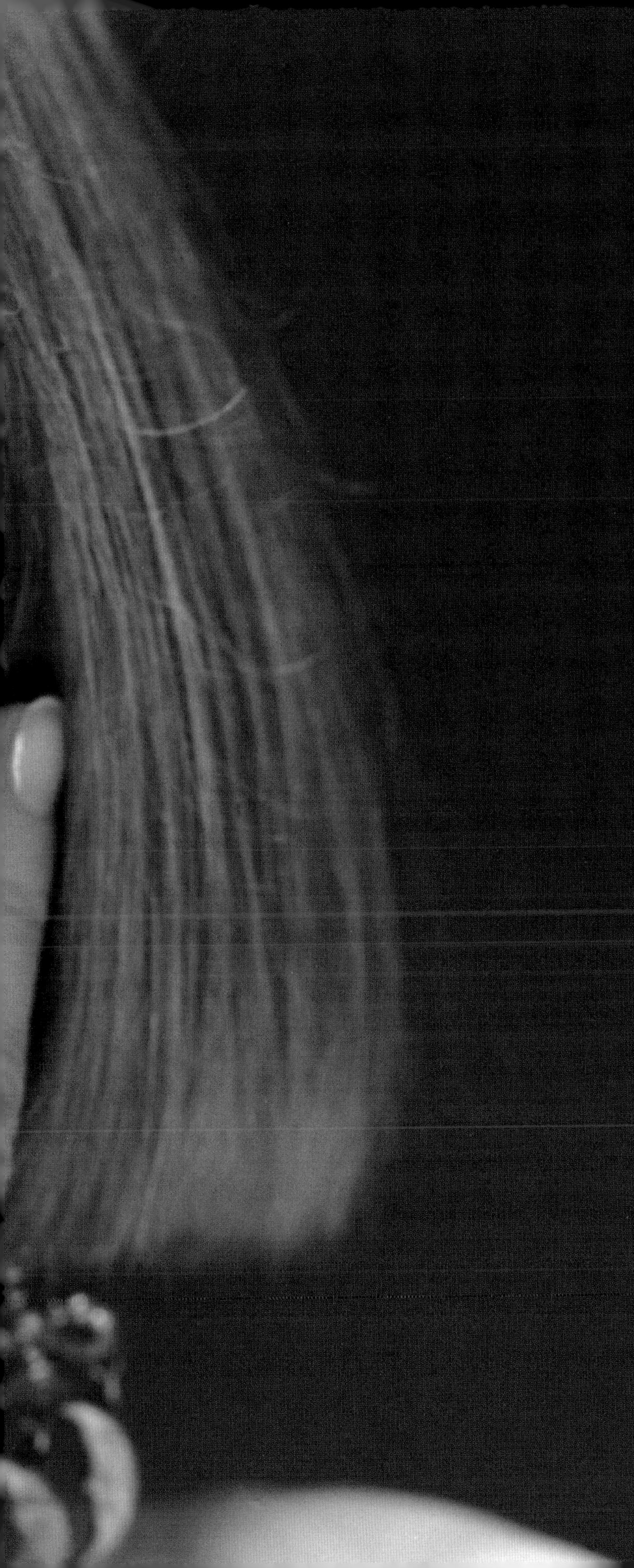

DOROTHY: I hate having my picture taken! *(struggling to get past him)* I hate it, hate it, hate it, hate it, hate it, hate it, hate it, hate it. . . . *Hate it, hate it, hate it, hate it!* . . . Why can't you set up your camera in my brain? Bore a hole in my skull and let 'er rip. . . . Click! *(tapping her temple)* Aim your camera here, Mr. Hugo. *This* is where beauty lies . . . Mysterious, inchoate and out of sight!

—FROM *THE DIVINE FALLACY*, A PLAY BY TINA HOWE

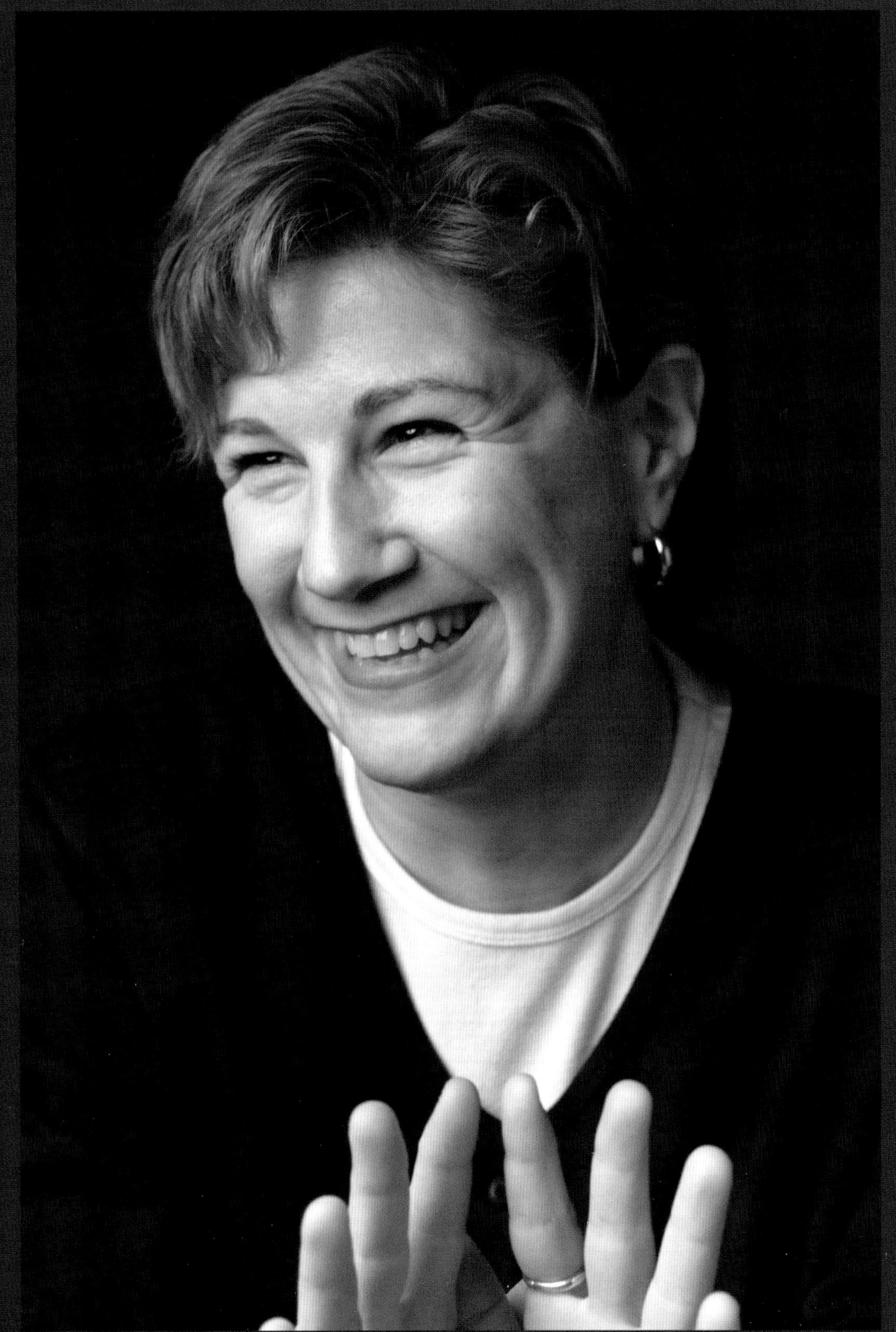

ACKNOWLEDGMENTS

Since the beginning of this series, I have been helped along the way by a small army of wonderful people starting with photographer Timothy Greenfield-Sanders, who inspired me, was my only teacher, and has been a mentor for the last twenty-five years. Always in the midst of a demanding schedule, he was never too busy to return a call or email. Brandon Judell gave me an assignment to photograph my first playwright, Christopher Durang, and so, accidentally launched the series. Alexandra C. Anderson, arts editor, first featured the portraits in *Smart* magazine and later in *The Argonaut*. She has supported and encouraged my efforts continually over the length of the project. Elisabeth Lewis Corley was invaluable in shaping the interviews from the beginning with gentle but firm editing that kept me on track. Sonja Karlsen sat beside me, editing and coaxing me through the end game.

Thanks to my agents: Judy Boals of Judy Boals Agency, Tony Gardner at the Tantleff Office, and Laura Blake-Peterson at Curtis-Brown. Through Laura, I got such a favorable rejection from Jacqueline Onassis at Doubleday that her praise of the project kept me going for years.

I am lastingly grateful to Jim O'Quinn, editor of *American Theatre*, who never stops giving me assignments to shoot playwrights and uses those photos and interviews in the magazine; Terence Nemeth, publisher for Theatre Communications Group, who used the portraits on the covers of books and so helped the cause; Cathy Mather, photo editor of Arts and Leisure at the *New York Times*, who remembered to call me when she needed a portrait of a playwright (I loved the last-minute, mad dash to the Public Theater to shoot Sam Shepard); James Houghton, founding Artistic Director of Signature Theatre, who supported the project and must be thanked for his brilliant theater devoted to playwrights. Houghton kept me busy doing the production stills for Signature and used and displayed the prints from the playwright series and then invited me to come to the O'Neill Playwrights Conference to present the slide presentation, *Focus on Playwrights*. Also at Signature were James Morrison, a wonderful publicist, who suggested playwrights and made sure I didn't starve during a few lean years; and our beloved Tom Proehl, the first General Manager at Signature, whose dazzling smile and enthusiasm encouraged me to go on—and who left us much too soon.

Thank you to Todd London at New Dramatists, who made a space there for me, as he does for playwrights, where I did the first *Focus on Playwrights*, and to Lee Melahn, who helped run that slide show. Thanks to Ann

Lisa Kron (opposite)

Shumard at the Smithsonian's National Portrait Gallery, who included my playwright portraits in several of their exhibitions; to Beverly Adler, who hosted a lobby show of the playwright portraits at Ogilvy-Mather in New York City; to Carol Fineman at the New York Public Theater for helping me get access to many playwrights; and to Ed Henredeen at the Contemporary American Theatre Festival, who put up a gallery show. Thanks to the Tryon Fine Arts Center for including me in their *Explore the Arts* series. Also in Tryon, my thanks to Julia Williams and Tracy Daniels.

Thanks to the endlessly patient Tom Morgan at Blue Design for his skills and his aesthetics in designing the book.

This project was shot on a special Kodak film—Technical Pan—and it would have been impossible to have the prints look so good without master printer Chuck Kelton, and all those at Kelton Labs who make the finest negatives and prints in the world.

Some portions of the interviews appeared previously in *American Theatre*, published by Theatre Communications Group, and are reprinted by permission: George Abbott (April 1995), Garson Kanin (August 1999), Nicky Silver (October 1996), and August Wilson (August 1996). I am grateful to both Tina Howe and Joan Schenkar for permission to include selections from "The Divine Fallacy," from *Shrinking Violets and Towering Tiger Lilies*, by Tina Howe (Samuel French, 2009), and from the Preface to *Signs of Life: Six Comedies of Menace*, by Joan Schenkar (Wesleyan, 1997).

There are so many people who encouraged me over these many years. I have tried to remember them all and still fear there will be significant omissions. They introduced me to playwrights, suggested playwrights, and gave me tickets to plays. Most important, I wish to thank the playwrights themselves—especially Edward Albee, Christopher Durang, Marsha Norman, and Joan Schenkar. I have gained immeasurably from every contact with the playwrights—in the theater or in the studio where they lent me their valuable time. It was a privilege. I will continue to add to the archive as there will always be more playwrights I am eager to photograph.

Finally, thanks to my husband, Dallas, who was always patient and understood the importance of the work.

INDEX OF PLAYWRIGHTS

Birth and death years, when known. Year photograph was taken. Selected plays. Asterisk indicates a play awarded the Pulitzer Prize for Drama.

About Susan Johann

The work of award-winning photographer Susan Johann has been featured in galleries and cultural centers throughout the United States, including the Smithsonian Institution's National Portrait Gallery in Washington, D.C., the New York Public Theater, and the Contemporary American Theater Festival.

Johann's photographs are in public, corporate, and private collections; such as the Marriott Corporation, Shaver/Melahn, Gomez Associates, and Signature Theatre Company's Pershing Square Center. They have also been featured in numerous publications, including the *New York Times*, *Vogue*, *Harper's Bazaar*, the *New Yorker*, and *American Theater Magazine.* Penguin; Knopf: Pantheon; Simon & Schuster; Stewart, Tabori & Chang; University of South Carolina Press; and Theatre Communications Group published books that featured Johann's work.

Susan is married to theatre director and former Broadway performer, Dallas Johann. Her sons, Cameron Johann and Trevor Johann, live in Los Angeles where they work in the film industry.

Focus on Playwrights is also a live, multi-media presentation in which Susan narrates an inside look at creativity in the theater and in photography. It has been presented at such venues as the New Dramatists in New York and the Eugene O'Neill Theater Center.

www.susanjohann.com

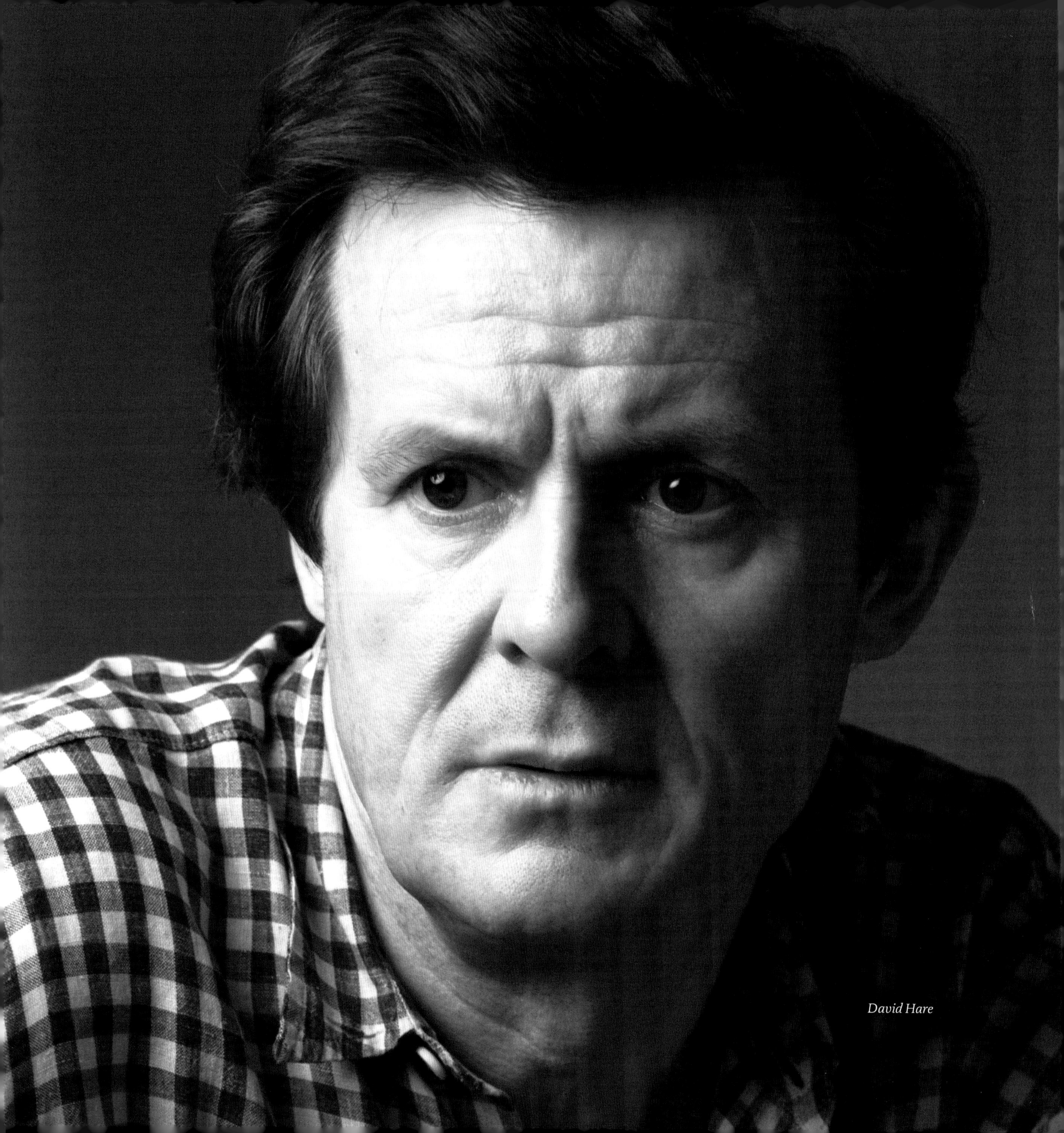

David Hare